ITALIAN

Verbs &

Essentials
of Grammar

Second Edition

Carlo Graziano

New York   Chicago   San Francisco   Lisbon   London   Madrid   Mexico City
Milan   New Delhi   San Juan   Seoul   Singapore   Sydney   Toronto

2 3 4 5 6 7 8 9 10 11 12 13 14 15 16 17 18 19   DIG/DIG   10

ISBN 978-0-07-149801-2
MHID   0-07-149801-X

McGraw-Hill books are available at special quantity discounts to use as premiums and sales promotions, or for use in corporate training programs. For more information, please write to the Director of Special Sales, Professional Publishing, McGraw-Hill, Two Penn Plaza, New York, NY 10121-2298. Or contact your local bookstore.

Preface

Italian Verbs and Essentials of Grammar presents to its users the major grammatical concepts of the Italian language. The book is divided into two parts. In Part I, the primary emphasis is placed on the mastery of verbs—their formation and uses, as well as their interconnections with other parts of speech. A chapter devoted to irregular verbs serves as a unique and comprehensive reference to these commonly used and often troublesome forms. Part II of this book offers concise explanations of the essential parts of Italian grammar—from the use of definite and indefinite articles to the numerous prefixes and suffixes that color Italian speech and writing. The last two chapters of Part II feature an extensive list of Italian idioms, as well as vocabulary lists organized according to the activities and objects of everyday life.

Examples illustrating grammar concepts were chosen for their authenticity, their frequency in everyday speech and writing, and their idiomatic quality. Each topic is treated separately, so that users of the book can either work on one topic at a time or quickly find the reference needed to help solve a particular difficulty. The synopses of verb forms in the simple, perfect, and subjunctive tenses should prove an especially valuable reference tool. The abundant tables and charts provide ample material for creative exercises and extended writing, as well as for oral practice. In addition, the pronunciation section at the beginning of the book provides a helpful key to the main characteristics of the Italian sound system.

Italian Verbs and Essentials of Grammar is a thorough handbook that lends itself to a variety of uses. Because its basic approach is to provide simple, concise explanations, it can be used by language learners at all levels of proficiency—from those who have completed one semester's work to those who have attained a high level of mastery but who, from time to time, need a convenient reference to consult on difficult points of grammar. This book can be used for study and review, for individual or group work, as part of a refresher course, or for business, travel, or research. The commanding importance of Italy in music, literature, history, and the arts also enhances the cultural significance of a knowledge of the Italian language.

Italian Verbs and Essentials of Grammar is a unique and effective language-learning tool. We are confident that this comprehensive reference will prove indispensable to all those teaching and studying Italian.

Contents

Part One: Italian Verbs

1. Pronunciation   3
2. Regular Verbs—The Simple Tense Forms   8
3. Regular Verbs—Auxiliary Verbs and the Perfect Tenses   27
4. Reflexive Verbs   37
5. Formation of Subjunctive Tenses—Regular Verbs   41
6. Uses of the Subjunctive   46
7. Orthographic-Changing Verbs   54
8. Irregular Verbs   57
9. Impersonal and Defective Verbs   77
10. Sequence of Tenses   83
11. Auxiliary Verbs   88
12. Past Infinitive, Gerund, and Participle   92
13. Active and Passive Voices   95
14. Verbs Followed by a Preposition   98

Part Two: Essentials of Grammar

15. Articles   105
16. Nouns   113
17. Adjectives and Adverbs   120
18. Possessive Adjectives and Pronouns   131
19. Demonstrative Adjectives and Pronouns   134
20. Comparison of Adjectives and Adverbs   138
21. Personal Pronouns   149
22. Relative Pronouns   164
23. Interrogatives and Exclamations   168

24. Negatives   171

25. Indefinite Adjectives and Pronouns   175

26. Prepositions   181

27. Conjunctions   186

28. Numbers and Units of Measure   191

29. Time   199

30. Prefixes and Suffixes   204

31. Letters   213

32. Idioms and Expressions   216

33. Vocabulary Lists   221

Index   237

Part One:
Italian Verbs

1. Pronunciation

The Alphabet

The Italian alphabet has twenty-one letters (16 consonants and 5 vowels). In the list below, the name of each letter is indicated in italics.

LETTERS	NAMES OF THE LETTERS	
	Italian	**English**
a	*a*	as in English **ah**
b	*bi*	as in English **bee**
c	*ci*	as in English **chee**
d	*di*	as in English **dee**
e	*e*	as in English **ay**
f	*effe*	as in English **ayffay**
g	*gi*	as in English **gee**
h	*acca*	as in English **akka**
i	*i*	as in English **ee**
l	*elle*	as in English **ayllay**
m	*emme*	as in English **aymmay**
n	*enne*	as in English **aynnay**
o	*o*	as in English **oh**
p	*pi*	as in English **pea**
q	*cu*	as in English **coo**
r	*erre*	as in English **ayrray**
s	*esse*	as in English **ayssay**
t	*ti*	as in English **tee**
u	*u*	as in English **oo**
v	*vu*	as in English **voo**
z	*zeta*	as in English **zaytah**

The following five letters are used in foreign words or obsolete Italian words.

j	**i lungo (i lunga)**
k	**cappa**
y	**ipsilon** or **i greco (i greca)**
w	**doppia vu (vu doppia)**
x	**ics**

In modern Italian *j* has largely been replaced by *i*, but it remains in proper names (*Jacopo, Jolanda, Rajna, Jemolo, Ojetti*) and in foreign words (*jazz, jolly*).

The letter *k* is used in some abbreviations (*kg.* for *chilogrammo, km.* for *chilometro, kw.* for *chilowàtt*) and in foreign words (*poker, danke*).

The letter *y* sounds like *i* and is found in foreign words *(brandy, yacht, yogurt)* or in surnames (*Cybo*).

The letter *w* sounds like the *u* in words derived from English (*week-end, clown, wafer*) and sounds like *v* in words derived from German (*wagneriano*).

The letter *x* sounds like *cs* or *gs* and is found in words derived from Latin (*uxoricida*), from Greek (*xenofobìa*), or other languages (*texano*).

Vowels

The five Italian vowels have a clear-cut sound; they are never drawn out or slurred as in English. Italian vowels correspond approximately to the following English sounds.

a	as "a" in "father":	**casa, ama, lana**
e (*closed*)	as "a" in "make":	**sera, mele, vedere**
e (*open*)	as "e" in "let":	**sedia, festa, bene**
i	as "ee" in "feet":	**liti, tini, piccolo**
o (*closed*)	as "o" in "note":	**coda, molto, conto**
o (*open*)	as "o" in "for":	**cosa, toro, donna**
u	as "oo" in "mood":	**luna, uno, lupo**

Consonants

b	like English *b* in "boy": **bello, bianco, abete**
c	before *a, o,* and *u,* like English *k* in "kind": **cura, come, casa**
c	before *e* and *i,* like English *ch* in English "cherry": **cento, celeste, baci**
cc	before *e* and *i,* like a double *ch:* **accento, accidenti**
ch	(used only before *e* or *i*) like English *k* in "kick": **perchè, chiaro, bianchi**
ci	before *a, o,* and u, like *ch* in "cherry": **ciao, cioccolata, ciuffo**
d	like English *d* in "dance": **dedalo, davanti, dove**
g	before *a, o,* and *u,* like English *g* in "go": **gara, lago, gufo**
g	before *e* and *i,* like English *g* in "gem": **gelo, giro, vagito.** If the *i* is unstressed and followed by another vowel, its sound is unheard, as in English "joke": **giovane, giacca, giocare, giugno**
gh	(used only before *e* and *i*) like English *g* in "go": **ghirlanda, fughe, laghi**

gli   sounds somewhat like *-lli-* in "million": **egli, migliore, figlia.** However *gli* is pronounced hard like English "negligence" 1) when it is initial (except in the article *gli*) as in *glioma,* 2) when it is preceded by a consonant as in *ganglio,* and 3) when it is followed by a consonant as in *negligenza.*

gn   sounds approximately like *ni* in "onion": **lavagna, signore, legno.**

gu   sounds like English *gw* in "Gwen": **guerra, guida, guasto.**

h   is always silent: *ho, hai, ha, ah.*

l   like English *l* in "lamb": **lana, lavoro, levare**

m   like English *m* in "money": **male, merito, moto**

n   like English *n* in "net": **nano, nebbia, nido**

p   like English *p* in "pot," but without the aspiration that sometimes accompanies the English sound: **porta, ape, lupa**

qu   like English *qu* in "quart": **questo, quasi, quinto**

r   is well trilled and pronounced with the tip of the tongue against the upper front teeth: **rosa, mare, ora.**

s   has two sounds: 1) when it is followed by a vowel, it is called "pure" and sounds like English hard *s* in "some": **sale, falso;** 2) when it is followed by a consonant (except *p*), especially at the beginning of a word, it is called "impure" and sounds like English soft *s* in "rose" or *z* in "zero": **sbaglio, svenire, snello.**

sc   before *a, o,* and *u,* like English *sk* in "skip": **scatola, scopo, scusa**

sc   before *e* or *i,* like English *sh* in "ship": **scena, scelta, scivolare**

sch   has the sound of English *sc* in "scope" or English *sch* in "school": **schiavo, dischi, mosche, schema, maschio.**

t   like English *t* in "table": **tale, tutto, patire**

z   sometimes sounds like English *ts* in "nuts": **grazia, forza, zucchero;** sometimes like English *dz* in "adze": **zero, mezzo, zelo.**

Double Consonants

In Italian, double consonants are longer and more emphatic than single consonants, it takes much more time and force to pronounce them: **mamma fratello battaglia cappello atto pelle bocca tetto.**

Stress

Generally, Italian words are stressed on the last syllable but one, that is, the penultimate syllable: cu**ci**na vo**ta**re col**la**na ma**ti**ta.

Sometimes the words are stressed on the last syllable but two, that is ante-penultimate syllable: *ma*gico *lo*gico *al*bero dif*fi*cile.

In certain cases the words are stressed on the last syllable but three: *co*llocano por*ta*temelo *ec*cotelo and an*dan*dosene.

In certain cases the words are stressed on the last syllable: cit*tà* volon*tà* caf*fè* vir*tù*.

Rhythm and Intonation

Intonation in Italian is dictated by the speaker's feelings. However, as a general rule, intonation can be:

  a. rising at the end of a "yes"/"no" question: **Sei stato promosso?**

  b. falling at the end of an affirmative or a negative sentence, or interrogative sentence introduced by an interrogative word:

  Carlo legge sempre i giornali.

  c. unchanged in the everyday expressions: **Mi lasci passare** or **Grazie tante.**

Accents

l'accento acuto indicates the closed sound of *e* and *o:* **caténa, méla, concórso, ancóra.**

l'accento grave indicates the open sound of *e* and *o:* **cancellò, modèstia, nòtte, còro**

l'accento circonflesso is seldom used, except in poetry. It indicates contraction or syncope: **amâr,** instead of **amarono; vizî,** instead of **vizii.**

Punctuation Marks

,	la virgola
.	il punto fermo
:	i due punti
;	il punto e virgola
...	i puntini sospensivi (i puntini di sospensione)
?	il punto interrogativo
!	il punto esclamativo
( )	le parentesi tonde
[ ]	le parentesi quadre
" "	le virgolette
« »	le virgolette
'	l'apostrofo
-	il tratto d'unione (trattino)
___	la lineetta (stanghetta)
=	le lineette
¨	la dieresi
*	l'asterisco (stelletta)

2. Regular Verbs—
The Simple Tense Forms

Subject Pronouns

The following are the subject pronouns in Italian:

Singular		Plural	
1. **io**	I	1. **noi**	we
2. **tu**	you (*familiar*)	2. **voi**	you (*familiar*)
3. **Lei**	you (*polite*)	3. **Loro**	you (*polite*)
egli, lui, esso	he, it (*m*).	**essi, loro**	they (*m.*)
ella, lei, essa	she, it (*f.*)	**esse, loro**	they (*f.*)

The infinitives of Italian verbs have one of three possible endings: *-are* (first conjugation), *-ere* (second conjugation), or *ire* (third conjugation). Each of these infinitive endings displays a characteristic vowel (*vocale tematica*): *a,* indicating the first conjugation; *e,* the second conjugation; and *i,* the third conjugation.

parlare	to speak	**vend**ere	to sell
sentire	to listen	**cap**ire	to understand

An infinitive without its ending is called the *stem.* To conjugate a verb in the simple tenses, drop the endings of the infinitive and add the appropriate endings to the stem.

parlare	**egli parl**a	he speaks
vendere	**noi vend**iamo	we sell
capire	**io capirò**	I will understand

Simple Tenses of the Indicative Mood

1. Present	*Il presente dell'indicativo*
	(L'indicativo presente)
2. Imperfect	*L' imperfetto*
3. Simple past	*Il passato remoto*
4. Future	*Il futuro*

Conditional Mood

Present Conditional	*Il presente del condizionale*
	(Il condizionale presente)

Imperative Mood

Imperative

*Il presente dell'imperativo
(L'imperativo presente)*

Participle

Participle

*Il presente del participio
(Il participio presente)*

Gerundive

Gerund

*Il presente del gerundio
(Il gerundio presente)*

The Present Tense

The present tense expresses an action or a state that is taking place at the moment of speech. It is formed by adding the appropriate endings to the stem of the infinitive. Note that the Italian present tense not only expresses the English simple present but also the emphatic and the progressive present tenses. Therefore **io lavoro** may mean:

I work.
I do work.
I am working.

First Conjugation, *-are* Verbs

To form the present tense of first conjugation verbs, the following endings are added to the verb stem.

parlare, to speak
I speak, do speak, am speaking, etc.

io	parl*o*	noi	parl*iamo*
tu	parl*i*	voi	parl*ate*
Lei	parl*a*	Loro	parl*ano*
egli, lui, esso	parl*a*	essi, loro	parl*ano*
ella, lei, essa	parl*a*	esse, loro	parl*ano*

Io parl*o* italiano.	I am speaking Italian.
	or I speak Italian.
I ragazzi parl*ano* male.	The boys speak badly.
Tu e Carlo parl*ate* spagnolo.	You and Carl speak Spanish.
Anna parl*a* bene.	Anne speaks well.

Sample Verbs of the First Conjugation

abitare	to live, to reside	**desiderare**	to wish, to desire
aiutare	to help	**domandare**	to ask
amare	to love	**entrare**	to enter
arrivare	to arrive	**guardare**	to look at
ascoltare	to listen (to)	**imparare**	to learn
aspettare	to wait	**incontrare**	to meet
baciare	to kiss	**insegnare**	to teach
ballare	to dance	**lavare**	to wash
cambiare	to change	**lavorare**	to work
camminare	to walk	**mandare**	to send
cantare	to sing	**mangiare**	to eat
cenare	to have supper	**pagare**	to pay
cercare	to seek, to look for	**salutare**	to greet
chiamare	to call	**studiare**	to study
comprare	to buy	**visitare**	to visit

Second Conjugation, *-ere* Verbs

vendere, to sell
I sell, do sell, am selling, etc.

io	vend*o*	noi	vend*iamo*
tu	vend*i*	voi	vend*ete*
Lei	vend*e*	Loro	vend*ono*
egli, lui, esso	vend*e*	essi, loro	vend*ono*
ella, lei, essa	vend*e*	esse, loro	vend*ono*

Il macellaio vend*e* la carne.	The butcher sells meat.
Noi vend*iamo* la nostra casa.	We are selling our house.
Tu e Giovanni vend*ete* i giornali	You and John are selling newspapers.
Maria e Lisa vend*ono* i fiori.	Mary and Lisa sell flowers.
Io vend*o* i libri.	I sell books.
Tu vend*i* le caramelle.	You sell candies.

Sample Verbs of the Second Conjugation

accendere	to light, to turn on	**prendere**	to take
battere	to hit, to beat, to knock	**promettere**	to promise
chiedere	to ask	**proteggere**	to protect
chiudere	to close	**ricevere**	to receive
comprendere	to understand	**ripetere**	to repeat
conoscere	to know	**rispondere**	to respond
correre	to run	**rompere**	to break
credere	to believe	**scendere**	to descend
decidere	to decide	**scrivere**	to write
dividere	to divide	**spendere**	to spend
godere	to enjoy	**temere**	to fear
leggere	to read	**vedere**	to see
mettere	to put	**vincere**	to win
perdere	to lose	**vivere**	to live, to reside

Third Conjugation, *-ire* Verbs

The verbs of the third conjugation fall into two groups: 1. those that are conjugated like *sentire* and 2. those conjugated like *capire.* The endings for both groups are identical, but verbs of the *capire* type insert *isc* between the stem and all endings of the singular and the third-person plural.

sentire, to feel, to hear, to listen to, to smell
I feel, I do feel, I am feeling, I hear, I do hear, I am hearing, etc.

Singular		Plural	
io	sent*o*	noi	sent*iamo*
tu	sent*i*	voi	sent*ite*
Lei	sent*e*	Loro	sent*ono*
egli, lui, esso	sent*e*	essi, loro	sent*ono*
ella, lei, essa	sent*e*	esse, loro	sent*ono*

Sent*o* un odore di pizza.	I smell pizza.
Non sent*i* il rumore del traffico?	Don't you hear the noise of the traffic?
Sent*iamo* un disco di Pavarotti.	We are listening to a Pavarotti record.
Sent*ono* il maestro spiegare la lezione.	They are listening to the teacher explain the lesson.
Lui non sent*e* il mio consiglio.	He doesn't listen to my advice.
Non sent*ite* quello che diciamo.	You aren't listening to what we're saying.

Sample Verbs of the Third Conjugation—*Sentire-Type*

aprire	to open	partire	to depart, to leave
bollire	to boil	scoprire	to discover
coprire	to cover	seguire	to follow
dormire	to sleep	servire	to serve
fuggire	to flee	soffrire	to suffer
offrire	to offer	vestire	to dress

capire, to understand
I understand, I do understand, I am understanding, etc.

io	cap*isco*	noi	cap*iamo*
tu	cap*isci*	voi	cap*ite*
Lei	cap*isce*	Loro	cap*iscono*
egli, lui, esso	cap*isce*	essi, loro	cap*iscono*
ella, lei, essa	cap*isce*	esse, loro	cap*iscono*

Io cap*isco* quello che dici.	I understand what you are saying.
Cap*iscono* la poesia di Dante.	They understand Dante's poetry.
Cap*isci* il nostro libro di biologia?	Do you understand our biology book?
Maria non cap*isce* Giacomo.	Maria doesn't understand James.
Noi non cap*iamo* perchè ridono.	We don't understand why they are laughing.
Non cap*ite* quello che leggete.	You don't understand what you're reading.

Sample Verbs of the Third Conjugation—*Capire-Type*

ardire	to dare to	**preferire**	to prefer
costruire	to build	**proibire**	to forbid
disobbedire	to disobey	**pulire**	to clean
fornire	to furnish	**punire**	to punish
guarire	to heal	**spedire**	to send, to mail
obbedire	to obey	**suggerire**	to suggest

The present tense is often used:

1. Instead of the future, to describe an action in the future that is considered certain or to give the action greater vividness;

La cerimonia comincia alle nove.	The ceremony will start at nine o'clock.
Stasera lo vedo e gli parlo.	Tonight I'll see him and I'll speak to him.

2. To replace the preterite to make the past more vivid and graphic;

Egli ascolta, non capisce niente e si mette subito a dormire.	He listened, understood nothing, and soon fell asleep.
Arrivano i pompieri e domano l'incendio.	The firemen arrived and got the fire under control.

3. To express an action or state that began in the past and continues in the present.

Lavoro qui da maggio.	I have been working here since May.
Studio l'italiano da tre mesi.	I have been studying Italian for three months.

Note: The preposition *da* translates as both "since" and "for."

Negative Form

To form the negative in Italian, *non* is placed before the verb.

Io *non* parlo italiano.	I don't speak Italian.
Tu *non* parli bene.	You don't speak well.

However, when an object pronoun precedes the verb, *non* is placed before the object pronoun and *not* before the verb.

Non lo **mando a scuola.**	I don't send him to school.
Non la **rimprovero spesso.**	I don't scold her often.

Interrogative Form

There are 3 possible ways to form a question in Italian:

1. Place the subject after the verb.

Studia *Lei* molto?	Do you study a lot?

2. If the sentence is short, you may place the subject at the end of the question.

Studia molto *Lei?*	Do you study a lot?

3. In spoken Italian, you may also raise the inflection of the voice at the end of a statement.

Lei **studia molto?**	Do you study a lot?

Negative Interrogative Form

To form the negative interrogative, place *non* before the verb.

Non **studia Lei molto?**	
Non **studia molto Lei?**	Aren't you studying a lot?
Lei *non* **studia molto?**	
Non **rispetti più il tuo maestro?**	Don't you respect your teacher any longer?

Note: An affirmative or negative sentence can be changed into a question by adding to it expressions such as *vero?, non è vero?, è vero?, no?, va bene?, intesi?, d'accordo?.*

Lui è venuto, *non è vero?*	He did come, didn't he?
Giovanni non va più in città, *vero?*	John does not go to the city anymore, does he?
Ci vediamo domani, *va bene?*	See you tomorrow, all right?

The Imperfect Tense

The imperfect tense (also called the *past descriptive)* is formed by adding the characteristic vowel (*a, e,* or *i*) to the respective stems and the following endings, which are the same for all three conjugations: *-vo, -vi, -va, -vamo, -vate, -vano.*

parlare, to speak
I was speaking, used to speak, etc.

io	parl*avo*	**noi**	parl*avamo*
tu	parl*avi*	**voi**	parl*avate*
Lei	parl*ava*	**Loro**	parl*avano*
egli, lui, esso	parl*ava*	**essi, loro**	parl*avano*
ella, lei, essa	parl*ava*	**esse, loro**	parl*avano*

vendere, to sell
I was selling, used to sell, etc.

io	vend*evo*	**noi**	vend*evamo*
tu	vend*evi*	**voi**	vend*evate*
Lei	vend*eva*	**Loro**	vend*evano*
egli, lui, esso	vend*eva*	**essi, loro**	vend*evano*
ella, lei, essa	vend*eva*	**esse, loro**	vend*evano*

capire, to understand
I was understanding, used to understand, etc.

io	cap*ivo*	noi	cap*ivamo*
tu	cap*ivi*	voi	cap*ivate*
Lei	cap*iva*	Loro	cap*ivano*
egli, lui, esso	cap*iva*	essi, loro	cap*ivano*
ella, lei, essa	cap*iva*	esse, loro	cap*ivano*

The imperfect tense is used to describe:

1. Physical, mental, emotional states that existed in the past and other past conditions such as weather, time, and age.

Egli *soffriva* **un mal di testa.**	He had a headache.
Faceva **molto freddo.**	It was very cold.
Aveva **quindici anni.**	He was fifteen years old.
Erano **le undici di sera.**	It was 11:00 P.M.
Il mare *era* **calmo, la spiaggia** (*era*) **deserta.** *Regnava* **dappertutto un silenzio assoluto.**	The sea was calm and the beach (was) deserted. Absolute silence prevailed.

2. A customary, habitual, or repeated action in the past, not what happened, but what *used to happen,* or *would happen regularly.* This is ordinarily expressed in English by "used to" + the infinitive or "would" + the verb.

Giorgio *studiava* **la lezione tutti i giorni.**	George studied (*or* used to study) the lesson every day.
Giuseppe *andava* **al cinema ogni sabato.**	Joseph went (*or* would go) to the movies every Saturday.
Mio padre *usciva* **di casa alle sette del mattino.**	My father left (*or* used to leave) the house at 7:00 A.M.

3. An action that was going on in the past when something else happened or was happening.

Mentre io *leggevo,* **essi** *studiavano.*	While I was reading, they were studying.
Pranzavo **quando lui è entrato.**	I was having dinner when he entered.

The Simple Past Tense *(Passato Remoto)*

The simple past tense (also called *past absolute)* describes an action or event that took place at a specific time in the past.

Michelangelo *scolpì* **la Pietà.**	Michelangelo sculpted the Pietà.
Cristoforo Colombo *salpò* **da Palos.**	Christopher Columbus sailed from Palos
Le rose *fiorirono* **nel giardino.**	The roses bloomed in the garden.
I soldati *attraversarono* **il ponte.**	The soldiers crossed the bridge.
I contadini *piantarono* **gli alberi.**	The farmers planted the trees.

It is used only in formal speech or writing and is usually found in literature. Its equivalent in conversation and informal writing is the present perfect *(passato prossimo)*. The simple past tense is formed by adding appropriate endings to the stem of the infinitive as follows:

parlare, to speak

I spoke, did speak, you spoke, did speak, etc.

Singular		Plural	
io	parl*ai*	noi	parl*ammo*
tu	parl*asti*	voi	parl*aste*
Lei	parl*ò*	Loro	parl*arono*
egli, lui, esso	parl*ò*	essi, loro	parl*arono*
ella, lei, essa	parl*ò*	esse, loro	parl*arono*

vendere, to sell

I sold, did sell, you sold, did sell etc.

Singular		Plural	
io	vend*ei* (vend*etti*)	noi	vend*emmo*
tu	vend*esti*	voi	vend*este*
Lei	vend*è* (vend*ette*)	Loro	vend*erono* (vend*ettero*)
egli, lui, esso	vend*è* (vend*ette*)	essi, loro	vend*erono* (vend*ettero*)
ella, lei, essa	vend*è* (vend*ette*)	esse, loro	vend*erono* (vend*ettero*)

Note: Most **-ere** verbs (except those ending in **-ttere** and **-ssere**) have an alternate set of endings for the first- and third-persons singular and the third-person plural.

I turisti god*erono* **la visita al museo.**	The tourists enjoyed the visit to the museum.

or:

I turisti god*ettero* **la visita al museo.**	The tourists enjoyed the visit to the museum.

capire, to understand
I understood, did understand, you understood,
did understand, etc.

Singular		Plural	
io	cap*ii*	noi	cap*immo*
tu	cap*isti*	voi	cap*iste*
Lei	cap*ì*	Loro	cap*irono*
egli, lui, esso	cap*ì*	essi, loro	cap*iróno*
ella, lei, essa	cap*ì*	esse, loro	cap*irono*

Note: The imperfect and the simple past may appear in the same sentence. The imperfect expresses action that was going on at the time another action took place.

Arrivai **a casa sua, mentre lui** *usciva.*	I arrived at his house while he was going out.
Poichè *aveva* **abbastanza denaro,** *comprò* **una macchina nuova.**	Since he had enough money, he bought a new car.
Mentre *leggevo,* **il campanello** *suonó.*	While I was reading, the doorbell rang.

The Future Tense

The future tense expresses an action that will occur *after* the present.

Io *ritornerò* **a casa domani mattina.**	I'll come back to my house tomorrow morning.
Noi *studieremo* **tutta l'estate.**	We'll study all summer.
Voi *lavorerete* **fino alle nove.**	You'll be working until nine o'clock.
Lui *metterà* **in ordine la casa.**	He will put the house in order.
Lo spettacolo *finirà* **alle undici.**	The show will end at eleven o'clock.

The future tense is formed by adding the appropriate future endings to the stem of the infinitive, as follows:

parlare, to speak
I will speak, you will speak, etc.

Singular		Plural	
io	parl*erò*	noi	parl*eremo*
tu	parl*erai*	voi	parl*erete*
Lei	parl*erà*	Loro	parl*eranno*
egli, lui, esso	parl*erà*	essi, loro	parl*eranno*
ella, lei, essa	parl*erà*	esse, loro	parl*eranno*

vendere to sell
I will sell, you will sell, etc.

	Singular		Plural
io	vender*ò*	noi	vender*emo*
tu	vender*ai*	voi	vender*ete*
Lei	vender*à*	Loro	vender*anno*
egli, lui, esso	vender*à*	essi, loro	vender*anno*
ella, lei, essa	vender*à*	esse, loro	vender*anno*

capire, to understand
I will understand, you will understand, etc.

	Singular		Plural
io	cap*irò*	noi	cap*iremo*
tu	cap*irai*	voi	cap*irete*
Lei	cap*irà*	Loro	cap*iranno*
egli, lui, esso	cap*irà*	essi, loro	cap*iranno*
ella, lei, essa	cap*irà*	esse, loro	cap*iranno*

Note: In addition to its usual function of expressing actions, the future tense is also used idiomatically to express uncertainty, probability, conjecture, deduction, or supposition concerning an action in the present (the *futuro anteriore* expresses probability in the past).

Chi *sarà?*	I wonder who he is. (Who can he be?)
Antonio *avrà* **quattordici anni.**	Anthony is probably fourteen years old.
Sento bussare alla porta. *Sarà* **il postino.**	I hear knocking at the door. I suppose it is the mailman.

The Conditional Mood

1. The conditional mood is formed by adding the appropriate endings to the infinitive stem; as follows:

parlare, to speak
I would speak, you would speak, etc.

io	parl*erei*	noi	parl*eremmo*
tu	parl*eresti*	voi	parl*ereste*
Lei	parl*erebbe*	Loro	parl*erebbero*
egli, lui, esso	parl*erebbe*	essi, loro	parl*erebbero*
ella, lei, essa	parl*erebbe*	esse, loro	parl*erebbero*

vendere, to sell
I would sell, you would sell, etc.

io	venderei	noi	venderemmo
tu	venderesti	voi	vendereste
Lei	venderebbe	Loro	venderebbero
egli, lui, esso	venderebbe	essi, loro	venderebbero
ella, lei, essa	venderebbe	esse, loro	venderebbero

capire, to understand
I would understand, you would understand, etc.

io	capirei	noi	capiremmo
tu	capiresti	voi	capireste
Lei	capirebbe	Loro	capirebbero
egli, lui, esso	capirebbe	essi, loro	capirebbero
ella, lei, essa	capirebbe	esse, loro	capirebbero

2. The conditional mood is used to express an action that may occur in the future. It usually corresponds to the English "would" + the verb.

Andrebbe, **se possibile.**	He would go if possible.
Visiteremmo **Napoli, ma non abbiamo tempo.**	We would visit Naples, but we don't have the time.
Avendo i soldi, *comprerei* **uno yacht.**	Having the money, I would buy a yacht.

Note: As stated, the conditional is normally expressed in English by "would" + the verb. However, when "would" actually means "used to," it is translated into Italian by the imperfect tense.

| *Scriveva* **una volta al mese.** | He would (*or* used to) write once a month. |

3. The conditional also translates the English modal auxiliaries "should" (conditional of *dovere*) and "could" (conditional of *potere*).

| *Dovrei* **studiare di più.** | I should study more. |
| *Potresti* **aggiustarlo?** | Could you fix it? |

4. The conditional is frequently used to express what *would happen* (result) if (*se*) something else *were true* right now (condition contrary-to-fact). In this kind of *se* sentence, there are generally two verbs: 1. the verb that follows *se,* which is in the subjunctive and 2. the other verb (in the result clause), which is in the conditional.

| Se *avessi* **più denaro,** *comprerei* **una macchina nuova.** | If I had more money, I would buy a new car. |
| Se **Lei** *m'invitasse,* **io** *verrei.* | If you invited me, I would come. |

These are "contrary-to-fact" sentences, since they describe conditions that are contrary to what actually exists. "If I had more money, I would buy a new car" implies that I am *not* buying a new car because I do *not* have enough money.

5. The conditional is often used instead of the present to soften a statement or a request, as well as to express wishes or preferences.

Non *saprei* **cosa dirvi.**	I do not know what to tell you.
Vorrei **parlare col direttore.**	I would like to speak to the manager.
Desidererei **un po' di denaro.**	I'd like some money.
Preferirei **una tazza di tè.**	I would prefer a cup of tea.

6. The conditional is also used to express a conjecture or a rumor.

Comprerebbe **una casa nuova?**	Is he actually going to buy a new house?
Il governo *aumenterebbe* **le tasse.**	It is rumored the government is going to raise taxes.

Note: The conditional of *fare meglio a* plus the infinitive translates the English "had better."

Farebbero **meglio a lavorare tutti i giorni.**	They had better work every day.
Faresti **meglio a studiare la grammatica italiana.**	You had better study Italian grammar.

7. Note that, when expressing a future action from the standpoint of the past, Italian uses the *past conditional,* unlike English which uses the present conditional.

Mario ha detto che *sarebbe andato* **al teatro con noi.**	Mario said that he would go to the theater with us.
Maria disse che *avrebbe fatto* **il viaggio.**	Maria said that she would take the trip.
Giorgio aveva promesso che *avrebbe lavorato* **di più.**	George had promised that he would work harder.

(For the formation and uses of the past conditional, see p. 33.)

The Imperative Mood

The imperative is a mood of action. It is used to command, persuade, exhort, wish, with the intent of getting a result. The imperative has five forms, corresponding to *tu, Lei, noi, voi,* and *Loro.* Here they are:

	parlare, to speak (Speak! Let's speak! Let them speak!)	*vendere,* to sell (Sell! Let's sell! Let them sell!)
(tu)	**parl***a*	**vend***i*
(Lei)	**parl***i*	**vend***a*
(noi)	**parl***iamo*	**vend***iamo*
(voi)	**parl***ate*	**vend***ete*
(Loro)	**parl***ino*	**vend***ano*

	capire, to understand (Understand! Let's understand! Let them understand!)	*sentire,* to feel, to listen, to hear (Feel! Let's feel! Let them feel!)
(tu)	cap*isci*	sen*ti*
(Lei)	cap*isca*	sen*ta*
(noi)	cap*iamo*	sent*iamo*
(voi)	cap*ite*	sent*ite*
(Loro)	cap*iscano*	sent*ano*

1. Strictly speaking only the second-person singular is imperative. The third-person singular and the third-person plural are forms of the present subjunctive, while the first- and second-person plural are forms of the present indicative.

2. The third-person singular and the third-person plural are called *polite command forms.* All the others are called *familiar command forms.* With the polite command forms, the direct and indirect object pronouns (except *Loro*) and the reflexive pronouns are placed before the verb.

Ecco il giornale; *lo* **legga!**	Here is the newspaper; read it!
Ecco mio fratello; *gli* **parli, per piacere.**	Here is my brother; please, speak to him!
Ecco i ragazzi; parli *loro!*	Here are the boys; talk to them!
Si **pettini i capelli!**	Comb your hair!

3. The subject pronouns are generally omitted with the imperative, unless one wants to add emphasis or call attention to the person.

Parla piano!	Speak slowly!
Aprite le finestre!	Open the windows!
Vendi la macchina a Paolo!	Sell your car to Paul!
Parli *Lei!*	*You* talk!
Lei **legga quello che vuole!**	*You* read what you want!

4. The first-person plural of the imperative (the *noi* form) is used to express commands or to make suggestions to a group of people of which the speaker is a member. It translates the English "Let's."

Finiamo **il lavoro!**	Let's finish the work!
Diamo **un'offerta alla chiesa!**	Let's give a donation to the church!
Facciamo **un passo avanti!**	Let's take a step forward!
Chiudiamo **la porta!**	Let's close the door!
Studiamo **la grammatica italiana!**	Let's study Italian grammar!

Negative Imperative

Generally the imperative is made negative by placing *non* before the affirmative imperative.

Non parlate **(voi) all'autista.**	Do not speak to the driver.
Non vendiamo **(noi) la casa.**	Let's not sell the house.
Non apra **(Lei) la finestra.**	Do not open the window.
Non ascoltino **(Loro) quel programma.**	Do not listen to that program.

However, the negative of the familiar singular *(tu)* imperative is formed by placing *non* before the infinitive.

Non parlare **(tu) a quel ragazzo.**	Do not talk to that boy.
Non vendere **(tu) la bicicletta.**	Do not sell the bicycle.
Non partire **(tu) adesso.**	Do not leave now.

The Infinitive

The endings of the simple (or *present*) infinitive are: *-are, -ere,* and *-ire.*

parlare	to speak	**vendere**	to sell
sentire	to hear, to listen, to feel.	**capire**	to understand

1. The infinitive is often used after an adjective or a verb to complete the meaning of the sentence.

E' bello *passeggiare* **lungo il fiume.**	It is beautiful to walk along the river.
Mi piace *ballare.*	I like to dance
Vuole (Lei) *venire* **in ufficio e** *parlare* **con il signor Rossi?**	Do you want to come in the office and (to) speak with Mr. Rossi?

2. In Italian, an infinitive is used to express an action after a preposition, whereas, in English, a present participle is used.

Prima di uscire, **(io) leggo il giornale.**	Before going out, I read the newspaper.
Nel leggere **quel libro, incontrai molte difficoltà.**	In reading that book, I found many difficulties.

3. The infinitive is also used in impersonal commands and suggestions, as on traffic signs or in recipes.

Moderare **la velocità.**	Moderate your speed.
Tagliare **a pezzi la carne.**	Cut the meat in pieces.

4. In Italian, the infinitive may be used as a verbal noun (with or without the article). In other words, it may be used as subject, object, or predicate nominative. In English, we use either the infinitive or the gerund to express a verbal noun.

(Il) viaggiare è **molto divertente.**   To travel (Traveling) is very
                                              amusing.
Lavorare è *guadagnare.*   Working is earning.

The Present Gerund

1. The Italian gerund form of the verb translates the English present participle (ending in -*ing*) if the present participle has a *verbal* function.

Camminando **per la strada**   Walk*ing* down the street, I met
   incontrai Giovanni.   John.

In Italian, the infinitive form of the verb is sometimes used to translate the English gerund (also ending in -*ing*). The English gerund has a *noun* function.

Mi piace *cantare.*   I like sing*ing.*

The present (or simple) gerund in Italian is formed by adding -*ando* to the stem of the verbs of the first conjugation and -*endo* to the stem of the verbs of the second and third conjugation.

parlare/parl*ando*   **vendere/vend***endo*   **sentire/sent***endo*

2. The present gerund is invariable. That is, it does not agree with the word it modifies. Its subject is normally the same as the subject of the main clause, unless a different subject is specified.

I ragazzi, *vedendo* **l'animale,**   The boys, seeing the animal, ran
   scapparono.   away.
Parlando **con i suoi amici,**   Talking to his friends, Robert
   Roberto apprese la verità.   learned the truth.

However, to avoid ambiguity when there are different subjects, a subordinate clause usually replaces the present gerund.

L'ho visto *che partiva.*   I saw him leave. *or* I saw him
                                       while he was leaving.

instead of:
L'ho visto *partendo.*

3. The present gerund may express the condition under which a principal action takes place.

Le ragazze passarono tutto il   The girls spent the whole day
   giorno *lavorando* **nel giardino.**   working in the garden.

4. The present gerund may also express an action that takes place at the same time as the action of the main clause. It then translates as "in," "upon," "by," "while," plus a verb form in *-ing.*

Ascoltando **la radio, imparo molte canzoni.**	By listening to the radio, I learn many songs.
Passeggiando **per il parco, vidi tuo fratello.**	Walking through the park, I saw your brother.

However, the action of the present gerund may occur *before* and not at the same time as the action of the main clause.

Uscì *lasciando* **la porta aperta.**	He went out leaving the door open.
Morì *perdonando* **ai suoi nemici.**	He died forgiving his enemies.

5. The present gerund is also used with the construction verb *stare* to stress the duration or continuation of an action. This construction is called the *progressive form,* and it is less common than the equivalent in English.

Il maestro *sta spiegando* **la lezione.**	The teacher is explaining the lesson.
Stavano cogliendo **le rose, quando cominciò a piovere.**	They were gathering roses, when it started to rain.

Note: a. This construction is not possible with any past tenses except the imperfect. Thus the English "I have been waiting all day" is translated as either *Ho aspettato tutto il giorno* or *Sono stato tutto il giorno ad aspettare.*

b. Similarly, the passive construction is avoided and is replaced either by a *si* construction or by the active form. Thus the English, "Dinner is being served," is translated as either *Si sta servendo il pranzo,* or *Stanno servendo il pranzo.*

The Participle

1. To form the simple (or *present)* participle, add *-ante* to the stem of first-conjugation infinitives and *-ente* to the stem of second- and third-conjugation infinitives.

parl*are***/parl***ante* speaking	**cred***ere***/cred***ente* be-lieving	**part***ire***/part***ente* leaving

2. The present participle is a verbal adjective. As such, it agrees in gender and number with the noun it modifies.

Il mio amico, *sorridente,* **aspettava alla stazione.**	My friend, smiling, was waiting at the station.
Gli uccelli, *tremanti,* **volarono via.**	The birds, trembling, flew away.
Nelle lezioni *seguenti* **studieremo i pronomi.**	In the following lessons, we will study the pronouns.

3. Sometimes the present participle is used as a noun.

Franco è il mio *aiutante.*	Frank is my helper.
I *cantanti* **italiani sono famosi.**	Italian singers are famous.
Gli *insegnanti* **e gli** *studenti* **vanno a scuola.**	The teachers and the students are going to school.

4. At times, the present participle is used as a preposition.

Lo vedrò *durante* **l'estate.**	I shall see him during the summer.
Nonostante **i suoi difetti, è un buon uomo.**	In spite of his faults, he is a good man.

5. Very rarely, the present participle is used as a verb. In such cases, it can be replaced by a temporal or relative clause.

Vedemmo l'uomo *errante* (or *mentre errava,* or *che errava*) **per le vie della città.**	We saw the man wandering through the streets of the city.
Vivente (or *Mentre visse,* or *Finchè visse)* **Antonio, la famiglia era tutta unita.**	While Anthony was alive, the whole family stayed together.

Endings of Simple Tenses

Indicative Mood

	-are		**-ere**	
Present	stem *o*	___ *iamo*	___ *o*	___ *iamo*
	___ *i*	___ *ate*	___ *i*	___ *ete*
	___ *a*	___ *ano*	___ *e*	___ *ono*
Imperfect	___ *avo*	___ *avamo*	___ *evo*	___ *evamo*
	___ *avi*	___ *avate*	___ *evi*	___ *evate*
	___ *ava*	___ *avano*	___ *eva*	___ *evano*
Simple Past	___ *ai*	___ *ammo*	___ *ei (etti)*	___ *emmo*
	___ *asti*	___ *aste*	___ *esti*	___ *este*
	___ *ò*	___ *rono*	___ *è (ette)*	___ *erono (ettero)*
Future	___ *erò*	___ *eremo*	___ *erò*	___ *eremo*
	___ *erai*	___ *erete*	___ *erai*	___ *erete*
	___ *erà*	___ *eranno*	___ *erà*	___ *eranno*

Conditional Mood

Present	___ *erei*	___ *eremmo*	___ *erei*	___ *eremmo*
	___ *eresti*	___ *ereste*	___ *eresti*	___ *ereste*
	___ *erebbe*	___ *erebbero*	___ *erebbe*	___ *erebbero*

Imperative Mood

Present	___ *a*	___ *i*
	___ *i*	___ *a*
	___ *iamo*	___ *iamo*
	___ *ate*	___ *ete*
	___ *ino*	___ *ano*

Indicative Mood

-ire

Present	____ o	____ iamo
	____ i	____ ite
	____ e	____ ono

Imperfect	____ ivo	____ ivamo
	____ ivi	____ ivate
	____ iva	____ ivano

Simple Past	____ ii	____ immo
	____ isti	____ iste
	____ ì	____ irono

Future	____ irò	____ iremo
	____ irai	____ irete
	____ irà	____ iranno

Conditional Mood

Present	____ irei	____ iremmo
	____ iresti	____ ireste
	____ irebbe	____ irebbero

Imperative Mood

Present	____ i
	____ a
	____ iamo
	____ ite
	____ ano

Verb Synopsis

In a synopsis, any form of the verb is given in all the tenses.

parlare — *io*

Indicative Mood

Present	io parlo	I speak, I am speaking, I do speak
Imperfect	io parlavo	I used to speak, was speaking
Simple Past	io parlai	I spoke, I did speak
Future	io parlerò	I will speak
Conditional present	io parlerei	I would speak
Imperative (*tu* form)	parla!	speak!

3. Regular Verbs— Auxiliary Verbs and the Perfect Tenses

1. The perfect (or *compound)* tenses are formed by a simple tense form of one of the auxiliary verbs (*avere* or *essere*) and the past participle. The perfect tenses are:

1. Present Perfect	*Passato prossimo*
2. Pluperfect (Past Perfect)	*Trapassato prossimo*
3. Preterite Perfect	*Trapassato remoto*
4. Future Perfect	*Futuro anteriore*
5. Past Subjunctive	*Congiuntivo passato*
6. Pluperfect Subjunctive	*Congiuntivo trapassato*
7. Past Conditional (Conditional Perfect)	*Condizionale passato*
8. Past Infinitive	*Infinito passato*
9. Past Gerund	*Gerundio passato*

2. The simple-tense forms of the two auxiliary verbs in Italian are as follows: **avere**   to have

Present	Imperfect	Simple Past	Future
io ho	**io avevo**	**io ebbi**	**io avrò**
tu hai	**tu avevi**	**tu avesti**	**tu avrai**
egli ha	**egli aveva**	**egli ebbe**	**egli avrà**
noi abbiamo	**noi avevamo**	**noi avemmo**	**noi avremo**
voi avete	**voi avevate**	**voi aveste**	**voi avrete**
essi hanno	**essi avevano**	**essi ebbero**	**essi avranno**

Present Subjunctive	Imperfect Subjunctive	Conditional	Infinitive Present
che io abbia	**che io avessi**	**io avrei**	**avere**
che tu abbia	**che tu avessi**	**tu avresti**	
che egli abbia	**che egli avesse**	**egli avrebbe**	Gerund present
che noi abbiamo	**che noi avessimo**	**noi avremmo**	
che voi abbiate	**che voi aveste**	**voi avreste**	**avendo**
che essi abbiano	**che essi avessero**	**essi avrebbero**	

essere   to be

Present	Imperfect	Simple Past	Future
io sono	io ero	io fui	io sarò
tu sei	tu eri	tu fosti	tu sarai
egli è	egli era	egli fu	egli sarà
noi siamo	noi eravamo	noi fummo	noi saremo
voi siete	voi eravate	voi foste	voi sarete
essi sono	essi erano	essi furono	essi saranno

Present Subjunctive	Imperfect Subjunctive	Conditional	Infinitive
che io sia	che io fossi	io sarei	essere
che tu sia	che tu fossi	tu saresti	
che egli sia	che egli fosse	egli sarebbe	Gerund present
che noi siamo	che noi fossimo	noi saremmo	
che voi siate	che voi foste	voi sareste	essendo
che essi siano	che essi fossero	essi sarebbero	

3. The auxiliary verb *avere* is used with:

   a. transitive verbs (verbs that take a direct object).

Ho mangiato **una mela.**	I ate an apple.
Abbiamo visto **tua madre.**	We have seen your mother.

   b. intransitive verbs (verbs not taking a direct object) that express an action (physical or mental).

Egli *ha sorriso.*	He smiled
La tua presenza mi *ha giovato* **molto.**	Your presence was a great help to me.
Il cane *ha abbaiato.*	The dog barked.

Here are some intransitive verbs (or verbs used as such) that take *avere* as an auxiliary verb.

camminare	to walk	pranzare	to dine
cenare	to have supper	respirare	to breathe
dormire	to sleep	riflettere	to reflect
gridare	to shout	russare	to snore
meditare	to meditate	sonnecchiare	to doze
parlare	to speak	vegliare	to keep awake
pensare	to think	viaggiare	to travel
piangere	to cry		

4. The auxiliary verb *essere* is used:

   a. with reflexive and reciprocal verbs.

Il nemico *si è arreso.*	The enemy has surrendered.
Appena *ci siamo visti, ci siamo* **salutati.**	As soon as we saw each other, we greeted each other.

   b. with most intransitive verbs expressing motion or being.

Maria *è partita* **alle nove.**	Mary left at nine o'clock.
Siamo stati **a casa per tutto il giorno.**	We have been home all day long.

c. with transitive verbs that are used intransitively, that is, in a context where they cannot take a direct object.

Sono diminuito **di peso.**	I have lost weight.
La festa è *finita* **alle undici.**	The party ended at eleven o'clock.

d. in general, with impersonal verbs.

E' piovuto.	It rained.

5. Some verbs take the auxiliary *avere* if they are used in an absolute sense and *essere* if they are followed by a complement, such as a prepositional phrase:

Ho avanzato.	I advanced.
Sono avanzato con lentezza.	I advanced slowly.
Ho saltato.	I jumped.
Sono saltato fuori dal letto.	I jumped out of bed.

Note: It is almost impossible to establish rules that capture all the cases in which *avere* and *essere* are employed. There is also a new optional use of *avere,* which sometimes replaces the traditional *essere,* in sentences such as *Ha piovuto* (traditional *É piovuto*) or *Ha annottato* (traditional *É annottato*).

As a result, it is best to consult a good dictionary for the correct uses of *avere* and *essere.* However, a list of verbs that are usually conjugated with *essere* in compound tenses may be found at the end of this chapter (page 36).

Past Participle

A past participle is formed by adding *-ato* to the stem of *-are* verbs, *-uto* to the stem of *-ere* verbs, and *-ito* to the stem of *-ire* verbs.

cantare	**canta***to*	sung
vendere	**vend***uto*	sold
dormire	**dorm***ito*	slept

Note: See Chapter 8, *Irregular Verbs,* for irregular past participles.

The Present Perfect Tense

The present perfect is formed by the present tense of *avere* and *essere* and the past participle.

vendere, to sell
I have sold, you have sold, etc.

io ho venduto	**noi abbiamo venduto**
tu hai venduto	**voi avete venduto**
egli (ella) ha venduto	**essi (esse) hanno venduto**

arrivare, to arrive

I have arrived, you have arrived, etc.

io sono arrivato *(a)*	noi siamo arrivati *(e)*
tu sei arrivato *(a)*	voi siete arrivati *(e)*
egli (ella) è arrivato *(a)*	essi (esse) sono arrivati *(e)*

The present perfect tense is used to describe an action or a state that happened in the past at a precise moment.

Ha venduto molti libri.	He has sold many books.
Il treno *è arrivato* in orario.	The train has arrived on time.
Mia madre e mia sorella *sono arrivate* a casa.	My mother and my sister came home.

Note: In compound tenses, the negative is placed before the auxiliary verb.

Noi *non abbiamo* venduto la casa.	We have not sold our home.

See Chapter 10, *Sequence of Tenses,* for an explanation of the *imperfetto* versus *passato prossimo.*

Agreement of Past Participles

Verbs Using *avere* as the Auxiliary Verb

1. If a verb is conjugated with *avere,* the past participle generally remains unchanged.

Abbiamo comprat*o* una casa nuova.	We bought a new house.
Hanno portat*o* il pianoforte in casa.	They carried the piano into the house.

2. The past participle *may* agree with the direct object, if the direct object *precedes* the verb.

I libri *che* hanno comprat*i* (or comprat*o)* erano inestimabili.	The books they bought were priceless.
La casa *che* abbiamo comprat*a* (or comprat*o)* è nuova.	The house we bought is new.

3. The past participle agrees with a third-person direct-object pronoun (*lo, la, li, le*), if the direct object pronoun *precedes* the verb.

Ho incontrat*o* una ragazza e *l'*ho (or *la* ho) salutat*a.*	I met a girl and I greeted her.
Ho lett*o* i libri. *Li* ho lett*i.*	I have read the books. I have read them.
Ho comprat*o* delle mele. *Le* ho pagat*e* troppo.	I bought some apples. I paid too much for them.

Note: With the direct object pronouns *mi, ti, ci, vi,* the agreement is optional.

Maria, non ti ho salutat*o* (or **salutat***a)* **perchè non ti ho vist***o* (or **vist***a).*	Mary, I did not greet you because I did not see you.
Ragazze, vi abbiamo sempre ammirat*o* (or **ammirat***e).*	Girls, we have always admired you.

Verbs Using *essere* as the Auxiliary Verb

If the verb is conjugated with *essere,* the past participle agrees with the subject of the verb.

Le ragazze sono partit*e* **per Roma.**	The girls have left for Rome.
Anna è andat*a* **dal dentista.**	Ann went to the dentist's.
I nonni sono arrivat*i* **stamane.**	Our grandparents arrived this morning.
Carlo è venut*o* **solo.**	Carl came alone.

The Pluperfect Tense *(Past Perfect)*

The pluperfect *(trapassato prossimo)* is formed by the imperfect of *avere* or *essere* plus the past participle.

parlare, to speak
I had spoken, etc.

io avevo parlato	**noi avevamo parlato**
tu avevi parlato	**voi avevate parlato**
egli (ella) aveva parlato	**essi (esse) avevano parlato**

partire, to leave
I had left, etc.

io ero partito *(a)*	**noi eravamo partiti** *(e)*
tu eri partito *(a)*	**voi eravate partiti** *(e)*
egli (ella) era partito *(a)*	**essi (esse) erano partiti** *(e)*

The pluperfect is used to express an action that occurred *before* another action in the past (which can be expressed or implied). It is indicated by *had* + the past participle in English ("had run," "had bought," "had seen," etc.).

Giorgio mi ha detto che *aveva parlato* **col maestro.**	George told me that he *had spoken* to the teacher.
Essi *erano partiti* **col treno delle nove quando arrivammo alla stazione.**	They *had left* on the nine o'clock train when we arrived at the station.
Mi *avevano promesso* **un regalo.**	They had promised me a gift.

The Preterite Perfect Tense

The preterite perfect *(trapassato remoto)* is formed by the simple past of *essere* or *avere* and the past participle.

finire, to finish
I finished, you finished, etc.

io ebbi finito	noi avemmo finito
tu avesti finito	voi aveste finito
egli (ella) ebbe finito	essi (esse) ebbero finito

arrivare, to arrive
I arrived, you arrived, etc.

io fui arrivato *(a)*	noi fummo arrivati *(e)*
tu fosti arrivato *(a)*	voi foste arrivati *(e)*
egli (ella) fu arrivato *(a)*	essi (esse) furono arrivati *(e)*

The preterite perfect tense is essentially a literary tense that functions much like the pluperfect to express an action that occurred *before* another action in the past. It is rarely used in conversation.

Quando *ebbero finito* di parlare, uscirono.	When they had finished talking, they went out.
Non appena *fummo* arrivati all'albergo, andammo a dormire.	As soon as we got to the hotel, we went to sleep.

The Future Perfect Tense

The future perfect *(futuro anteriore)* is formed by the future of *essere* or *avere* and the past participle.

imparare, to learn
I will have learned, you will have learned, etc.

io avrò imparato	noi avremo imparato
tu avrai imparato	voi avrete imparato
egli (ella) avrà imparato	essi (esse) avranno imparato

ritornare, to return
I will have returned, you will have returned, etc.

io sarò ritornato *(a)*	noi saremo ritornati *(e)*
tu sarai ritornato *(a)*	voi sarete ritornati *(e)*
egli (ella) sarà ritornato *(a)*	essi (esse) saranno ritornati *(e)*

The future perfect tense is used to express a future action that will occur *before* another future action. It is indicated by *will have* + the past participle in English.

Per domani mattina *avrò* *imparato* **i verbi italiani.**	I will have learned the Italian verbs by tomorrow morning.
Quando *sarò ritornato* **a casa, ti telefonerò.**	When I have returned home, I'll call you.

Note: The future perfect is also used to express probability or conjecture, referring to the past. (See p. 85.)

Egli *avrà telefonato* **alla mamma.**	He has probably called his mother.
Essi *saranno andati* **allo stadio.**	They probably went to the stadium.

The Past Conditional Tense

1. The past conditional *(condizionale passato)* is formed by the conditional of *avere* or *essere* and the past participle.

parlare, to speak
I would have spoken, you would have spoken, etc.

io avrei parlato	**noi avremmo parlato**
tu avresti parlato	**voi avreste parlato**
egli (ella) avrebbe parlato	**essi (esse) avrebbero parlato**

partire, to leave
I would have left, you would have left, etc.

io sarei partito *(a)*	**noi saremmo partiti** *(e)*
tu saresti partito *(a)*	**voi sareste partiti** *(e)*
egli (ella) sarebbe partito *(a)*	**essi (esse) sarebbero partiti** *(e)*

2. The past conditional is used much as it is in English to express an action that *would have happened* (but didn't) in the past.

Tu *avresti parlato* **per difendermi se il giudice non te lo avesse impedito.**	You would have spoken to defend me if the judge hadn't stopped you.
Noi *saremmo partiti* **prima di voi, ma abbiamo dovuto parlare con Giovanni.**	We would have left before you, but we had to speak to John.

3. In Italian, the past conditional is used to express a future action from the standpoint of the past, instead of the present conditional as in English.

Riccardo ha detto che *avrebbe parlato* **col maestro.**	Richard said that he would talk to the teacher.
Sapevo che tu *saresti arrivato* **tardi.**	I knew that you would arrive late.
Ha telefonato che non *sarebbe venuto.*	He telephoned that he would not come.

Note: The conditional perfect is also used to express probability or conjecture, referring to the past.

Lo *avrebbe visto* **martedì scorso.**	He had probably seen him last Tuesday.
Egli forse *sarebbe arrivato* **a farlo.**	He would perhaps have succeeded in doing it.

Perfect Tenses
Verbs with *avere*

Passato Prossimo	*ho* + past participle	*abbiamo* _____
	hai _____	*avete* _____
	ha _____	*hanno* _____
Trapassato Prossimo	*avevo* _____	*avevamo* _____
	avevi _____	*avevate* _____
	aveva _____	*avevano* _____
Trapassato Remoto	*ebbi* _____	*avemmo* _____
	avesti _____	*aveste* _____
	ebbe _____	*ebbero* _____
Futuro Anteriore	*avrò* _____	*avremo* _____
	avrai _____	*avrete* _____
	avrà _____	*avranno* _____
Condizionale Passato	*avrei* _____	*avremmo* _____
	avresti _____	*avreste* _____
	avrebbe _____	*avrebbero* _____

Verbs with *essere*

Passato Prossimo	*sono* + past participle	*siamo* _____	
	sei _____	*siete* _____	
	è _____	*sono* _____	
Trapassato Prossimo	*ero* _____	*eravamo* _____	
	eri _____	*eravate* _____	
	era _____	*erano* _____	
Trapassato Remoto	*fui* _____	*fummo* _____	
	fosti _____	*foste* _____	
	fu _____	*furono* _____	
Futuro Anteriore	*sarò* _____	*saremo* _____	
	sarai _____	*sarete* _____	
	sarà _____	*saranno* _____	
Condizionale Passato	*sarei* _____	*saremmo* _____	
	saresti _____	*sareste* _____	
	sarebbe _____	*sarebbero* _____	

Synopsis of the Perfect Tenses

parlare — *io*

Passato Prossimo	*io ho parlato*	I have spoken, I spoke
Trapassato Prossimo	*io avevo parlato*	I had spoken
Trapassato Remoto	*io ebbi parlato*	I had spoken
Futuro Anteriore	*io avrò parlato*	I will have spoken
Condizionale Passato	*io avrei parlato*	I would have spoken

ritornare — *io*

Passato Prossimo	*io sono ritornato (a)*	I have returned, I returned
Trapassato Prossimo	*io ero ritornato (a)*	I had returned
Trapassato Remoto	*io fui ritornato (a)*	I had returned
Futuro Anteriore	*io sarò ritornato (a)*	I will have returned
Condizionale Passato	*io sarei ritornato (a)*	I would have returned

Verbs Conjugated with *essere* in Compound Tenses

abbronzare, abbrunire, accadere, accedere, accorrere, addivenire, affievolire, afflosciare, affluire, aggradare, allibire, ammuffire, ammutolire, andare, annottare, apparentare, apparire, arrabbiare, arrivare, attempare, attenere, avvampare, avvenire, avvizzire

balenare, bastare, bisognare, brinare

cadere, capitare, cascare, coesistere, comparire, consistere, convenire, costumare, crepare, crescere

decadere, decorrere, decrescere, deperire, derivare, digradare, dilagare, dipendere, dissomigliare, distare

emergere, entrare, esistere

fioccare, fiorire, franare, fuggire

gelare, ghiacciare, giungere, grandinare

imbaldanzire, imbecillire, imbestialire, imbizzarrire, imbronciare, imbrunire, immalinconire, immigrare, impadronire, impallidire, impazientire, impazzire, impermalire, imputridire, inacidire, incagliare, incalvire, incancrenire, incanutire, incappare, incollerire, incorrere, increscere, incretinire, incrudelire, inerpicare, infittire, insorgere, intercorrere, intervenire, intisichire, invalere, inviperire, irrigidire, irrompere, isterilire

levitare

malandare, marcire, muffire

nascere

occorrere

partire, penetrare, perire, piacere, precedere, precorrere, preesistere, putrefare

quagliare

rabbuiare, raddolcire, radicare, raffrescare, raggelare, rampollare, rannuvolare, rasserenare, rassomigliare, restare, rimanere, rimbambire, rinascere, ringalluzzire, rinsavire, rintristire, rovinare, risultare, riuscire.

sbiadire, sbiancare, sbocciare, sbottare, sbucare, scadere, scappare, scarseggiare, scaturire, scavalcare, schiattare, scolare, scomparire, scoppiare, screpolare, sfiorare, sfogare, sfumare, sgorgare, sgusciare, smagrire, soccombere, sopraggiungere, sopravvivere, sorgere, sottostare, sparire, spettare, spiacere, spicciare, spiovere, sporgere, stare, stratificare, stupire, subentrare, svaporare, svenire, svignare.

tarlare, tintinnare, tornare, tracollare, tramontare, tramortire, trapelare, trasumanare.

uscire

venire

4. Reflexive Verbs

1. A verb is called *reflexive* when the subject does something to itself, either directly or indirectly.

Io *mi alzo* **alle sei.**	I get (myself) up at six o'clock.
Giovanni *si lava* **le mani.**	John washes his hands.
Roberto *si compra* **un libro.**	Robert buys a book (for himself).
Voi *vi preparate* **ad uscire.**	You are getting (yourselves) ready to go out.
Maria *si guarda* **allo specchio.**	Mary is looking at herself in the mirror.

2. A reflexive verb is always used with one of the reflexive pronouns: *mi, ti, si* (singular) and *ci, vi, si* (plural). The reflexive pronouns differ from the direct-object pronouns only in the third-person singular and plural.

In a dictionary, a reflexive verb is indicated by the pronoun *si,* which is attached to the infinitive (the final *-e* of the infinitive is omitted): *alzarsi* ("to get [oneself] up"), *ricordarsi* ("to remember [to oneself]"), or *divertirsi* ("to amuse onself").

3. In the present, the reflexive of *vestire* is conjugated as follows:

vestirsi, to get dressed
I get dressed (dress myself), you get dressed
(dress yourself), etc.

io mi vesto	**noi ci vestiamo**
tu ti vesti	**voi vi vestite**
egli si veste	**essi si vestono**

Position of the Reflexive Pronouns

1. The reflexive pronoun usually precedes a conjugated verb.

Mi **alzo presto.**	I wake up early
Antonio *si* **pettina i capelli.**	Anthony combs his hair.

2. However, in a direct affirmative command, a reflexive pronoun follows the verb and is attached to it.

Alzati! **E' tardi!**	Wake up! It's late!
Giuseppe, *asciugati* **le mani!**	Joseph, dry your hands!

3. Reflexive pronouns precede other object pronouns.

Me lo **compro subito.**	I will buy it immediately.
Ora *se lo* **ricorda.**	She remembers it now.

4. The reflexive pronoun follows and is attached to an infinitive or a gerund.

Giorgio non vuole *sedersi.*	George does not want to sit down.
Avvicinandomi **alla porta, ho visto il postino.**	Approaching the door, I saw the mailman.

Note: With a negative command of the *tu* form, the reflexive pronoun may be placed either *before* or *after* the verb.

Non *ti alzare* **troppo presto.**⎫ **Non** *alzarti* **troppo presto.** ⎭	Don't get up too early.

5. With the progressive tenses (*stare* + gerund), the reflexive pronoun may stand either *before* the verb *stare* or *after* the gerund (and be attached to it).

Mi **sto lavando le mani.**⎫ **Sto lavando***mi* **le mani.**⎭	I am washing my hands.

Reflexive Verbs and Compound Tenses

All reflexive verbs are conjugated with *essere* in compound tenses. The reflexive pronoun immediately precedes *essere,* while the past participle agrees in gender and number with the subject.

Anna, a che ora ti *sei alzata* **stamattina?**	Anne, at what time did you get up this morning?
Le ragazze *si sono annoiate.* **I miei fratelli** *si sono divertiti.*	The girls got bored. My brothers enjoyed themselves.

Reciprocal Verbs

A reflexive verb is called *reciprocal* when the action passes from one person or thing to another, or from one group to another. It is only used in the plural.

Si guardano.	They look at each other.
Ci aiutiamo.	We help each other.
Vi parlate di nuovo?	Are you speaking to each other again?

A reciprocal construction may have two meanings. For example, *Si guardano* may mean "They look at each other" or "They look at themselves." Ambiguity is avoided by adding the forms: *l'uno l'altro, l'un l'altra, fra loro, reciprocamente, a vicenda, fra noi.*

Si guardavano *l'un l'altro.*	They were looking at each other.
Ci aiutiamo *fra noi.*	We help each other.
Si odiano *a vicenda.*	They hate each other.
S'ingannano *reciprocamente.*	They deceive each other.

Uses of Reflexive Verbs

1. Generally, if a verb is reflexive in English, it is also reflexive in Italian.

appoggiarsi	to lean (oneself against)
divertirsi	to enjoy oneself
lavarsi	to wash oneself
pettinarsi	to comb one's hair
tagliarsi	to cut oneself
vestirsi	to get dressed

2. However, many reflexive verbs in Italian have no reflexive equivalent in English.

accorgersi	to notice
addormentarsi	to fall asleep
fermarsi	to stop
lamentarsi (di)	to complain about
pentirsi (di)	to repent about (of)
sentirsi	to feel
sposarsi	to get married

3. With parts of the body or clothing, a reflexive verb is used in Italian, not the possessive adjective.

Mi lavo **la faccia.**	I wash my face.
Ci togliamo **il cappotto.**	We take off our coats.

4. Reflexive verbs are also used:
   a. in commands or instructions of an impersonal nature:

Si giri **a destra.**	Turn to the right.
Si veda **a pagina 20.**	See on page 20.
Si seguano **le indicazioni.**	Follow the instructions.

   b. to translate the English indefinite subjects such as "one," "you," "they," "people."

Si chiude **alle 5 del pomeriggio.**	Closed at 5 PM (We close . . . .)
Si può **vedere ogni cosa.**	One can see everything.
Qui *si sta* **molto bene**	We are very comfortable here.

5. Some verbs in Italian change meaning when they are used reflexively. The most common of these are listed below.

Verb		Reflexive Verb	
adempiere	to accomplish	**adempiersi**	to come true
annoiare	to annoy	**annoiarsi**	to get bored
battere	to beat	**battersi**	to fight
chiamare	to call	**chiamarsi**	to be called, to be named
comportare	to bear, to entail	**comportarsi**	to behave
disdire	to cancel	**disdirsi**	to contradict oneself
dispensare	to dispense	**dispensarsi**	to excuse oneself from
erudire	to educate	**erudirsi**	to learn
frapporre	to interpose	**frapporsi**	to interfere
giocare	to play	**giocarsi**	to risk
guardare	to look	**guardarsi (da)**	to keep from
impiegare	to employ, to use	**impiegarsi**	to find a job
infuriare	to infuriate	**infuriarsi**	to get angry
lamentare	to lament	**lamentarsi**	to complain
licenziare	to dismiss	**licenziarsi**	to resign
montare	to mount	**montarsi**	to swell, to work oneself up
offendere	to offend	**offendersi**	to take offense at
onorare	to honor	**onorarsi**	to take pride (in)
perdere	to lose	**perdersi**	to get lost
recare	to bring	**recarsi**	to go
risparmiare	to save	**risparmiarsi**	to refrain from
scostare	to remove	**scostarsi**	to stand aside
scusare	to excuse	**scusarsi**	to apologize (for)
usare	to use	**usarsi**	to get used to
vantare	to praise	**vantarsi**	to boast
vincere	to win	**vincersi**	to master oneself

5. Formation of Subjunctive Tenses — Regular Verbs

The subjunctive is the mood of uncertainties, emotions, assumptions, possibilities, conditions, and is generally used to express the speaker's attitude. The subjunctive occurs most frequently in dependent clauses introduced by *che*.

(The varied uses of the subjunctive will be explained in Chapter 6, while the subjunctive forms of irregular verbs are included in Chapter 8.)

Tenses of the Subjunctive Mood

1. Present Subjunctive   **Il congiuntivo presente**
2. Past Subjunctive   **Il congiuntivo passato**
3. Imperfect Subjunctive   **Il congiuntivo imperfetto**
4. Pluperfect Subjunctive   **Il congiuntivo trapassato**

The four subjunctive tenses in Italian are commonly used in writing and everyday speech.

Present Subjunctive

The regular present subjunctive is formed by adding the appropriate endings to the stem of the infinitive.

parlare, to speak		*vendere,* to sell	
che io parl*i*	che noi parl*iamo*	che io vend*a*	che noi vend*iamo*
che tu parl*i*	che voi parl*iate*	che tu vend*a*	che voi vend*iate*
che egli parl*i*	che essi parl*ino*	che egli vend*a*	che essi vend*ano*

finire, to speak		*partire,* to leave	
che io fin*isca*	che noi fin*iamo*	che io part*a*	che noi part*iamo*
che tu fin*isca*	che voi fin*iate*	che tu part*a*	che voi part*iate*
che egli fin*isca*	che essi fin*iscano*	che egli part*a*	che essi part*ano*

E' importante che egli *parli* **con un dottore.**	It is important that he speak with a doctor.
Temo che essi *vendano* **la casa.**	I am afraid they will sell the house.
Voglio che tu *finisca* **il compito.**	I want you to finish your homework.
Credo che egli *parta* **domani.**	I believe that he is leaving tomorrow.

Past Subjunctive

The past subjunctive is formed with the present subjunctive of *avere* or *essere* and the past participle of the verb.

parlare, to speak
(*vendere,* to sell/*finire,* to finish)

che io abbia parlato (venduto/finito)	che noi abbiamo parlato (venduto/finito)
che tu abbia parlato (venduto/finito)	che voi abbiate parlato (venduto/finito)
che egli abbia parlato (venduto/finito)	che essi abbiano parlato (venduto/finito)

partire, to leave

che io sia partito *(a)*	che noi siamo partiti *(e)*
che tu sia partito *(a)*	che voi siate partiti *(e)*
che egli sia partito *(a)*	che essi siano partiti *(e)*

Sono contento che tu *abbia finito* **gli studi.**	I am happy that you have finished your studies.
E' possibile che egli *abbia venduto* **la macchina.**	It is possible that he sold his car.
Mi dispiace che essi *siano partiti* **così presto.**	I am sorry that they have left so early.

Imperfect Subjunctive

The imperfect subjunctive is formed by adding the appropriate endings to the stem of the infinitive.

parlare, to speak

che io parl*assi*	che noi parl*assimo*
che tu parl*assi*	che voi parl*aste*
che egli parl*asse*	che essi parl*assero*

vendere, to sell

che io vend*essi*	che noi vend*essimo*
che tu vend*essi*	che voi vend*este*
che egli vend*esse*	che essi vend*essero*

finire, to finish

che io fin*issi*	che noi fin*issimo*
che tu fin*issi*	che voi fin*iste*
che egli fin*isse*	che essi fin*issero*

Fu necessario che io *parlassi* **così.**	It was necessary that I spoke that way.
Luisa m'invitò a casa sua perchè io *vedessi* **i suoi quadri.**	Louise invited me to her house so that I could see her paintings.
Giovanni parlò ad alta voce perchè io *sentissi.*	John spoke aloud so I could hear.

Pluperfect Subjunctive

The pluperfect subjunctive is formed with the imperfect subjunctive of the auxiliary verbs *avere* or *essere* and the past participle.

parlare, to speak
(**vendere,** to sell/**finire,** to finish)

Che io avessi parlato (venduto/finito)	che noi avessimo parlato (venduto/finito)
che tu avessi parlato (venduto/finito)	che voi aveste parlato (venduto/finito)
che egli avesse parlato (venduto/finito)	che essi avessero parlato (venduto/finito)

partire, to leave

Che io fossi partito *(a)*	che noi fossimo partiti *(e)*
che tu fossi partito *(a)*	che voi foste partiti *(e)*
che egli fosse partito *(a)*	che essi fossero partiti *(e)*

Sarebbe stato possibile che *io* **non** *avessi amato* **Maria?**	Could it have been possible that I did not love Maria?
Non sapevo che *tu avessi venduto* **il tuo registratore.**	I did not know that you had sold your tape recorder.
Non avrei mai creduto che *tu fossi partito* **di notte.**	I would never have believed that you left at night.

Note: Since the first- and second-person singular are identical in the pluperfect subjunctive, the subject pronoun is usually used with these persons to avoid ambiguity.

Tenses of the Subjunctive Mood

-are

Present	____ i		____ iamo
	____ i		____ iate
	____ i		____ ino
Past	abbia ____ ato		abbiamo ____ ato
	abbia ____ ato		abbiate ____ ato
	abbia ____ ato		abbiano ____ ato
	sia ____ ato (a)		siamo ____ ati (e)
	sia ____ ato (a)		siate ____ ati (e)
	sia ____ ato (a)		siano ____ ati (e)
Imperfect	____ assi		____ assimo
	____ assi		____ aste
	____ asse		____ assero
Pluperfect	avessi ____ ato		avessimo ____ ato
	avessi ____ ato		aveste ____ ato
	avesse ____ ato		avessero ____ ato
	fossi ____ ato (a)		fossimo ____ ati (e)
	fossi ____ ato (a)		foste ____ ati (e)
	fosse ____ ato (a)		fossero ____ ati (e)

-ere

Present	____ a		____ iamo
	____ a		____ iate
	____ a		____ ano
Past	abbia ____ uto		abbiamo ____ uto
	abbia ____ uto		abbiate ____ uto
	abbia ____ uto		abbiano ____ uto
	sia ____ uto (a)		siamo ____ uti (e)
	sia ____ uto (a)		siate ____ uti (e)
	sia ____ uto (a)		siano ____ uti (e)
Imperfect	____ essi		____ essimo
	____ essi		____ este
	____ esse		____ essero
Pluperfect	avessi ____ uto		avessimo ____ uto
	avessi ____ uto		aveste ____ uto
	avesse ____ uto		avessero ____ uto
	fossi ____ uto		fossimo ____ uti (e)
	fossi ____ uto		foste ____ uti (e)
	fosse ____ uto		fossero ____ uti (e)

-ire

Present	_____ a	_____ iamo
	_____ a	_____ iate
	_____ a	_____ ano
Past	abbia _____ ito	abbiamo _____ ito
	abbia _____ ito	abbiate _____ ito
	abbia _____ ito	abbiano _____ ito
	sia _____ ito (a)	siamo _____ iti (e)
	sia _____ ito (a)	siate _____ iti (e)
	sia _____ ito (a)	siano _____ iti (e)
Imperfect	_____ issi	_____ issimo
	_____ issi	_____ iste
	_____ isse	_____ issero
Pluperfect	avessi _____ ito	avessimo _____ ito
	avessi _____ ito	aveste _____ ito
	avesse _____ ito	avessero _____ ito
	fossi _____ ito (a)	fossimo _____ iti (e)
	fossi _____ ito (a)	foste _____ iti (e)
	fosse _____ ito (a)	fossero _____ iti (e)

Note: The verbs in -*ire* that add -*isc*- in the present indicative also add -*isc*- in the present subjunctive, except in the first- and second-person plural.

Verb Synopsis of Subjunctive Tenses

parlare — *egli*

Present	*che egli parli*	he may speak
Past	*che egli abbia parlato*	he may have spoken
Imperfect	*che egli parlasse*	he might or should speak
Pluperfect	*che egli avesse parlato*	he might or should have spoken

arrivare — *egli*

Present	*che egli arrivi*	he may come
Past	*che egli sia arrivato*	he may have come
Imperfect	*che egli arrivasse*	he might or should come
Pluperfect	*che egli fosse arrivato*	he might or should have come

6. Uses of the Subjunctive

In Main and Independent Clauses

In Commands

In a main clause or in an independent clause, the subjunctive is used to express a command, a suggestion, a wish, or a regret. It is used most often in the third person.

Che nessuno *esca*!	No one can go out!
Che Dio vi *aiuti*!	May God help you!
Oh! Se lui non *fosse* **mai** *partito*!	If only he had never left!

In Fixed Expressions

The subjunctive is also used in some fixed expressions such as the following:

Viva **la libertà!**	Hurray for freedom!
Si salvi **chi può!**	Every man for himself!
Così *sia*!	So be it! Amen!
Dio vi *benedica*!	God bless you!
Succeda **quel che** *succeda*!	Come what may!

In Dependent Clauses

After Impersonal Expressions

1. Most impersonal expressions used to express the speaker's *will, desire,* or *judgment* are followed by the subjunctive in the dependent clause. These expressions, like all impersonal expressions, are followed by *che*.

E' poco probabile che Mario *venga*	It is hardly probable that Mario will come.
E' necessario che tu *aiuti* **i tuoi genitori.**	It is necessary that you help your parents.
E' preferibile che tu *smetta* **di fumare.**	It is preferable that you stop smoking.
Può darsi che *sia* **tardi.**	It may be late.

Below is a list of the most common impersonal expressions requiring the subjunctive.

E' bene	it is well	**E' preferibile**	it is preferable
E' meglio	it is better	**E' probabile**	it is probable
E' giusto	it is right	**E' naturale**	it is natural
E' ora	it is time	**E' strano**	it is strange
E' una vergogna	it is a shame	**E' raro**	it is rare
E' possibile	it is possible	**E' sufficiente**	it is sufficient
E' necessario	it is necessary	**E' importante**	it is important
E' utile	it is useful	**E' impossibile**	it is impossible
E' tempo	it is time	**Non importa**	never mind
Può darsi	it may be	**E' poco probabile**	it is hardly
E' peccato	it is a pity		probable
Bisogna	it is necessary	**Sembra**	it seems
		Basta	it suffices

2. Impersonal expressions that introduce a *fact* or a *certainty* are followed by the indicative in the dependent clause, if they are used *affirmatively* in the main clause.

E' evidente che egli non *ha* *studiato.*	It is evident that he did not study.
E' certo che la primavera *è* *arrivata.*	It is certain that spring has arrived.
E' vero che egli *è* **americano.**	It is true that he is an american.

Impersonal expressions indicating certainty include the following.

è certo	it is certain	**è vero**	it is true
è evidente	it is evident	**è sicuro**	it is sure
è palese	it is obvious	**è chiaro**	it is clear

3. If the impersonal expressions indicating certainty are used *negatively* in the main clause, the subjunctive is used in the dependent clause.

Non **è certo che essi** *siano* *partiti.*	It is not certain that they left.
Non **è vero che egli** *sia povero.*	It is not true that he is poor.

4. Impersonal expressions take the subjunctive if the verb of the dependent clause has a definite subject that is expressed or implied; if not, the infinitive is used.

E' importante che *Lei impari* **l'italiano.**	It is important that you learn Italian.
E' importante *imparare* **l'italiano.**	It is important to learn Italian.
E' necessario che *tu* **lo** *faccia.*	It is necessary that you do it.
E' necessario *farlo.*	It is necessary to do it.

After Verbs of Volition

The subjunctive is used in dependent clauses after verbs expressing the speaker's mind or will *(volition)*. These verbs express volitional qualities such as desire, preference, command, advice, judgment, or forbidding.

Voglio che Lei *venga* **con me.**	I want you to come with me.
Permetta che io *saluti* **sua sorella**	Allow me to greet your sister.
Desidero che Lei *vada* **in vacanza.**	I want you to go on vacation.
Suggerisco che tu e Pietro *lavoriate* **un po' di più.**	I suggest that you and Peter work a little harder.
Lascia che *vada* **per la sua strada.**	Let him go his way.

Here is a partial list of verbs of volition.

comandare	to command	**permettere**	to permit
consigliare	to advise	**preferire**	to prefer
desiderare	to wish	**pregare**	to beg
dire	to tell	**proibire**	to prohibit
domandare	to ask, to demand	**proporre**	to propose
esigere	to require	**suggerire**	to suggest
giudicare	to judge	**vietare**	to forbid
impedire	to prevent	**volere**	to want
insistere	to insist		
lasciare	to let, to allow		
ordinare	to order		

Note: Verbs that express permitting or forbidding, advising or ordering may also use the infinitive in the dependent clause.

Non ti permetto di uscire.	I don't permit you to go out.

After Verbs of Emotion

The subjunctive is also used after expressions of *emotion* (fear, joy, hope, regret, sorrow, surprise).

Ho paura che non *venga.*	I am afraid he won't come.
Mi dispiace che tu non *stia* **bene.**	I am sorry that you are not feeling well.

The most common expressions of emotion are as follows:

avere paura	to be afraid	**essere rammaricato**	to regret
dispiacersi	to feel sorry	**lamentarsi**	to complain
dolersi	to be sorry	**rallegrarsi**	to rejoice
essere contento	to be happy, to be pleased		
essere desolato	to be sorry, to be distressed		
essere meravi-gliato	to be surprised		

After Verbs of Doubt and Denial

The subjunctive is also used after expressions of doubt, denial, disbelief, uncertainty, expectation, or opinion.

Aspetto che egli *arrivi*.	I am waiting for him to come.
Mi chiedo cosa *voglia*.	I wonder what he wants.
Ho l'impressione che non *voglia* **venire.**	I have the impression that he does not want to come.
Crediamo che *sia stato* **uno sbaglio.**	We believe it was a mistake.
Sperava che i genitori lo *aiutassero*.	He hoped his parents would help him.

The most common verbs of this type are the following.

aspettare	to wait	**negare**	to deny
aspettarsi	to expect	**pensare**	to think
avere l'impressione	to have the feeling	**sperare**	to hope
chiedersi	to wonder	**supporre**	to suppose
credere	to believe		
dubitare	to doubt		

Note: If the verb in the main clause expresses certainty, the subjunctive is *not* used in the dependent clause.

Sono sicuro che *sono arrivati*.	I am sure that they arrived.
Vedo che *stai* **bene**.	I see that you are well.

After Conjunctions

The subjunctive is used after the following conjunctions:

TIME		CONDITIONS	
prima che*	before	**a meno che non**	unless
dopo che**	after	**senza che**	without
appena che	as soon as	**purchè**	
finchè (non)**	until	**a patto che**	provided that
		a condizione che	

*Prima che + the subjunctive are used only if the subject of the independent clause is different from the subject of the dependent clause. If the subjects are the same, *prima di* + the infinitive are used.

Parlami prima che io *parta*.	Talk to me before I leave.
Parlami prima di *partire*.	Talk to me before you leave.

**The subjunctive is used only when uncertainty (possibility, probability, or expectation) is implied. When certainty is implied, the indicative is used.

Gli potrò parlare solo dopo che io l'*abbia visto*. (possibility)	I will talk to him if I see him.
Gli parlai dopo che tu *uscisti*. (accomplished certainty)	I spoke to him after you left.

Sometimes either the subjunctive or the indicative can be used.

Non ti darò tregua finchè non mi *abbia* (*avrai*) **accontentato.**	I will not stop pressuring you until you please me.

PURPOSE		CONCESSION	
affinchè	in order that	**benchè**	
perchè	in order that	**sebbene**	although
in maniera	so that	**quantunque**	
(modo) che		**nonostante che**	in spite of the fact
		malgrado che	
		anche se	even if

SUPPOSITION		EMOTION	
supponiamo che	supposing that	**per paura (timore) che**	for fear that
nel caso che	in the event that	**nella speranza che**	in the hope that

OTHERS

chiunque	whoever
qualunque	whatever
sia che ... sia che	either that ... or that
dovunque	wherever
comunque	however
per quanto	no matter how much
in qualunque modo	no matter how

Note the use of the subjunctive after these conjunctions in the following examples.

Benchè avesse **ragione, tacque.**	Although he was right, he kept quiet.
Anche se **gli** *scrivessi,* **non verrebbe lo stesso.**	Even if I wrote to him, he still won't come.
Ricordati di me, *dovunque* **tu** *sia.*	Remember me wherever you are.
Per quanto **ricco tu** *sia,* **non potrai comprarlo.**	However rich you are, you can never buy it.
Supponiamo che sia **vero.**	Let's suppose it is true.
Ti presto il libro, *a condizione che* **me lo** *restituisca* **subito.**	I will lend you the book, provided that you return it to me soon.
Le diedi il denaro *perchè comprasse* **il libro.**	I gave her the money so that she might buy the book.
Gli darò la lettera, *nel caso che* **lo** *veda.*	I will give him the letter if I see him.

Note: After *prima che* and *senza che,* the subjunctive is used only when there is a change of subject in the sentence. If the subject remains the same, then *prima di* (or *senza)* + the infinitive is used.

Prima che tu esca, **voglio sapere dove vai.**	Before you leave, I want to know where you are going.
Prima di uscire, **mettiti il cappotto.**	Before you leave, put your coat on.
Senza che tu **me lo** *dica,* **so dove vai.**	I know where you are going, without your telling me.
Partì *senza dirmelo.*	He left without telling me.

After the Conjunction *Se (if)*

1. The subjunctive is used after the conjunction *se*, if the clause that follows expresses a condition that cannot be true under the circumstances, *or* if it refers to something merely imagined or impossible to realize in the future. The *se* clause is expressed in the imperfect (or pluperfect) subjunctive and the main clause in the conditional present (or past).

Se avessi **il denaro, comprerei una casa.**	If I had the money, I would buy a house.
Se avessimo studiato **di più, avremmo superato l'esame.**	If we had studied more, we would have passed the exam.
Se **Lei** *fosse venuto* **prima, avrebbe visto mio zio.**	If you had come earlier, you would have seen my uncle.
Ti avrei portato un bel regalo, *se fossi stato invitato* **alla festa.**	I would have brought you a beautiful gift, if I had been invited to the party.
Se **tu me lo** *avessi detto,* **t'avrei telefonato.**	If you had told me, I would have called you.

2. When the condition is an accepted fact, the *se* clause is followed by a tense in the indicative mood, and the main clause by the indicative or the imperative.

Se non presti attenzione, non capirai niente.	If you don't pay attention, you won't understand anything.
Se leggi, impari molte cose.	If you read, you will learn many things.
Se hai fame, mangia.	If you are hungry, eat.
Se vedi il professore, salutalo.	If you see the professor, greet him.

3. A gerund can be used as a substitute for a *se* clause.

Avendo **tempo, lo farei.**	If I had time, I would do it.
Avendo avuto **tempo, lo avrei fatto.**	If I had had time, I would have done it.

A gerund can also be used as a substitute for a subjunctive. However, this replacement is less desirable, because it does not convey the exact meaning of the subjunctive. The best alternative is to master the rules that govern the Italian subjunctive.

Avendo **Lei** *detto* **questo, sono felice.**	Your having said this makes me happy.
But preferably: **Sono felice che Lei** *abbia detto* **questo.**	I am happy that you said this.

In Relative Clauses

1. The subjunctive is used in a relative clause introduced by a superlative or adjectives such as *solo, primo, ultimo, unico,* and *supremo.*

E' l'uomo più divertente che io *abbia* **mai** *incontrato.*	He is the most amusing man that I ever met.
Tu sei l'unico che *abbia risposto* **al mio invito.**	You are the only one who answered my invitation.

2. The subjunctive is also used in relative clauses introduced by certain negatives: *niente, nessuno, non c'è.*

Non c'è niente che *possa* **spaventarlo.**	Nothing can scare him.
Non trovo nessuno che mi *ascolti.*	I can't find anybody who listens to me.
Non c'è un libro che mi *piaccia.*	There is not one book that I like.

3. The subjunctive also comes after an indefinite expression such as *un (uno, una), qualcuno, qualcosa.*

Cerchiamo una dattilografa che *conosca* **l'inglese.**	We are looking for a typist who knows English.
Hai qualcosa che m'*aiuti* **a dormire?**	Do you have anything that will help me sleep?

Note: a) The replacement of the subjunctive by the indicative in both spoken and written Italian is sometimes tolerated.

Credo che *è venuto* **ieri sera.**	I think he came last night.
Mi sembra che tu *stai* **bene.**	You seem to be fine.

b) Sometimes the indicative replaces *both* the subjunctive and the conditional.

Se venivi, mi trovavi **a casa.**	If you had come, you would have found me at home.

instead of:
Se fossi venuto, mi avresti trovato a casa.

Subjunctive versus Infinitive

1. If the subject of the independent and the subject of the dependent clause are the same, *di* + infinitive (or the infinitive alone after verbs of wishing) is used instead of the subjunctive.

Dubito *di farcela.*	I doubt I can make it.

But:

Dubito che *tu* **ce la** *faccia.*	I doubt you can make it.

2. The *di* + infinitive construction may be used with verbs expressing a command, even though the subject of the dependent clause is not the same as the subject of the main clause.

Ti ordino *di uscire.*	I order you to leave.
Ti prego *di scrivermi.*	I beg you to write to me.
Vi dico *di lavorare* **di più.**	I tell you to work harder.

7. Orthographic-Changing Verbs

Orthographic-changing verbs are those that change spelling in order to preserve the sound of the last consonant of the stem.

1. Verbs whose infinitives end in -*care* or -*gare* add an *h* between the stem and those endings that start with an *i* or *e*.

indicare	to indicate
Present Indicative	io indico, tu indichi, egli indica, noi indichiamo, voi indicate, essi indicano
Future	io indicherò, tu indicherai, egli indicherà, noi indicheremo, voi indicherete, essi indicheranno
Imperative	—, indica tu, indichi egli, indichiamo noi, indicate voi, indichino essi
Conditional	io indicherei, tu indicheresti, egli indicherebbe, noi indicheremmo, voi indichereste, essi indicherebbero
Present Subjunctive	(che) io indichi, tu indichi, egli indichi, noi indichiamo, voi indichiate, essi indichino

Other verbs of this type:

asciugare	to dry	moltiplicare	to multiply
cercare	to look for, to search for	negare	to deny
		nevicare	to snow
dimenticare	to forget	obbligare	to oblige
giocare	to play	pagare	to pay
impiegare	to employ	pescare	to fish
investigare	to investigate	piegare	to fold
litigare	to quarrel	placare	to placate
mancare	to fail, to be missing	pregare	to pray
		significare	to mean
masticare	to chew	spiegare	to explain
		sprecare	to waste
		toccare	to touch

2. Verbs whose infinitives end in *-ciare, -giare,* and *-sciare* drop the *i* of the stem whenever the ending starts with an i or an e.

cominciare	to begin
Present Indicative	**io comincio, tu cominc*i*, egli comincia, noi cominc*iamo*, voi cominciate, essi cominc*iano***
Future	**io comincerò, tu comincerai, egli comincerà, noi cominceremo, voi comincerete, essi cominceranno**
Imperative	**comincia tu, cominc*i* egli, cominc*iamo* noi, cominciate voi, cominc*ino* essi**
Conditional	**io comincerei, tu cominceresti, egli comincerebbe, noi cominceremmo, voi comincereste, essi comincerebbero**
Present Subjunctive	**(che) io cominc*i*, tu cominc*i*, egli cominc*i*, noi cominc*iamo*, voi cominciate, essi cominc*ino***

Other verbs of this type include:

assaggiare	to taste	**lasciare**	to let, to leave
baciare	to kiss	**lisciare**	to smooth
bruciare	to burn	**mangiare**	to eat
falciare	to mow	**passeggiare**	to stroll
fasciare	to wrap, to swaddle	**viaggiare**	to travel
incoraggiare	to encourage		
lampeggiare	to flash lightning		

Note: The verb *sciare* ("to ski") is *not* an orthographic-changing verb. It retains the i of its stem: *tu scìi, che io scìi, che essi scìino.*

3. Before an ending that starts with *i,* verbs whose infinitives end in *-iare* drop the *i* of the stem if it is not stressed, but they retain it if it is stressed. Note the differences in the verbs below.

invidiare	to envy	**inviare**	to send

Present Indicative	**io invidio, tu invid*i*, egli invidia, noi invidiamo, voi invidiate, essi invidiano**
	io invio, tu invìi, egli invia, noi inviamo, voi inviate, essi inviano
Present Subjunctive	**(che) io invid*i*, tu invid*i*, egli invid*i*, noi invidiamo, voi invidiate, essi invid*ino***
	(che) io invìi, tu invìi, egli invìi, noi inviamo, voi inviate, essi invìino

Other verbs of this type include:

avviare   to start, to set in motion
obliare   to forget

4. Verbs whose infinitive end in *-chiare, -ghiare, -gliare,* drop the i of the stem before the endings starting with an *i.*

sbagliare	to mistake, to miss, to get something wrong
Present Indicative	**io sbaglio, tu sbagl*i*, egli sbaglia, noi sbagliamo, voi sbagliate, essi sbagliano**
Present Subjunctive	**(che) io sbagl*i*, tu sbagl*i*, egli sbagl*i*, noi sbagliamo, voi sbagliate, essi sbagl*ino***

Other verbs of this type include:

avvinghiare	to claw	**sbrigliare**	to unbridle
imbrigliare	to bridle	**sbrogliare**	to untangle
macchiare	to stain, to soil	**tagliare**	to cut
ridacchiare	to giggle	**vivacchiare**	to manage to make
sbadigliare	to yawn		a living

5. Verbs whose infinitive end in *-gnare* generally keep the *i* of the indicative or subjunctive ending *-iamo: noi sogniamo, che noi bagniamo.* However, in modern usage some authors drop the *i,* while some others keep it in the subjunctive and drop it in the indicative.

6. Verbs whose infinitive end in *-cere* or *-scere* add an *i* before the past participle ending in *-uto.*

Infinitive		*Past Participle*
conoscere	to know, recognize	**conosc*iuto***
crescere	to grow	**cresc*iuto***
pascere	to graze	**pasc*iuto***
piacere	to like	**piac*iuto***
tacere	to keep quiet	**tac*iuto***

8. Irregular Verbs

Only irregular verb forms are given here. The remaining tenses of the verbs are regular. Check regular tense formation in Chapter 2 (simple tenses), Chapter 3 (perfect tenses), and Chapter 5 (subjunctive mood). The *gerund* and *past participle* follow the infinitive directly in this summary of irregular forms.

accendere to light	**accendendo**	**acceso** (*aux.* avere)
Simple Past	**accesi, accendesti, accese, accendemmo, accendeste, accesero**	

accorgersi to become aware of	**accorgendosi**	**accortosi** (*aux.* essere)
Simple Past	**mi accorsi, ti accorgesti, si accorse, ci accorgemmo, vi accorgeste, si accorsero**	

andare to go	**andando**	**andato** (*aux.* essere)
Present	**vado, vai, va andiamo, andate, vanno**	
Present Subjunctive	**vada, vada, vada, andiamo, andiate, vadano**	
Imperative	**vai (va') vada, andiamo, andate, vadano**	
Future	**andrò, andrai, andrà, andremo, andrete, andranno**	
Conditional	**andrei, andresti, andrebbe, andremmo, andreste, andrebbero**	

apparire to appear	**apparendo**	**apparso** (*aux.* **essere**)
Present	**apparisco (appaio), apparisci (appari), apparisce (appare), appariamo, apparite, appariscono (appaiono)**	
Simple Past	**apparvi (apparii), apparisti, apparve (apparì, apparse), apparimmo, appariste, apparvero (apparirono, apparsero)**	
Present Subjunctive	**apparisca (appaia), apparisca (appaia), apparisca (appaia), appariamo, appariate, appariscano (appaiano)**	
Imperative	**apparisci (appari), apparisca (appaia), apparite, appariscano (appaiano)**	

Other verbs of this type:

disapparire
scomparire } to disappear
sparire

---

appendere to hang (up)	**appendendo**	**appeso** (*aux.* **avere**)
Simple Past	**appesi, appendesti, appese, appendemmo, appendeste, appesero**	

Other verbs of this type:

dipendere   to depend
sospendere   to suspend

---

aprire to open	**aprendo**	**aperto** (*aux.* **avere**)
Simple Past	**aprii (apersi), apristi, aprì (aperse), aprimmo, apriste, aprirono (apersero)**	

Other verbs of this type:

riaprire   to reopen
ricoprire   to cover again
scoprire   to discover

assistere to assist	**assistendo**	**assistito** (*aux.* **avere**)

Simple Past **assistei (assistetti), assistesti, assistè (assistette), assistemmo, assisteste, assisterono (assistettero)**

Other verbs of this type:

resistere to resist

---

bere to drink	**bevendo**	**bevuto** (*aux.* **avere**)

Present **bevo, bevi, beve, beviamo, bevete, bevono**

Future **berrò, berrai, berrà, berremo, berrete, berranno**

Imperfect **bevevo, bevevi, beveva, bevevamo, bevevate, bevevano**

Conditional **berrei, berresti, berrebbe, berremmo, berreste, berrebbero**

Simple Past **bevvi (bevei), bevesti, bevve (bevè, bevette), bevemmo, beveste, bevvero (beverono, bevettero)**

Present Subjunctive **beva, beva, beva, beviamo, beviate, bevano**

Imperfect Subjunctive **bevessi, bevessi, bevesse, bevessimo, beveste, bevessero**

Imperative **—, bevi, beva, —, bevete, bevano**

---

cadere to fall	**cadendo**	**caduto** (*aux.* **essere**)

Future **cadrò, cadrai, cadrà, cadremo, cadrete, cadranno**

Simple Past **caddi, cadesti, cadde, cademmo, cadeste, caddero**

Conditional **cadrei, cadresti, cadrebbe, cadremmo, cadreste, cadrebbero**

Other verbs of this type:

accadere to happen *(impersonal)*
ricadere to fall back, to fall again, to relapse
scadere to fall due

chiedere to ask	**chiedendo**	**chiesto** (*aux.* **avere**)
Simple Past	**chiesi, chiedesti, chiese, chiedemmo, chiedeste, chiesero**	

Other verbs of this type:

richiedere, to require, to request

---

chiudere to close	**chiudendo**	**chiuso** (*aux.* **avere**)
Simple Past	**chiusi, chiudesti, chiuse, chiudemmo, chiudeste, chiusero**	

Other verbs of this type:

racchiudere, to include
schiudere to open
rinchiudere, to shut in, to enclose

---

cogliere to gather, to catch	**cogliendo**	**colto** (*aux.* **avere**)
Present	**colgo, cogli, coglie, cogliamo, cogliete, colgono**	
Simple Past	**colsi, cogliesti, colse, cogliemmo, coglieste, colsero**	
Present Subjunctive	**colga, colga, colga, cogliamo, cogliate, colgano**	

Other verbs of this type:

raccogliere to pick up, to gather

---

compiere to accomplish, to fulfill	**compiendo**	**compiuto** (*aux.* **avere**)
Present	**compio, compi, compie, compiamo, compite, compiono**	

| Simple Past | **compii, compisti, compì, compimmo, compiste, compirono** |

| Present
Subjunctive | **compia, compia, compia, compiamo, compiate, compiano** |

| Imperative | **—, compi, compia, —, compite, compiano** |

Other verbs of this type:

adempiere to
accomplish,
to fulfill
empiere to fill
riempire to fill, to
stuff

| **comprimere** to
compress | **comprimendo** | **compresso** (*aux.*
avere) |

| Simple Past | **compressi, comprimesti, compresse, comprimemmo, comprimeste, compressero** |

Other verbs of this type:

deprimere to depress
imprimere to imprint
reprimere to repress
sopprimere to suppress

| **conoscere** to
know | **conoscendo** | **conosciuto** (*aux.*
avere) |

| Simple Past | **conobbi, conoscesti, conobbe, conoscemmo, conosceste, conobbero** |

Other verbs of this type:

riconoscere, to recognize

| **correre** to run | **correndo** | **corso** (*aux.* **avere
and essere)** |

| Simple Past | **corsi, corresti, corse, corremmo, correste, corsero** |

Other verbs of this type:

accorrere to run, to rush
concorrere to concur, to converge
discorrere to talk, to chat
incorrere to incur
occorrere to be necessary
scorrere to flow
soccorrere to aid
trascorrere to pass, to spend
percorrere to run through (or across)

---

costruire to build, to construct	**costruendo**	**costruito** (*aux.* **avere**)
Simple Past	**costruii (costrussi), costruisti, costruì (costrusse), costruimmo, costruiste, costruirono (costrussero)**	

Other verbs of this type:

istruire to instruct, to train

---

crescere to grow	**crescendo**	**cresciuto** (*aux.* **avere** and **essere**)
Simple Past	**crebbi, crescesti, crebbe, crescemmo, cresceste, crebbero**	

Other verbs of this type:

accrescere to increase
rincrescere to be sorry, to regret

---

dare to give	**dando**	**dato** (*aux.* **avere**)
Present	**do, dai, dà, diamo, date, danno**	
Future	**darò, darai, darà, daremo, darete, daranno**	
Conditional	**darei, daresti, darebbe, daremmo, dareste, darebbero**	
Simple Past	**diedi (detti), desti, diede, demmo, deste, diedero (dettero)**	
Present Subjunctive	**dia, dia, dia, diamo, diate, diano**	
Imperfect Subjunctive	**dessi, dessi, desse, dessimo, deste, dessero**	
Imperative	**—, dai (da', dà), dia, —, date, diano**	

Other verbs of this type:

ridare   to give back

---

decidere to decide	**decidendo**	**deciso** (*aux.* **avere**)
Simple Past	**decisi, decidesti, decise, decidemmo, decideste, decisero**	

Other verbs of this type:

incidere   to cut

---

difendere to defend	**difendendo**	**difeso** (*aux.* **avere**)
Simple Past	**difesi, difendesti, difese, difendemmo, difendeste, difesero**	

Other verbs of this type:

offendere   to offend

---

dire to say	**dicendo**	**detto** (*aux.* **avere**)
Present	**dico, dici, dice, diciamo, dite, dicono**	
Imperfect	**dicevo, dicevi, diceva, dicevamo, dicevate, dicevano**	
Simple Past	**dissi, dicesti, disse, dicemmo, diceste, dissero**	
Future	**dirò, dirai, dirà, diremo, direte, diranno**	
Present Subjunctive	**dica, dica, dica, diciamo, diciate, dicano**	
Imperfect Subjunctive	**dicessi, dicessi, dicesse, dicessimo, diceste, dicessero**	
Conditional	**direi, diresti, direbbe, diremmo, direste, direbbero**	
Imperative	**—, di' (dì), dica, —, dite, dicano**	

Other verbs of this type:

benedire   to bless
contraddire   to contradict
predire   to predict
ridire   to say again, to object to
maledire   to curse

dirigere to
direct

dirigendo

diretto (*aux.* **avere**)

Simple Past

**diressi, dirigesti, diresse, dirigemmo, dirigeste,
diressero**

Other verbs of this type:

erigere to
erect, to
build

———————

discutere to
discuss

discutendo

discusso (*aux.*
avere)

Simple Past

**discussi (discutei), discutesti, discusse (discutè),
discutemmo, discuteste, discussero (discuterono)**

———————

distinguere to
distinguish

distinguendo

distinto (*aux.*
avere)

Simple Past

**distinsi, distinguesti, distinse, distinguemmo,
distingueste, distinsero**

———————

dividere to di-
vide

dividendo

diviso (*aux.* **avere**)

Simple Past

divisi, dividesti, divise, dividemmo, divideste, divisero

———————

dovere to owe,
must

dovendo

dovuto (*aux.* **avere**
and **essere**)

Present

**debbo (devo), devi, deve, dobbiamo, dovete, debbono
(devono)**

Future

dovrò, dovrai, dovrà, dovremo, dovrete, dovranno

Present
Subjunctive

**debba (deva), debba (deva), debba (deva), dobbiamo,
dobbiate, debbano (devano)**

fare to do, to make	**facendo**	**fatto** (*aux.* **avere**)

Present

faccio (fo), fai, fa, facciamo, fate, fanno

Future

farò, farai, farà, faremo, farete, faranno

Imperfect

facevo, facevi, faceva, facevamo, facevate, facevano

Conditional

farei, faresti, farebbe, faremmo, fareste, farebbero

Simple Past

feci, facesti, fece, facemmo, faceste, fecero

Present
Subjunctive

faccia, faccia, faccia, facciamo, facciate, facciano

Imperfect
Subjunctive

facessi, facessi, facesse, facessimo, faceste, facessero

Imperative

—, fai (fa', fà), faccia, —, fate, facciano

Other verbs of this type:

rifare   to do again, to make again
soddisfare   to satisfy
sopraffare   to overcome

---

giungere to join, to arrive	**giungendo**	**giunto** (*aux.* **avere** and **essere**)

Simple Past

giunsi, giungesti, giunse, giungemmo, giungeste, giunsero

Other verbs of this type:

aggiungere   to add
congiungere   to join
disgiungere   to disjoin
raggiungere   to overtake, to reach
soggiungere   to add

---

leggere to read	**leggendo**	**letto** (*aux.* **avere**)

Simple Past

lessi, leggesti, lesse, leggemmo, leggeste, lessero

Other verbs of this type:

eleggere   to elect
rileggere to reelect

mettere to put	**mettendo**	**messo** (*aux.* **avere**)
Simple Past	**misi, mettesti, mise, mettemmo, metteste, misero**	

Other verbs of this type:

ammettere to admit
commettere to commit
emettere to emit
rimettere to put again (or back)
scommettere to bet
smettere to cease
sottomettere to subdue
trasmettere to transmit, to send

---

mordere to bite	**mordendo**	**morso** (*aux.* **avere**)
Simple Past	**morsi, mordesti, morse, mordemmo, mordeste, morsero**	

Other verbs of this type:

rimordere to bite again, to feel remorse

---

morire to die	**morendo**	**morto** (*aux.* **essere**)
Present	**muoio, muori, muore, moriamo, morite, muoiono**	
Future	**morirò (morrò), morirai (morrai), morirà (morrà), moriremo (morremo), morirete (morrete), moriranno (morranno)**	
Present Subjective	**muoia, muoia, muoia, moriamo, moriate, muoiano**	
Imperative	**—, muori, muoia, —, morite, muoiano**	

---

muovere to move	**movendo**	**mosso** (*aux.* **avere** and **essere**)
Simple Past	**mossi, movesti, mosse, movemmo, moveste, mossero**	

Other verbs of this type:

commuovere to move, to affect
promuovere to promote
rimuovere to remove

nascere to be born	**nascendo**	**nato** (*aux.* **essere**)
Simple Past	**nacqui, nascesti, nacque, nascemmo, nasceste, nacquero**	

Other verbs of this type:

rinascere to be born again

---

nascondere to hide	**nascondendo**	**nascosto** (*aux.* **avere**)
Simple Past	**nascosi, nascondesti, nascose, nascondemmo, nascondeste, nascosero**	

---

offrire to offer	**offrendo**	**offerto** (*aux.* **avere**)
Simple Past	**offrii (offersi), offristi, offrì (offerse), offrimmo, offriste, offrirono (offersero)**	

Other verbs of this type:

soffrire to suffer

---

parere to seem	**parendo**	**parso** (*aux.* **essere**)
Present	**paio, pari, pare, pariamo (paiamo), parete, paiono**	
Future	**parrò, parrai, parrà, parremo, parrete, parranno**	
Past	**parvi, paresti, parve, paremmo, pareste, parvero**	
Present Subjunctive	**paia, paia, paia, pariamo, pariate (paiate), paiano**	
Imperative	*(Lacking)*	

---

perdere to lose	**perdendo**	**perduto** (**perso**) (*aux.* **avere**)
Simple Past	**persi (perdetti), perdesti, perse (perdette, perdè), perdemmo, perdeste, persero (perdettero, perderono)**	

---

persuadere to persuade	**persuadendo**	**persuaso** (*aux.* **avere**)
Simple Past	**persuasi, persuadesti, persuase, persuademmo, persuadeste, persuasero**	

piacere to please	**piacendo**	**piaciuto** (*aux.* **essere**)
Present	piaccio, piaci, piace, piacciamo, piacete, piacciono	
Simple Past	piacqui, piacesti, piacque, piacemmo, piaceste, piacquero	
Present Subjunctive	piaccia, piaccia, piaccia, piacciamo, piacciate, piacciano	

Other verbs of this type:

compiacere to gratify, to please
dispiacere to dislike, to displease

---

piangere to cry	**piangendo**	**pianto** (*aux.* **avere**)
Simple Past	piansi, piangesti, pianse, piangemmo, piangeste, piansero	

Other verbs of this type:

compiangere to pity
rimpiangere to regret

---

porre to put	**ponendo**	**posto** (*aux.* **avere**)
Present	pongo, poni, pone, poniamo, ponete, pongono	
Future	porrò, porrai, porrà, porremo, porrete, porranno	
Simple Past	posi, ponesti, pose, ponemmo, poneste, posero	
Present Subjunctive	ponga, ponga, ponga, poniamo, poniate, pongano	
Imperative	—, poni, ponga, —, ponete, pongano	

Other verbs of this type:

anteporre to place before
comporre to compose
deporre to lay (down), to depose
disporre to dispose
esporre to expose
imporre to impose
opporre to oppose
proporre to propose
riporre to put back (away)
supporre to suppose

potere can, may, to be able	**potendo**	**potuto** (*aux.* **aver** and **essere**)

Present   **posso, puoi, può, possiamo, potete, possono**

Future   **potrò, potrai, potrà, potremo, potrete, potranno**

Present Subjunctive   **possa, possa, possa, possiamo, possiate, possano**

Imperative   *(Lacking)*

---

prendere to take	**prendendo**	**preso** (*aux.* **avere**)

Simple Past   **presi, prendesti, prese, prendemmo, prendeste, presero**

Other verbs of this type:

apprendere to learn
comprendere to understand
intraprendere to undertake
riprendere to take again
sorprendere to surprise

---

proteggere to protect	**proteggendo**	**protetto** (*aux.* **avere**)

Simple Past   **protessi, proteggesti, protesse, proteggemmo, proteggeste, protessero**

---

ridere to laugh	**ridendo**	**riso** (*aux.* **avere**)

Simple Past   **risi, ridesti, rise, ridemmo, rideste, risero**

Other verbs of this type:

deridere to deride
sorridere to smile

---

rimanere to remain	**rimanendo**	**rimasto** (*aux.* **essere**)

Present   **rimango, rimani, rimane, rimaniamo, rimanete, rimangono**

Future   **rimarrò, rimarrai, rimarrà, rimarremo, rimarrete, rimarranno**

Simple Past	**rimasi, rimanesti, rimase, rimanemmo, rimaneste, rimasero**	
Present Subjunctive	**rimanga, rimanga, rimanga, rimaniamo, rimaniate, rimangano**	
Imperative	**—, rimani, rimanga, —, rimanete, rimangano**	

rispondere to
  respond
	rispondendo	**risposto** (*aux.*
		  avere)

Simple Past	**risposi, rispondesti, rispose, rispondemmo, rispondeste, risposero**	

Other verbs of this type:

corrispondere to correspond

rompere to break	**rompendo**	**rotto** (*aux.* **avere**)
Simple Past	**ruppi, rompesti, ruppe, rompemmo, rompeste, ruppero**	

Other verbs of this type:

corrompere to corrupt
irrompere to rush upon
interrompere to interrupt

salire to rise,
  to go up
	salendo	**salito** (*aux.* **avere**
		  and **essere**)

Present	**salgo, sali, sale, saliamo, saliate, salgono**	
Present Subjunctive	**salga, salga, salga, saliamo, salite, salgano**	
Imperative	**—, sali, salga, —, salite, salgano**	

sapere to know	**sapendo**	**saputo** (*aux.* **avere**)
Present	**so, sai, sa, sappiamo, sapete, sanno**	

Future	**saprò, saprai, saprà, sapremo, saprete, sapranno**
Simple Past	**seppi, sapesti, seppe, sapemmo, sapeste, seppero**
Present Subjunctive	**sappia, sappia, sappia, sappiamo, sappiate, sappiano**
Imperative	**—, sappi, sappia, —, sappiate, sappiano**

---

scegliere to choose	**scegliendo**	**scelto** (*aux.* **avere**)
Present	**scelgo, scegli, sceglie, scegliamo, scegliete, scelgono**	
Simple Past	**scelsi, scegliesti, scelse, scegliemmo, sceglieste, scelsero**	
Present Subjunctive	**scelga, scelga, scelga, scegliamo, scegliate, scelgano**	
Imperative	**—, scegli, scelga, —, scegliete, scelgano**	

Other verbs of this type:

prescegliere to prefer

---

scendere to descend, to go down	**scendendo**	**sceso** (*aux.* **avere** and **essere**)
Simple Past	**scesi, scendesti, scese, scendemmo, scendeste, scesero**	

Other verbs of this type:

accondiscendere to condescend
ascendere to ascend
condiscendere to condescend
discendere to descend, to go down

---

scrivere to write	**scrivendo**	**scritto** (*aux.* **avere**)
Simple Past	**scrissi, scrivesti, scrisse, scrivemmo, scriveste, scrissero**	

Other verbs of this type:

circoscrivere   to circumscribe
descrivere   to describe
iscrivere to inscribe
prescrivere   to prescribe
proscrivere   to proscribe
riscrivere   to rewrite
trascrivere   to transcribe

---

sedere to sit	**sedendo**	**seduto** (*aux.* essere)
Present	**siedo (seggo), siedi, siede, sediamo, sedete, siedono (seggono)**	
Simple Past	**sedei (sedetti), sedesti, sedè (sedette), sedemmo, sedeste, sederono (sedettero)**	
Present Subjunctive	**sieda (segga), sieda (segga), sieda (segga), sediamo, sediate, siedano (seggano)**	
Imperative	**—, siedi, sieda (segga), —, sedete, siedano (seggano)**	

---

stare to stay, to stand	**stando**	**stato** (*aux.* essere)
Present	**sto, stai, sta, stiamo, state, stanno**	
Future	**starò, starai, starà, staremo, starete, staranno**	
Simple Past	**stetti, stesti, stette, stemmo, steste, stettero**	
Present Subjunctive	**stia, stia, stia, stiamo, stiate, stiano**	
Imperfect Subjunctive	**stessi, stessi, stesse, stessimo, steste, stessero**	
Imperative	**—, stai (sta', sta), stia, —, state, stiano**	

Note: The compound verbs **contrastare** (to contrast), **costare** (to cost), **prestare** (to lend), **restare** (to remain), **sovrastare** (to tower over) do not follow the model verb *stare*. They are conjugated regularly.

---

tacere to be si-lent	**tacendo**	**taciuto** (*aux.* avere)
Present	**taccio, taci, tace, tacciamo, tacete, tacciono**	

Simple Past	**tacqui, tacesti, tacque, tacemmo, taceste, tacquero**
Present Subjunctive	**taccia, taccia, taccia, tacciamo, tacciate, tacciano**
Imperative	**—, taci, taccia, —, tacete, tacciano**

tenere to hold, to have	**tenendo**	**tenuto** (*aux.* **avere**)
Present	**tengo, tieni, tiene, teniamo, tenete, tengono**	
Future	**terrò, terrai, terrà, terremo, terrete, terranno**	
Simple Past	**tenni, tenesti, tenne, tenemmo, teneste, tennero**	
Present Subjunctive	**tenga, tenga, tenga, teniamo, teniate, tengano**	
Imperative	**—, tieni, tenga, —, tenete, tengano**	

Other verbs of this type:

appartenere to belong
contenere to contain
mantenere to maintain
ritenere to retain
sostenere to support
trattenere to detain

trarre to draw, to pull	**traendo**	**tratto** (*aux.* **avere**)
Present	**traggo, trai, trae, traiamo, traete, traggono**	
Future	**trarrò, trarrai, trarrà, trarremo, trarrete, trarranno**	
Imperfect	**traevo, traevi, traeva, traevamo, traevate, traevano**	
Simple Past	**trassi, traesti, trasse, traemmo, traeste, trassero**	
Present Subjunctive	**tragga, tragga, tragga, traiamo, traiate, traggano**	
Imperative	**—, trai, tragga, —, traete, traggano**	

Note: All regular forms derive from the infinitive form **traere**.

Other verbs of this type:

attrarre   to attract
contrarre   to contract
distrarre   to distract
sottrarre   to subtract

---

uccidere to kill	**uccidendo**	**ucciso** (*aux.* **avere**)
Simple Past	**uccisi, uccidesti, uccise, uccidemmo, uccideste, uccisero**	

---

udire to hear	**udendo**	**udito** (*aux.* **avere**)
Present	**odo, odi, ode, udiamo, udite, odono**	
Future	**udirò (udrò), udirai (udrai), udirà (udrà), udiremo (udremo), udirete (udrete), udiranno (udranno)**	
Present Subjunctive	**oda, oda, oda, udiamo, udiate, odano**	
Imperative	**—, odi, oda, —, udite, odano**	

---

uscire to go out	**uscendo**	**uscito** (*aux.* **essere**)
Present	**esco, esci, esce, usciamo, uscite, escono**	
Present Subjunctive	**esca, esca, esca, usciamo, usciate, escano**	
Imperative	**—, esci, esca, —, uscite, escano**	

Other verbs of this type:

riuscire   to succeed

---

valere to be worth	**valendo**	**valso** (*aux.* **essere**)
Present	**valgo, vali, vale, valiamo, valete, valgono**	
Future	**varrò, varrai, varrà, varremo, varrete, varranno**	

Simple Past	valsi, valesti, valse, valemmo, valeste, valsero
Present Subjunctive	valga, valga, valga, valiamo, valiate, valgano
Imperative	—, vali, valga, —, valete, valgano

Other verbs of this type:

prevalere   to prevail

---

vedere to see	**vedendo**	**veduto (visto)** **(aux. avere)**
Simple Past	vidi, vedesti, vide, vedemmo, vedeste, videro	
Future	vedrò, vedrai, vedrà, vedremo, vedrete, vedranno	

---

venire to come	**venendo**	**venuto (aux. essere)**
Present	vengo, vieni, viene, veniamo, venite, vengono	
Future	verrò, verrai, verrà, verremo, verrete, verranno	
Simple Past	venni, venisti, venne, venimmo, veniste, vennero	
Present Subjunctive	venga, venga, venga, veniamo, veniate, vengano	
Imperative	—, vieni, venga, —, venite, vengano	

Other verbs of this type:

avvenire   to happen
convenire   to convene
divenire   to become
pervenire   to attain
provenire   to proceed from, to stem
rinvenire   to find, to revive
svenire   to faint

---

vincere to win	**vincendo**	**vinto (aux. avere)**
Simple Past	vinsi, vincesti, vinse, vincemmo, vinceste, vinsero	

Other verbs of this type:

avvincere　to fascinate
convincere　to convince
rivincere　to win back

---

vivere　to live	**vivendo**	**vissuto**　(*aux.* essere and avere)

Simple Past　**vissi, vivesti, visse, vivemmo, viveste, vissero**

Future　**vivrò, vivrai, vivrà, vivremo, vivrete, vivranno**

Other verbs of this type:

convivere　to live together
rivivere　to live again

---

volere　to want	**volendo**	**voluto**　(*aux.* avere)

Present　**voglio, vuoi, vuole, vogliamo, volete, vogliono**

Future　**vorrò, vorrai, vorrà, vorremo, vorrete, vorranno**

Simple Past　**volli, volesti, volle, volemmo, voleste, vollero**

Present Subjunctive　**voglia, voglia, voglia, vogliamo, vogliate, vogliano**

Imperative　**—, vogli, voglia, —, vogliate, vogliano**

---

volgere　to turn	**volgendo**	**volto**　(*aux.* avere)

Simple Past　**volsi, volgesti, volse, volgemmo, volgeste, volsero**

Other verbs of this type:

avvolgere　to wrap
coinvolgere　to involve
sconvolgere　to overturn, to upset
travolgere　to overpower

9. Impersonal and Defective Verbs

Impersonal Verbs

Impersonal verbs (better called *unipersonal)* are verbs used *only* in the third-person singular, with no definite subject. Included in this category are:

1. Verbs that describe weather conditions such as: *nevica* ("it is snowing"), *piove* ("it is raining"), *grandina* ("it is hailing"), *gela* ("it is freezing"), *tuona* ("it is thundering"), *lampeggia* ("it is lightning"), *fiocca* ("it is snowing"), *balena* ("it is lightning"), *diluvia* ("it is pouring"), *pioviggina* ("it is drizzling"), *tira vento* ("it is windy"), *albeggia* ("it is dawning"), *annotta* ("it is getting dark"), *fa caldo* ("it is warm"), *fa freddo* ("it is cold"), *fa fresco* ("it is cool"), *fa bel tempo* ("the weather is fine"), *fa cattivo tempo* ("the weather is bad").

In compound tenses, these verbs (except *fare)* are conjugated with the auxiliary *essere,* because they are intransitive. However, when these verbs express the duration of an action, they may also take *avere* as their auxiliary. In colloquial Italian, *avere* is widely used with weather verbs in *all* circumstances.

Qui *si gela!*	It is freezing here!
Non *è piovuto* **da un mese.**	It has not rained in a month.
E' nevicato.	It snowed.
Ha nevicato **tutta la notte.**	It snowed all night.
La settimana scorsa *ha fatto* **molto** *caldo.*	Last week it was very warm.
Ha fatto freddo **per tutto l'inverno.**	It has been cold all winter.

Note: Many of these verbs may also be used personally, that is, to refer to a definite subject.

Tuonarono **i cannoni.**	The cannons thundered.
Le lacrime gli *piovevano* **sul volto.**	Tears poured down his cheeks.
Una buona idea mi *è balenata* **nella mente.**	A good idea flashed into my mind

2. Verbs expressing a necessity, an occurrence, or the appearance of fact, such as: *occorre* ("must"), *bisogna ("must")*, *pare* ("it seems"), *importa* ("it matters"), *accade* ("it happens"), *risulta* ("it appears"), *sembra* ("it seems").

Accade **solo a te.**	It only happens to you.
Succedono **tante cose tristi.**	So many sad things happen.
Sembra **facile scrivere questa lettera.**	It seems easy to write this letter.
Occorre **che tu parta subito.**	You must leave at once.
Risulta **che Giorgio sta per sposarsi.**	It appears that George is getting married.
Non importa **che tu venga.**	It is not necessary for you to come.

Note: The infinitive, prepositional phrase, or subordinate clause that follows an impersonal verb acts as subject, thus justifying the use of the third-person singular. Note also that these verbs may be used personally as well.

Tu sembri ricco *(personally).* = You seem to be rich.
Sembra che tu sia ricco *(impersonally).* = It seems that you are rich.

Che tu sia ricco is the subject of *sembra.*

3. Forms of the verb *essere* plus an adjective: *è facile* ("it is easy"), *è difficile* ("it is difficult"), *è vero* ("it is true"), *è falso* ("it is false"), *è probabile* ("it is probable"), *è necessario* ("it is necessary"), *è possibile* ("it is possible").

E' **più** *facile* **dirlo che farlo.**	It is easier said than done.
E' necessario **far presto.**	We must hurry.
Non *è possibile* **vedere il malato oggi.**	It is not possible to see the patient today.

Impersonal Construction with *si*

1. All verbs that are normally used personally may also be used impersonally, that is, in the third-person singular, with no definite subject, and preceded by the impersonal (not reflexive) pronoun *si*.

Si raccomanda **di stare attenti.**	You are advised to pay attention.
Si teme **che gli operai sciopereranno ancora.**	It is to be feared that the workers will strike again.
Si sente **che è italiano.**	You can tell that he is Italian.
Si vieta **di fumare.**	No smoking.

Note: Reflexive and pronominal verbs that already use *si* as reflexive pronoun, use *ci* before it as an impersonal pronoun (*ci si,* instead of *si si).* Examples: *ci si pente* ("one is sorry"), *ci si assicura* ("we are assured"), *ci si rallegra* ("we are happy").

2. An impersonal action may also be expressed: 1) with the verb in the third-person singular passive, 2) in the third-person plural without a subject, or 3) in the second-person singular.

Ci *fu detto* **di partire.**	We were told to leave.
Penseranno **che siamo ricchi.**	One may think we are rich.
Tu dirai **che è un bel film.**	One can say that it is a beautiful movie.

The Impersonal Use of *piacere*

1. The irregular verb *piacere* ("to please," "to give pleasure to") has all the personal forms, like any other verb. For example, here are the present-tense forms:

Singular	*Plural*
piaccio	**piacciamo**
piaci	**piacete**
piace	**piacciono**

2. However, *piacere* is most often used *impersonally,* that is, in the third-person singular or plural, to translate the English verb "to like."

Present Indicative	**piace, piacciono**
Future	**piacerà, piaceranno**
Imperfect	**piaceva, piacevano**
Simple Past	**piacque, piacquero**
Present Perfect	**è piaciuto *(a)*, sono piaciuti *(e)***

3. In an Italian sentence where *piacere* is used impersonally, the thing that is pleasing is the subject of the sentence, while a person who is pleased is the indirect object. In English, on the other hand, the person is the subject and a thing is the direct object. Therefore, to express the idea "to like" in Italian (which has no verb meaning "to like"), one must reword the English sentence, using the verb "to please."

English Sentence	*Rewording of English Sentence*	*Resulting Italian Sentence*
I like roses.	Roses are pleasing to me.	**Mi piacciono le rose.**
He likes roses.	Roses are pleasing to him.	**Gli piacciono le rose.**
She likes roses.	Roses are pleasing to her.	**A lei (or le) piacciono le rose.**
You *(sing.)* like roses.	Roses are pleasing to you.	**Ti piacciono le rose.**
We like roses.	Roses are pleasing to us.	**Ci piacciono le rose.**
You *(pl.)* like roses.	Roses are pleasing to you.	**Vi piacciono le rose.**
They like roses.	Roses are pleasing to them.	**A loro piacciono le rose.**

Notice that the object of the English sentence ("roses") becomes the subject of the Italian sentence while the subject of the English sentence ("I") becomes the indirect object of the Italian sentence (*mi, gli,* etc.).

Notice also that the subject of the Italian sentence comes at the end of the sentence and that *piacere* agrees with it in number.

4. If what is liked is expressed by an infinitive, the verb *piacere* is in the singular even if the infinitive has a plural object.

Mi piace cantare. I like to sing. ("To sing is pleasing to me.")
Mi piace cantare le vecchie canzoni. I like to sing old songs. ("To sing old songs is pleasing to me").

5. If the subject of the verb "to like" is a noun instead of a pronoun, that noun is preceded by *a* (or *a* + article) in Italian, because it functions as an indirect object.

A Tommaso piace la pizza.	Thomas likes pizza.
Ai bambini piace giocare.	Children like to play.

6. In compound tenses *piacere* is conjugated with *essere*. The past participle agrees in gender and number with the subject.

Ti è piaciut*o* quel romanzo francese?	Did you like that French novel?
Mi è piaciut*a* la partita di calcio.	I liked the soccer game.
Gli sono piaciut*i* i biscotti.	He liked cookies.
A Mario sono piaciut*e* le riviste italiane.	Mario liked the Italian magazines

Note: Other verbs of this type are: *dispiacere* ("to be sorry, to mind"), *mancare* ("to lack," "to miss," "to be short"), *occorrere* ("to need"), *restare* ("to have . . . left").

Mi dispiace **se La disturbo.**	I'm sorry to trouble you.
Ti dispiacerebbe **impostare questa lettera?**	Would you mind mailing this letter?
Gli mancavano **le parole.**	He lacked words.
Vi occorre **altro?**	Do you need anything else?
Non *ti resta* **più niente.**	You have nothing left.

Defective Verbs

Verbs are called *defective* when they are used only in certain tenses. Defective verbs have forms only in the third-person singular.

Here is a list of the most commonly used defective verbs in the tenses in which they are used.

addirsi   to be suitable
  Present   **si addice, si addicono**
  Imperfect   **si addiceva, si addicevano**
  Present Subjunctive   **si addica, si addicano**
  Imperfect Subjunctive   **si addicesse, si addicessero**

aggradare   to please
  Present   **aggrada**

calere   to matter
  Present   **cale**
  Future   **calerà (carrà)**

consumere   to wear out
  Simple Past   **consunsi, consunsero**
  Past Participle   **consunto**

fallare   to lack, to be short of
  Present   **falla**
  Past Participle   **fallato**

fervere   to be fervent, to boil
  Present   **ferve, fervono**
  Imperfect   **ferveva, fervevano**
  Present Participle   **fervente**
  Gerund   **fervendo**

lucere   to shine
  Present   **luce, lucono**
  Imperfect   **luceva, lucevano**
  Present Subjunctive   **luca, lucano**
  Imperfect Subjunctive   **lucesse, lucessero**
  Present Participle   **lucente**
  Gerund   **lucendo**

prudere   to itch
  Present   **prude, prudono**
  Imperfect   **prudeva prudevano**
  Future   **pruderò, pruderanno**
  Present Subjunctive   **pruda, prudano**
  Imperfect Subjunctive   **prudesse, prudessero**
  Conditional   **pruderebbe, pruderebbero**
  Gerund   **prudendo**

solere   to be accustomed to
Present   **soglio, suoli, suole, sogliamo, solete, sogliono**
Imperfect   **solevo, solevi, soleva, solevamo, solevate, solevano**
Present Subjunctive   **soglia, soglia, soglia, sogliamo, sogliate, sogliano**
Imperfect Subjunctive   **solessi, solessi, solesse, solessimo, soleste, solessero**
Past Participle   **solito**
Gerund   **solendo**

vertere   to concern, to be about
Present   **verte, vertono**
Imperfect   **verteva, vertevano**
Simple Past   **vertè, verterono**
Future   **verterà, verteranno**
Present Subjunctive   **verta, vertano**
Imperfect Subjunctive   **vertesse, vertessero**
Present Participle   **vertente**
Gerund   **vertendo**

10. Sequence of Tenses

The action described in a dependent clause can occur in the same time, earlier or later than the action expressed in the main (independent) clause. In Italian, this is true of sentences in the indicative, conditional, or subjunctive moods.

> I see that they like to read. *(same time)*
> I saw that they had eaten dinner. *(earlier)*
> I saw to it that they would come on time. *(later)*

The chart below shows a sequence of tenses in time. The tense most removed in past time is the preterite perfect *(trapassato remoto);* the farthest in the future is the future *(futuro).*

Tenses of the Indicative

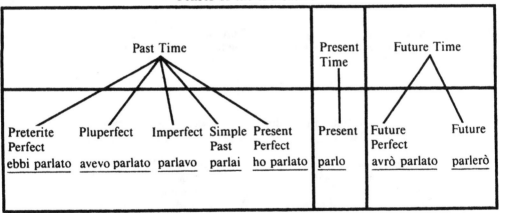

Past Time					Present Time	Future Time	
Preterite Perfect	Pluperfect	Imperfect	Simple Past	Present Perfect	Present	Future Perfect	Future
ebbi parlato	avevo parlato	parlavo	parlai	ho parlato	parlo	avrò parlato	parlerò

Present Time

When the present indicative is used in the independent clause, the tense used in the dependent clause depends on whether the action takes place at the same time, before, or after the action in the independent clause.

So che *legge* **molto.**	I know he reads a lot. *(same time)*
Antonio *dice* **che Anna** *è partita* **alle sei.**	Anthony says that Ann left at six o'clock. *(before)*
Credo **che** *studierà* **di più.**	I think that he will study more *(after).*

Past Time

Imperfect vs. Present Perfect vs. Simple Past

In order to understand when to use either the imperfect, the present perfect, or the simple past, keep in mind that:

1. Actions that were begun but not completed in the past *and* descriptions are generally expressed by the imperfect.

Tutti i giorni *leggeva* **il giornale e poi** *faceva* **una passeggiata.**	Every day he used to read the newspaper and then go for a walk.
Era **mezzogiorno; non** *tirava* **vento; il sole** *splendeva* **ed il mare** *sembrava* **calmo.**	It was noon; it was not windy; the sun was shining and the sea seemed to be calm.

2. Actions completed in the recent past or connected with the present by the speaker are expressed by the present perfect.

Stamattina *ho visto* **Alfredo.**	This morning I saw Alfred.
L'anno scorso *abbiamo visitato* **i nostri parenti in Italia.**	Last year, we visited our relatives in Italy.

3. Actions completed in the past without any connection with the present (therefore called "remote") are described in the simple past (or *passato remoto*).

Dante *nacque* **a Firenze.**	Dante was born in Florence.
I cacciatori *uccisero* **una volpe.**	The hunters killed a fox.

Future Time

1. The choice of tense in the dependent clause depends upon the time of its action in relation to the future-time action of the main clause.

Quando *sarò* **solo,** *penserò* **a te.**	When I'm alone, I'll think of you.
Penserà **che io** *sia andato* **allo stadio quel pomeriggio.**	He will think that I went to the stadium that afternoon.
Quando *avrò avuto* **il passaporto,** *andrò* **in Italia.**	When I get the passport, I will go to Italy.
Scriverò **quella lettera perchè tu me l'hai chiesto.**	I'll write that letter because you have asked me.

2. In modern usage there is a tendency to replace the Future Perfect *(Futuro Anteriore)* with the Future *(Futuro Semplice)*, or with the Present *(Presente)*.

Quando *sarò* **arrivato a Roma, ti telefonerò.**	
Quando *arriverò* **a Roma, ti** *telefonerò.*	When I arrive in Rome, I'll call you.
Quando *arrivo* **a Roma, ti** *telefono.*	

3. Sometimes the *Futuro Anteriore* expresses probability in the past.

Sarà stato (= *può darsi che sia* *stato)* **un bel romanzo, ma io** **non l'ho letto.**	It might have been a beautiful novel, but I haven't read it.
Cosa *sarà accaduto?*	What could have happened?

Conditional Sentences

Note the sequence of actions in the following table and the corresponding examples.

Dependent Clause	Main Clause
1. *Se* plus the present tense.	a. Present c. Imperative b. Future
Se *esco,* **mi** *metto* **il cappotto.** **Se** *prendi* **la medicina, ti** *sentirai* **meglio.** **Se** *esci, comprami* **il giornale.**	If I go out, I put on my coat. If you take the medicine, you'll feel better. If you go out, buy me the newspaper.
2. *Se* plus the future tense	a. Future
Se lo *incontrerò,* **lo** *saluterò.* **Se** *preparerai* **la cena,** *porterò* **il vino.**	If I see him, I'll greet him. If you make dinner, I'll bring the wine.
3. *Se* plus the present perfect or imperfect tense.	a. Present d. Present Perfect b. Future e. Imperative c. Imperfect
Se *hai letto* **il giornale,** *sai* **le notizie.** **Se** *avete fatto* **bene il compito,** *avrete* **un buon voto.** **Se** *ha risposto* **male, non** *voleva* **offendere nessuno.** **Se non ti** *ha salutato* **è perchè non ti** *ha visto.* **Se** *hai visto* **il film,** *dimmi* **di che si tratta.**	If you read the newspaper, you know the news. If you have done your homework well, you'll get a good grade. If he gave the wrong answer, he did not mean to offend anyone. If he did not greet you, it is because he did not see you. If you saw the movie, tell me what it is all about.

4. *Se* plus the imperfect tense.	a. Present	c. Present Perfect
	b. Imperfect	

Se *studiava* **sempre, perchè non** *ricorda* **più niente?**	If he was always studying, why doesn't he remember anything anymore?
Se non *capivate,* **perchè** *ridevate?*	If you didn't understand, why were you laughing?
Se il quadro *era* **bello, perchè non l'***avete* **comprato?**	If the picture was beautiful, why didn't you buy it?

5. *Se* plus the imperfect subjunctive.	a. Conditional
Se *avessi* **il denaro,** *comprerei* **una macchina nuova.**	If I had the money, I would buy a new car.

6. *Se* plus the pluperfect subjunctive.	a. Conditional
	b. Past Conditional
Se tu m'*avessi scritto,* **ora** *saprei* **cosa fare.**	If you had written to me, I would know what to do now.
Se *fosse andato* **alla festa,** *avrebbe rivisto* **i suoi amici.**	If he had gone to the party, he would have seen his friends.

Sentences Requiring the Subjunctive

In a dependent clause with a subjunctive verb, the tense of that verb is determined by the tense of the verb in the independent clause, that is, by the relationship of the dependent clause with the main clause.

Main Clause	**Dependent Clause**
1. Present, Future, or Imperative	Present or Past Subjunctive
Dubito che venga.	I doubt that he is coming.
Dubito che sia venuto	I doubt that he came.
Andremo alla spiaggia, a meno che non piova.	We'll go to the beach, unless it rains.
Quando penserò che tu abbia fatto i compiti, ti porterò al cinema.	When I think that you have finished your homework, I'll take you to the movies.
Sii felice che essi ti scrivano.	Be happy that they write to you.
Sii felice che essi ti abbiano scritto.	Be happy that they wrote to you.

2. Present Perfect

Ho pensato che essi abbiano fame.

Ho pensato che essi abbiano avuto fame.

Ho pensato che essi avessero fame.

Ho pensato che essi avessero avuto fame.

Present, Past, Imperfect, or Pluperfect Subjunctive

I thought they were *(and still are)* hungry.

I thought they have been hungry *(from time to time)*.

I thought they were hungry *(at that time)*.

I thought they had been hungry *(at a specific moment in the past)*.

3. Simple Past, Imperfect, or Pluperfect

Temei (temevo, avevo temuto) che non arrivassero.

Temei (temevo, avevo temuto) che non fossero arrivati.

Imperfect or Pluperfect Subjunctive

I was afraid they wouldn't come.

I was afraid they wouldn't have come.

4. Present Conditional

Vorrei che tu mi scrivessi più spesso.

Vorrei che tu fossi pagato meglio.

Non vorrei che tu abbia torto in questo caso.

Non penserei che tu sia stato solo tutto il giorno.

Imperfect or Pluperfect Subjunctive*

I would like you to write to me more often.

I would like you to get better pay.

I wouldn't want you to be wrong in this case.

I wouldn't think that you have been alone all day.

5. Past Conditional

Non avrei mai creduto che tu fossi infelice.

Avremmo comprato la casa, se avessimo avuto il denaro.

Imperfect or Pluperfect Subjunctive

I would never have believed that you were unhappy.

We would have bought the house, if we had had the money.

*Sometimes Present or Past Subjunctive

11. Auxiliary Verbs

In addition to the auxiliary verbs *avere* and *essere,* which are used in the perfect tense, there are other verbs that have a similar function when followed by an infinitive.

The most common auxiliary verbs are: *volere, potere,* and *dovere.* These verbs, when they are not followed by an infinitive, are all conjugated with the auxiliary *avere.* However, when they *are* followed by an infinitive, they are conjugated with the auxiliary verb required by that particular infinitive. Thus, since *leggere* requires the auxiliary *avere:*

Egli *aveva* **voluto (potuto, dovuto) leggere.**	He had wanted (had been able, had had) to read.

And since *venire* requires the auxiliary *essere:*

Egli *era* **voluto (potuto, dovuto) venire.**	He had wanted (had been able, had had) to come.

In modern usage and in conversational Italian, the auxiliary *avere* often replaces the auxiliary *essere.* Thus:

Non *ho* **potuto venire.**	I wasn't able to come.
Ho **dovuto partire.**	I had to leave.

volere

Volere translates the English "to want," "to wish," but has many other meanings, depending on the tense in which it is used.

Voleva venire a visitarci.	He *intended* to come see us.
Vorrei leggere un giornale italiano.	I *would like* to read an Italian newspaper.
Non credo che essi vogliano partire.	I don't think they *want to* leave.

potere

Potere translates the English "to be able," "to be allowed," but has many other meanings, depending on the tense in which it is used. Note that, in Italian, there is no distinction between "can" and "may."

Non posso venire.	I *can't* come.
Posso parlare?	*May* I speak?
Non siamo potuti arrivare a tempo. (or Non abbiamo potuto . . .)	We *couldn't* arrive on time.
Avrei potuto telefonargli dall' ufficio.	I *could have* phoned him from the office.
Dubitiamo che egli possa venire domani.	We doubt that he *can* come tomorrow.

Note: The present and perfect conditional of *potere* translates the English "could" or "might" and "could have" or "might have" respectively.

Potrei comprarlo.	I *could* buy it.
Avrei potuto comprarlo.	I *could have* bought it.

dovere

Dovere has many meanings, depending on the sense in which it is used.

Devo partire adesso.	I *must* leave now.
Doveva lavorare fino alle cinque del pomeriggio.	He *had to* work until 5 PM.
Dovrebbe arrivare da un momento all'altro.	He *should be* in any minute.
Avresti dovuto scrivergli una lettera.	You *should have* written him a letter.
Credo che tu debba mangiare di meno.	I think you *should* eat less.
Temevo che essi dovessero partire immediatamente.	I was afraid that they *might have* to leave immediately.
Dovresti mangiare di più.	You *ought to* eat more.

Note: *Dovere* + a direct object means "to owe."

Tu mi devi centomila lire	You *owe* me one hundred thousand lire.
Devo a te la mia promozione.	I *owe* you my promotion.

sapere

Sapere can be translated as "to be able," "can," "could," etc. when it is used in the sense of "to know how to do something."

Non seppero rispondere.	They *couldn't* (or *didn't know how to*) answer.
Non so nuotare.	I *can't* (or *don't know how to*) swim.

parere, sembrare

Mi sembra di sognare.	It *seems* as if I'm dreaming.
Il vento pare giocare con le foglie.	It *seems* as if the wind is playing with the leaves.

solere

Maria suole partire alle sette.	Maria *is used to* leaving at seven o'clock.

cominciare, finire, continuare, cessare

Il maestro cominciò ad insegnare.	The teacher *began to* teach.
Finiscila di fare rumore!	*Stop* making noise.
Continuò a lavorare.	He *kept on* working.
Non abbiamo mai cessato di scrivergli.	We never *stopped* writing to him.

desiderare, preferire, cercare di

Desidero fargli una visita.	I *would like to* visit him.
Preferiamo stare da soli.	We *prefer to* be alone.
Egli cerca d'imparare l'italiano.	He *is trying to* learn Italian.

essere sul punto di

This verbal phrase expresses the meaning "to be about to," or "to be on the verge of."

Siamo sul punto di partire.	We *are about* to leave.
E' sul punto di morire.	He *is about* to die.

fare + infinitive

1. The verb *fare* followed by an infinitive expresses the idea of *having* something done or *causing* someone else to do something. In the latter case, the thing acted upon is the direct object and the person who has to act is the indirect object.

Faccio riparare le *scarpe.* (D.O.)	I am having my shoes repaired
Il maestro fa studiare la *lezione agli alunni.* (D.O./I.O.)	The teacher makes the students study the lesson.

2. Noun objects *follow* the infinitive (the direct preceding the indirect).

La mamma fa mangiare *la pera al bambino.* (D.O./I.O.)	Mother is having her son eat the pear.

3. Pronoun objects generally *precede* forms of *fare* (except for *loro*, which always follows the infinitive).

Farò correggere gli errori. *Li* **farò correggere.**	I will have the errors corrected. I will have them corrected.
Farò ascoltare la musica agli invitati. Farò ascoltare *loro* **la musica.**	I will have my guests listen to the music. I will have them listen to the music.

Pronoun objects are attached to *fare* only when *fare* is in the

a. infinitive form

Se n'è andato? Avresti dovuto far*lo* aspettare.	Is he gone? You should have made him stay.

b. gerund form

Facendo*lo* aspettare, l'hai offeso.	You offended him by making him wait.

c. past participle form

Fatto*lo* sedere, gli parlai del contratto.	Having him seated, I spoke to him about the contract.

d. imperative form

La macchina è sporca; fate*la* lavare.	The car is dirty; have it washed.

4. If the action is done *on behalf of* the subject that is, "to have *(or* get) something done for oneself by someone else, the reflexive *farsi* is used.

Mi feci pettinare **i capelli da Maria.**	I *had* my hair combed by Mary.

lasciare

Lasciare means "to let someone do something" or "to let something happen." Just like *fare,* the verb *lasciare* is followed directly by the infinitive.

Lascialo dormire	Let him sleep.
Vivi e lascia vivere.	Live and let live.
Lasciami entrare!	Let me in!

Note: *Lasciare* may also be followed by *che* + the subjunctive.

Lascia *che vada* (= **Lascialo andare).**	Let him go.

12. Past Infinitive, Gerund, and Participle

1. The past (or *compound*) infinitive is formed by *avere* or *essere* plus the past participle of the main verb.

aver(e) parlato "to have talked"
aver(e) capito "to have understood"
aver(e) venduto "to have sold"

essere caduto *(a,i,e)* "to have fallen"
essere ritornato *(a,i,e)* "to have returned"
essere fuggito *(a,i,e)* "to have fled"

Note that the *e* of *avere* can be dropped.

2. The past infinitive is used when the action of the main clause takes place after the action described in the dependent clause.

Sono contento di *essere ritornato* **a casa.**
I'm happy that I came back home.

Disse di *aver capito* **la lezione.**
He said he understood the lesson.

3. If the past infinitive is reflexive, the pronoun is attached to *essere,* and the past participle agrees with the subject in gender and number.

Dopo *essermi vestito,* **sono uscito di casa.**
After dressing up, I went out.

Dopo *essersi pettinata,* **Maria scese giù in cucina.**
After combing her hair, Mary went down to the kitchen.

Dopo *esserci lavati* **ci sedemmo a tavola.**
After washing up, we sat down at the table.

Note: The preposition *dopo* ("after") and the verb *ringraziare* ("to thank") are always followed by the past infinitive.

Dopo *esserti asciugate* **le mani, scrivi questa lettera.**
After drying your hands, write this letter.

Ti *ringrazio* **di** (or **per**) *avermi avvisato.*
I thank you for informing me.

Vi *ringrazio* **per** *essere accorsi* **in mio aiuto.**
I thank you for coming to my aid.

Past Gerund

1. The past (or *compound*) gerund is used to express an action performed by the subject *before* the action of the main verb.

Essendo arrivato **in ritardo alla stazione, persi il treno.**	Having arrived late to the station, I missed the train.
Avendo ottenuto **il passaporto, posso partire per l'Italia.**	Having obtained the passport, I can leave for Italy.

2. Note that the use of the past gerund is not determined by the tense of the main verb.

Avendogli parlato molte volte, so come la pensa.	Having spoken to him many times, I know how he thinks.
Avendo studiato molto, superai l'esame.	Having studied hard, I passed the exam.

3. With the progressive construction (*stare* + gerund), reflexive and object pronouns are either placed before *stare* or are attached to the gerund.

Mi **stavo lavando** (or **Stavo lavando***mi*) **quando tu arrivasti.**	I was washing up when you arrived.
Ti **stiamo aspettando** (or Stiamo aspettando*ti*) **da ieri sera.**	We have been waiting for you since last night.

Past Participle

(For the formation of the past participle and its use in compound tenses, see Chapter 3.)

1. The past participle can be used either as a noun or an adjective (in this latter case, it must agree in gender and number with the noun it modifies).

Guai *ai vinti!* (noun)	Woe to the vanquished!
Onoriamo *i morti* **di tutte le guerre!** (noun)	Let us honor the dead of all wars!
Questo è un lavoro ben *fatto.* (adjective)	This is a job well done.
Ecco i fiori *raccolti* **nel giardino.** (adjective)	Here are the flowers that I gathered in the garden.

2. The past participle can be used independently in what is called an absolute construction. This can replace the past gerund or *dopo* + past infinitive.

Arrivato (or *Essendo arrivato, Dopo essere arrivato)* **a casa, mi misi a leggere.**	Having arrived home, I started to read.
Superato (or *Avendo superato, Dopo aver superato)* **l'esame, andai in vacanza.**	Having passed the exam, I went on vacation.

In this construction, the past participle agrees with the subject of the sentence if the verb is conjugated with *essere.*

Tornat*a* **al parco,** *Anna* **si sedette sotto un oleandro.**	Ann went back to the park and sat under an oleander.
Arrivat*i* **a Milano,** *i turisti* **andarono in albergo.**	Having arrived in Milan, the tourists went to a hotel.

If the verb is conjugated with *avere,* the past participle agrees in gender and number with its direct object.

Finit*a la lezione,* **il maestro tornò a casa.**	Having finished the lesson, the teacher came home.
Vist*o il padre,* **la ragazza gli corse incontro.**	Having seen her father, the girl ran to meet him.

When reflexive or object pronouns depend on a past participle, they follow and are attached to it.

Alzato*si* **in piedi, Roberto cominciò a cantare.**	Robert rose to his feet and started to sing.
Incontrata*la,* **la salutai.**	Having met her, I greeted her.

3. The past participle is used after certain adverbs and conjunctions, including *appena (non appena)* and *dopo.*

Appena arrivato, gli telefonai.	As soon as I arrived, I phoned him.
Dopo dormito, ti sentirai meglio.	After you sleep, you'll feel better.

Note: The Italian past participle often translates the English present participle.

Appeso alla parete, c'era un quadro di Michelangelo.	Hanging on the wall, there was a painting by Michelangelo.
Mia nonna è seduta vicino al camino.	My grandmother is sitting by the fireplace.

13. Active and Passive Voices

If a subject performs an action, the verb is *active*. If the subject receives the action or is acted upon, the verb is *passive*. In Italian the passive voice is much less common than in English.

Active:	**Giovanni** *firma* **la lettera.**	John signs the letter.
Passive:	**La lettera** *è firmata* **da Giovanni.**	The letter is signed by John.

The passive construction (also called the *passive voice*) is formed by the desired tense of the verb *essere* and the past participle of the verb. The past participle always agrees in number and gender with the subject. If the agent (the person or thing performing the action) is expressed, it is preceded by *da* (with or without the article).

Carlo *rispetta* **i genitori.** *(active)*	Carl respects his parents.
I genitori *sono rispettati* **da Carlo.** (passive).	The parents are respected by Carl.
Il maestro *loda* **Teresa e Cristina.** (active)	The teacher praises Theresa and Christine.
Teresa e Cristina *sono lodate* **dal maestro.** (passive)	Theresa and Christine are praised by the teacher.
Il fuoco *distrusse* **la casa.** (active)	The fire destroyed the house.
La casa *fu distrutta* **dal fuoco.** (passive).	The house was destroyed by the fire.

Conjugation of the Passive Voice

Simple Tenses		Perfect Tenses	
Present	**io sono lodato** *(a)*	Past Perfect	**io sono stato** *(a)* **lodato** *(a)*
Imperfect	**io ero lodato** *(a)*	Pluperfect	**io ero stato** *(a)* **lodato** *(a)*
Future	**io sarò lodato** *(a)*	Future Perfect	**io sarò stato** *(a)* **lodato** *(a)*
Past Absolute	**io fui lodato** *(a)*	Preterite Perfect	**io fui stato** *(a)* **lodato** *(a)*

Present Subjunctive	(che) io sia lodato *(a)*	Past Subjunctive	(che) io sia stato *(a)* lodato *(a)*
Present Conditional	io sarei lodato *(a)*	Past Conditional	io sarei stato *(a)* lodato *(a)*
Infinitive	essere lodato *(a)*	Past Infinitive	essere stato *(a)* lodato *(a)*
Present Gerund	essendo lodato *(a)*	Past Gerund	essendo stato *(a)* lodata *(a)*

Other Passive Constructions

1. In simple tenses only, *essere* may be replaced by *venire* in passive constructions. This substitution is preferable *only* when the action expressed by the verb is taking place at the moment of speech.

Il motore viene avviato.	The motor is being started. *(the action is in progress)*
Il motore è avviato.	The motor is on. *(before I started to talk)*
L'erba viene tagliata.	The grass is being cut. *(the action is in progress)*
L'erba è tagliata.	The grass is cut. *(before I started to talk)*

In all other cases, it is preferable to use *essere*.

Tu sarai lodato dal maestro.	You will be praised by the teacher.

2. If the passive verb expresses the idea of necessity or obligation, *essere* may be replaced by *andare*.

Le regole *vanno* (or *devono essere)* **rispettate.**	Rules must be respected.
Il lavoro *va* (or *deve essere)* **fatto in questo modo.**	The work has to be done this way.

Note: Even when the idea of necessity or obligation is not implied, *andare* may be used with verbs like *perdere, disperdere, smarrire.*

La lettera è andata smarrita.	The letter went astray.
L'indirizzo è andato perduto.	The address got lost.

3. Sometimes *essere* is replaced by *rimanere.*

La casa rimase danneggiata dal fuoco.	The house was damaged by the fire.

4. The passive construction can be made by placing *si* before the third-person singular or plural of any simple tense or by attaching it to the

infinitive or gerund. This construction may only be used when the agent is not expressed. (Usually, the subject will be a thing or things.) Note that the subject usually *follows* the verb.

Si vendono **molti libri. (Molti libri sono venduti.)**	Many books are sold.
Negli Stati Uniti *si parlano* **molte lingue straniere. (Molte lingue straniere** *sono parlate* **negli Stati Uniti.)**	Many foreign languages are spoken in the United States.
Queste sono le cose da *farsi.* **(Queste sono le cose che devono** *essere fatte.*)	These are the things that have to be done.

Note that in compound tenses *si* is placed before the passive form of the correspondent simple tense.

I libri *si* **sono venduti in gran numero.**	Books were sold in great number.

14. Verbs Followed by a Preposition

1. The following verbs require the preposition *a* when followed by an infinitive. The preposition is not always translated into English.

abituarsi	to get used to	**insegnare**	to teach
affrettarsi	to hurry	**invitare**	to invite
aiutare	to help		
andare	to go	**mandare**	to send
		mettersi	to begin, to set about
cominciare	to begin		
condannare	to condemn	**obbligare**	to oblige
continuare	to continue		
correre	to run	**passare**	to stop by
costringere	to compel	**pensare**	to think of
		persuadere	to persuade
decidersi	to make up one's mind	**preparare**	to prepare
		provare	to try
dedicarsi	to devote oneself		
divertirsi	to enjoy oneself	**rinunciare**	to renounce
		riprendere	to resume
fare meglio	to be better off	**riuscire**	to succeed
fare presto	to be quick, to hurry up		
		sbrigarsi	to hurry
fermarsi	to stop	**seguitare**	to continue
forzare	to force	**servire**	to be good for
		stare	to stay, to stand
imparare	to learn		
incoraggiare	to encourage	**tornare**	to return
		venire	to come

Il professore mi costrinse *a* studiare la lezione.	The professor compelled me to study the lesson.
Cominciò *a* ridere.	He started to laugh.
Sono venuto *a* trovarti.	I have come to see you.
Cominciammo *a* lavorare presto.	We began to work early.
Dopo cena ripresi *a* leggere il giornale.	After supper I resumed reading the newspaper.

2. The following verbs require the preposition *di* when followed by an infinitive.

accettare	to accept	**lamentarsi**	to complain
accorgersi	to notice		
ammettere	to admit	**meravigliarsi**	to be surprised
aspettare	to wait for	**minacciare**	to threaten
aspettarsi	to hope, to expect to		
augurare	to wish	**offrire**	to offer
augurarsi	to hope	**ordinare**	to order
avere bisogno	to need		
avere fretta	to be in a hurry	**pensare**	to plan
avere il tempo	to have the time to	**pentirsi**	to repent
avere l'impressione	to have the feeling	**permettere**	to permit
avere intenzione	to intend	**pregare**	to beg
avere paura	to be afraid	**proibire**	to prohibit
avere vergogna	to be ashamed	**promettere**	to promise
avere voglia	to feel like	**proporre**	to propose
cercare	to try	**rendersi conto**	to realize
cessare	to cease	**ricordarsi**	to remember
chiedere	to ask	**rifiutarsi**	to refuse
comandare	to command		
consigliare	to advise to	**sapere**	to know
credere	to believe	**sentirsela**	to feel up to
		smettere	to stop
decidere	to decide	**sognare**	to dream
dimenticare	to forget	**sperare**	to hope
dire	to say, to tell	**stabilire**	to decide
domandare	to ask	**stancarsi**	to get tired
dubitare	to doubt	**stupirsi**	to be amazed
		suggerire	to suggest
fare a meno	to do without		
fingere	to pretend	**temere**	to fear
finire	to finish	**tentare**	to try, to attempt
impedire	to prevent	**vergognarsi**	to be ashamed
		vietare	to forbid

Non ha intenzione *di* sposarla.	He has no intention of marrying her.
Non ho voglia *di* scherzare.	I am not in the mood for joking.
Non possiamo fare a meno *di* fumare.	We cannot give up smoking.
Fingeva *di* essere ammalato.	He pretended to be sick.
Non mi sento *di* dormire adesso.	I don't feel like sleeping just now.

3. Some verbs can be followed by both *a* (followed by a person) and *di* (followed by the infinitive).

chiedere a ... di	to ask ... to
comandare a ... di	to order ... to
consigliare a *(qualcuno)* di *(fare qualcosa)*	to advise *(someone)* to *(do something)*
dire a ... di	to ask ... to
domandare a ... di	to ask ... to
impedire a ... di	to forbid ... to
ordinare a ... di	to order ... to
permettere a ... di	to permit ... to
proibire a ... di	to forbid ... to
promettere a ... di	to promise ... to
proporre a ... di	to propose ... to
ricordare a ... di	to remind ... to
suggerire a ... di	to suggest to ... to
vietare a ... di	to forbid ... to

Consiglio *a* **Pietro** *di* **cambiare idea.**	I advise Peter to change his mind.
Chiedemmo *al* **maestro** *di* **venire al concerto con noi.**	We asked the teacher to come to the concert with us.
Il papà non permise *a* **Rosa** *di* **uscire.**	The father did not permit Rose to go out.
Ricorda *a* **Mario** *di* **comprare il giornale italiano.**	Remind Mario to buy the Italian newspaper.
Il maestro proibì *agli* **studenti** *di* **parlare.**	The teacher forbade the students to speak.

4. Some verbs can be followed *directly* by an infinitive.

amare	to love	parere	to seem
bastare	to suffice	piacere	to like
bisognare	to need	potere	to be able
desiderare	to desire	preferire	to prefer
dovere	to have to	sapere	to know how
fare	to make	sembrare	to seem
giovare	to be useful	sentire	to hear
gradire	to appreciate	solere	to be accustomed to
lasciare	to allow		
occorrere	to be necessary	udire	to hear
osare	to dare	vedere	to see
		volere	to want

Bisogna scrivere di nuovo la lettera.	The letter needs to be rewritten.
Non osammo andare alla festa.	We did not dare to go to the party.
Preferisco restare qui.	I prefer to stay here.
L'ho visto passare pochi minuti fa.	I saw him go by a few minutes ago.
Vogliamo fare come ci piace.	We will do as we like.

5. The following verbs require the preposition *su*.

contare su	to count on	**riflettere su**	to ponder on
giurare su	to swear on	**scommettere su**	to bet on

Puoi contare *su* di me.

You can rely on me.

Abbiamo riflettuto *sulle* ragioni di questo fallimento.

We have pondered on the reasons for this failure.

Ho scommesso molto denaro *su* quel cavallo.

I bet a lot of money on that horse.

Part Two:
Essentials of
Grammar

15. Articles

As in English, articles in Italian can be either definite or indefinite: **il** *ragazzo*, **the** boy; **un** *ragazzo*, **a** boy. The table below provides the forms of the definite and indefinite articles:

		Definite	Indefinite
Masculine	Singular	il, lo, (l')	un, uno
	Plural	i, gli, (gl')	—, —
Feminine	Singular	la, (l')	una, un'
	Plural	le	—, —

il and **i**   are used before masculine nouns beginning with a consonant (except *x, z, gn, ps,* or *s impura,* that is, an *s* followed by another consonant).

il **libro,** *i* **libri;** *il* **sarto,** *i* **sarti;** *il* **treno,** *i* **treni**

lo and **gli**   are used before masculine nouns beginning with a vowel, *x, z, gn, ps,* or *s impura.* Note that *lo* drops the *o* before masculine singular nouns that begin with a vowel and an apostrophe takes its place. *Gli* drops the *i* and takes an apostrophe only before masculine plural nouns beginning with an *i.*

lo **zio,** *gli* **zii;** *lo* **gnomo,** *gli* **gnomi;** *lo* **studente,** *gli* **studenti;** *lo* **psicanalista,** *gli* **psicanalisti;** *l'* **onore,** *gli* **onori;** *l'* **albero,** *gli* **alberi;** *l'* **Italiano,** *gl'* **Italiani**

la and **le**   are used before feminine nouns.

la **casa,** *le* **case;** *la* **mela,** *le* **mele**

Note that *la* drops the *a* and takes an apostrophe before feminine singular nouns starting with a vowel.

l' **anima,** *le* **anime;** *l'* **alba,** *le* **albe;** *l'* **estasi,** *le* **estasi;** *l'* **entità,** *le* **entità**

Before words beginning with *i* followed by a vowel (*iodio, iugoslavo),* either *il* or *lo* may be used. In modern usage, the article *lo* is preferred.

Before feminine nouns beginning with *i* followed by a vowel *(iena, ionosfera),* the article *la* never becomes *l': la iena, la ionosfera.*

un   is used before masculine nouns beginning either with a consonant or with a vowel.

un **cane**, *un* **gatto**, *un* **albero**, *un* **animale**

uno   is used before masculine nouns beginning with *s impura* or *x, z, gn, ps.*

uno **studente**, *uno* **xenofobo**, *uno* **zaino**, *uno* **gnomo**, *uno* **psichiatra**

una   is used before feminine nouns.

una **casa**, *una* **penna**, *una* **gomma**

If the noun starts with a vowel *una* becomes *un.'*

*un'***opera**, *un'***automobile**, *un'***aria**, *un'***impresa**

Uses of the Definite Article

The definite article is used with:

1. Geographical names (continents, countries, rivers, states, regions).

*L'***Europa è un vecchio continente.**	Europe is an old continent.
*L'***Italia è una penisola.**	Italy is a peninsula.
Il **Po è il fiume più lungo d'Italia.**	The Po is the longest Italian river.
La **Toscana è molto bella.**	Tuscany is very beautiful.

However, the definite article is omitted when these geographical names are preceded by the preposition *in* or *di.*

Ho passato le vacanze *in Austria.*	I spent my vacation in Austria.
Conosci la storia *d'Italia?*	Do you know the history of Italy?

Note: Names of cities, towns, and villages do not take an article, except those that are modified by an adjective or a phrase and those that already have an article as an integral part of their name *(La Spezia, il Cairo, l'Aquila, l'Aia, il Pireo, la Mecca).* Thus:

Milano è una città industriale.	Milan is an industrial city.
La **Roma dei Papi.**	The Rome of the Popes.
La **vecchia Napoli.**	Old Naples.
*L'***anno scorso ho visitato** *il* **Cairo.**	Last year I visited Cairo.

2. Nouns (abstract or concrete) used in a general sense and collective nouns.

*L'***oro è prezioso.**	Gold is precious.
La **perseveranza è una virtù.**	Perseverance is a virtue.
La **gente è contenta.**	People are happy.
Il **tempo è denaro.**	Time is money.

3. Parts of the body and articles of clothing (in place of the English possessive "my," "your," "his," "her," etc.).

Si lava *la* **faccia.**	He washes his face.
Si mette *il* **cappotto.**	He puts on his coat.

4. Days of the week, to indicate a *repeated* action or event occurring on a certain day.

Vado al cinema *il* **sabato.**	I go to the movies on Saturday. *(every Saturday)*

However, it is omitted when referring to a *specific* action or event occurring on a specific day.

La cartolina è arrivata martedì.	The postcard arrived on Tuesday. *(just once)*

5. Titles.

Il **dottor Rossi è un cardiologo.**	Doctor Rossi is a cardiologist.
Il **professor Graziosi ha finito la lezione.**	Professor Graziosi has finished his lesson.
Il **signor Brambilla è di Milano.**	Mr. Brambilla is from Milan.

However, in direct address, the article is omitted.

Buon giorno, signor Cardillo.	Good morning, Mr. Cardillo
Benvenuto, dottor Miletti.	Welcome, doctor Miletti.

Note: The definite article is omitted in numerical titles of monarchs.

Carlo Quinto	Charles the Fifth.

6. Names of languages and other subjects of study.

Noi apprendiamo *l'* **italiano.**	We learn Italian.
Mi piace *la* **storia.**	I like history.

Note: The definite article is *not* used after *di* or *in* and sometimes after the verbs *parlare, insegnare, studiare.*

Ho perduto il mio libro di latino.	I lost my Latin book.
La lettera è scritta in inglese.	The letter is written in English.
Qui si parla *(l')* **italiano.**	Italian spoken here.
Il professor Dupont insegna *(il)* **francese.**	Professor Dupont teaches French.
Noi studiamo *(il)* **latino e** *(il)* **greco.**	We study Latin and Greek.

7. Adjectives and verbs used as nouns.

Lui preferisce *il* **giallo.**	He prefers yellow.
Il **mangiare e** *il* **bere.**	Food and drinks.

8. Names of seasons.

Mi piace *l'* **estate.**	I like summer.

9. Units of weight or measure, instead of the English "a" or "an."

Queste pere costano duemila lire *la* **libbra.**	These pears cost 2 thousand lire a pound.

10. Certain time expressions.

*l'*anno prossimo	next year
il mese scorso	last month
la settimana passata	last week
sono *le* quattro	it is four o'clock

11. Surnames of very famous people or, colloquially, before given names of women.

Il **Carducci ed** *il* **Pascoli sono due poeti famosi.**	Carducci and Pascoli are two famous poets.
Conosci *il* **Fogazzaro?**	Do you know Fogazzaro?
Dove abita *la* **Teresa?**	Where does Theresa live?

12. After the verb *avere,* with parts of the body, in such expressions as:

Lisa ha *i* **capelli lunghi.**	Lisa has long hair.
Giorgio ha *le* **mani sporche.**	George has dirty hands.

Omission of the Definite Article

The definite article is omitted:

1. Before a masculine name (also when it is followed by a surname), unless modified by an adjective.

Raffaello nacque ad Urbino.	Raphael was born in Urbino.
Dante Alighieri scrisse la Divina Commedia.	Dante Alighieri wrote the Divine Comedy.

But:

Il **grande Galileo nacque a Pisa.**	The great Galileo was born in Pisa.
Il **divino Michelangelo scolpì il Mosè.**	The divine Michelangelo sculptured "the Moses."

2. Before a surname.

Marconi inventò la radio.	Marconi invented the radio.

However, the article *is* used before a surname that refers to a woman.

La **Serao scrisse molti romanzi.**	Serao wrote many novels.
La **Duse fu un'attrice famosa.**	Duse was a famous actress.

3. Before a noun in mere parenthetical apposition, *i.e.,* not necessary for purposes of identification or differentiation.

Roma, capitale d'Italia, è una città antica.	Rome, the capital of Italy, is an old city.

But:

Roma, *la* **capitale, m'interessa meno di Firenze.**	Rome, the capital, interests me less than Florence.

4. In an enumeration, if the nouns are understood to be all in the same category.

Abbiamo invitato parenti, amici e conoscenti.	We have invited relatives, friends and acquaintences.

5. Before days, months, time of day, and some holidays.

Partirò sabato.	I will leave Saturday.
Gennaio è un mese freddo.	January is a cold month.
Suona mezzogiorno.	It is noon.
Natale cade il 25 dicembre.	Christmas falls on December 25.

Note: The article *is* used with *La Pentecoste, la Candelora, l'Ascensione, il Corpus Domini.*

6. In a partitive construction.

Ho comprato pere mature ed uva squisita.	I bought some ripe pears and delicious grapes.

7. Before the names of some islands such as *Candia, Capri, Cipro, Malta, Rodi.*

Malta non è molto lontana *dalla* **Sicilia.**	Malta is not so far from Sicily.

8. In some common expressions following the prepositions: *a, in, per, da.*

a destra	to (on) the right	**per regalo**	as a gift
in campagna	in (to) the country	**da sinistra**	from the left

Omission of the Indefinite Article

The indefinite article is omitted:

1. Before unmodified nouns that designate professions, nationalities, ranks, religions, etc.

Giovanni è medico.	John is a doctor.
Antonio è americano.	Anthony is American (an American).
Roberto è capitano	Robert is a captain.
Lui è cattolico.	He is a Catholic.

However, when such nouns are modified, the indefinite article is used.

Antonio è *un* americano che vive in Italia.	Anthony is an American who lives in Italy.

2. Before a noun in apposition:

Orvieto, piccola città dell'Umbria, ha un duomo bellissimo.	Orvieto, a little town in Umbria, has a very beautiful cathedral.

3. Before the numbers *cento* and *mille.*

Te l'ho detto cento volte.	I told you a hundred times.
Avevo mille cose da fare.	I had a thousand things to do.

4. After the exclamatory adjectives *che* and *quale.*

Che viaggio!	What a trip!
Quale onore!	What an honor!

5. After the preposition *da* meaning "as" or "like."

A volte Paolo agisce da bambino.	Paul sometimes acts like a child.

Contractions of Prepositions with the Definite Article

When the prepositions *di* (of, by, from, about), *a* (to, at, in), *da* (from, by, to, at, in, with), *in* (in, into, to), *su* (on, above) are followed by a definite article, the preposition and article combine to form a single word, as follows:

	il	*lo*	*l'*	*la*	*i*	*gli*	*le*
di	del	dello	dell'	della	dei	degli	delle
a	al	allo	all'	alla	ai	agli	alle
da	dal	dallo	dall'	dalla	dai	dagli	dalle
in	nel	nello	nell'	nella	nei	negli	nelle
su	sul	sullo	sull'	sulla	sui	sugli	sulle

Note:

1. The prepositions *tra* ("among," "between") and *fra* ("among," "between") never contract.

Mi sento *tra* amici.	I feel myself among friends.

2. In compound prepositions like *davanti a, vicino a,* the *a* combines with the article.

Davanti *al* banco.	In front of the desk.
Davanti *all'*ufficio.	In front of the office.
Vicino *all'*albergo.	In front of the hotel.

3. The preposition *da* (+ the article) often means "at the place (house, office, etc.) of"

Lisa va *dal* **dentista.**	Lisa is going to the dentist's (office).
Caterina va *dalla* **nonna.**	Catherine is going to her grandmother's (house).

However, with first names, pronouns, and names of cities, the article is omitted.

Vado da Paolo.	I am going to Paul's (house).
Carlo sta da noi.	Carl is staying with us.
Ritorniamo da Venezia.	We are returning from Venice.

4. The combined forms of *per* ("for," "through"): *pel, pei, pegli,* etc. are practically obsolete.

5. The contracted forms of *con* ("with"), except *col* and *coi,* are seldom used. In modern usage the separate forms are preferred.

Maria va a scuola *con la* **sorella.**	Mary goes to school with her sister.

Possession

Possession is indicated in Italian by a phrase with *di* or *di* + the article. *Di* becomes *d'* before words beginning with *i*. With the other vowel the elision is optional.

La matita *di* **Bernardo.**	Bernard's pencil.
L'orologio *d'***Alberto** (or *di* **Alberto).**	Albert's watch.
I fiumi *d'***Italia.**	The rivers of Italy.
I guanti *del* **ragazzo.**	The boy's gloves.
La penna *dello* **studente.**	The student's pen.
La moglie *dell'***avvocato.**	The lawyer's wife.
La porta *della* **scuola.**	The door of the school.
Lo stipendio *dei* **maestri.**	The teacher's salary.
Le scarpe *delle* **ragazze.**	The girls' shoes.

Partitive Construction

1. The English "some" or "any" is usually expressed in Italian in affirmative sentences by the partitive construction of *di* + the definitive article.

Compriamo *della* **carne dal macellaio.**	We are buying some meat at the butcher's.
Abbiamo *dei* **parenti in Italia.**	We have some relatives in Italy.
Vuoi *del* **formaggio?**	Do you want any cheese?

This partitive construction may be considered as the plural form of the indefinite article.

2. The partitive "any" is not normally expressed in negative sentences. It is optional in interrogative sentences.

Non abbiamo libri.	We do not have any books.
Non mangio carne.	I do not eat any meat.
Hai ricevuto *(del)* **denaro da tuo padre?**	Did you receive any money from your father?
Prendi *(del)* **latte o** *(del)* **caffè?**	Do you take (some) coffee or (some) milk?

3. The partitive idea of "some" or "any" can also be rendered in Italian by *qualche, alcuni, alcune* meaning "a few," or by *un poco di, un po' di,* to mean "a bit of" or "a little."

Noi abbiamo *qualche* **libro** (or *alcuni* **libri**).	We have some books.
C'erano *alcune* **mele sulla tavola.**	There were some apples on the table.
Metti *un po' di* **burro sul pane.**	Put some butter on the bread.
Mangia *un poco di* **frutta.**	Eat some fruit.

16. Nouns

Gender

All nouns in Italian are either masculine or feminine.

1. A singular noun that ends in *-o* is generally masculine.

il **maestro,** the teacher il **treno,** the train il **quaderno,** the notebook

2. A singular noun that ends in *-a* is generally feminine.

la casa, the house **la penna,** the pen **la ragazza,** the girl

3. A singular noun that ends in *-e* or *-i* may be either masculine or feminine.

il **padre** *(m.)*, the father	la **stazione** *(f.)*, the station
la **madre** *(f.)*, the mother	l'**estate** *(f.)*, the summer
il **cane** *(m.)*, the dog	l'**automobile** *(f.)*, the automobile
il **leone** *(m.)*, the lion	l'**esame** *(f.)*, the examination
il **caffè** *(m.)*, the coffee	la **crisi** *(f.)*, the crisis
l'**arte** *(f.)*, the art	la **tesi** *(f.)*, the thesis
la **lezione** *(f.)*, the lesson	il **brindisi** *(m.)*, the toast

4. Some nouns ending in *-o* are feminine.

la **mano,** the hand	la **dinamo,** the dynamo
l'**eco,** the echo	la **moto,** the motorcycle
la **radio,** the radio	

5. Some nouns ending in *-a* are masculine.

il **poeta,** the poet	il **clima,** the climate	il **problema,** the problem
il **dramma,** the drama	il **programma,** the program	il **pianeta,** the planet
il **telegramma,** the telegram	il **vaglia,** the money order	

6. Some nouns ending in *-ù* are feminine.

la gioventù, the youth **la virtù,** the virtue

Some nouns ending in -*a*, or -*e* are either masculine or feminine.

il **turista** *(m.)*, the tourist	la **turista** *(f.)*, the tourist
il **pianista** *(m.)*, the pianist	la **pianista** *(f.)*, the pianist
il **giornalista** *(m.)*, the journalist	la **giornalista** *(f.)*, the journalist
il **cantante** *(m.)*, the singer	la **cantante** *(f.)*, the singer
il **nipote** *(m.)*, the nephew	la **nipote** *(f.)*, the niece

Note: Determining the gender of Italian nouns is not always easy. It is therefore advisable to memorize the article of each noun.

Masculine Nouns with Feminine Counterparts

1. Some masculine nouns ending in -*o* end in -*a* in the feminine.

il **maestro**	la **maestra**	teacher
il **gatto**	la **gatta**	cat
il **contadino**	la **contadina**	peasant
il **sarto**	la **sarta**	tailor, dressmaker

2. Some masculine nouns ending in -*e* end in -*a* in the feminine.

l'**infermiere**	l'**infermiera**	nurse
il **cameriere**	la **cameriera**	waiter, waitress
il **signore**	la **signora**	gentleman, lady

3. Some masculine nouns ending in -*a* or -*e* end in -*essa* in the feminine.

il **professore**	la **professoressa**	professor
il **poeta**	la **poetessa**	poet
il **dottore**	la **dottoressa**	doctor
il **leone**	la **leonessa**	lion
il **principe**	la **principessa**	prince, princess

Note: The following masculine nouns have a totally different form for the feminine:

il **babbo**, dad	la **mamma**, mom
il **cane**, male dog	la **cagna**, female dog
il **dio**, god	la **dea**, goddess
il **fratello**, brother	la **sorella**, sister
il **gallo**, rooster	la **gallina**, hen
il **genero**, son-in-law	la **nuora**, daughter-in-law
il **marito**, husband	la **moglie**, wife
il **maschio**, male	la **femmina**, female
il **padre**, father	la **madre**, mother
l'**uomo**, man	la **donna**, woman

4. Some masculine nouns ending in *-tore* end in *-trice* in the feminine.

l'at*tore*	l'at*trice*	actor, actress
il pit*tore*	la pit*trice*	painter
lo scrit*tore*	la scrit*trice*	writer
l'impera*tore*	l'impera*trice*	emperor, empress

But:

l'impos*tore*	l'impos*tora*	impostor
il pas*tore*	la pas*tora*	shepherd
il tin*tore*	la tin*tora*	dyer, cleaner

5. Some nouns have the same form in both masculine and feminine forms.

l'artista *(m.)*	l'artista *(f.)*	artist
il violinista *(m.)*	la violinista *(f.)*	violinist
il turista *(m.)*	la turista *(f.)*	tourist

6. Some nouns change the meaning when changing gender.

il **baleno,**	flash of lightning	la **balena,**	whale
il **ballo,**	dance	la **balla,**	bale
il **busto,**	bust	la **busta,**	envelope
il **caso,**	case	la **casa,**	house
il **cavo,**	cable	la **cava,**	quarry
il **collo,**	neck	la **colla,**	glue
il **corso,**	course	la **corsa,**	race
il **foglio,**	sheet of paper	la **foglia,**	leaf
il **lotto,**	lottery	la **lotta,**	struggle
il **manico,**	handle	la **manica,**	sleeve
il **modo,**	manner	la **moda,**	fashion
il **pasto,**	meal	la **pasta,**	noodles; pastry
il **pianto,**	weeping	la **pianta,**	plant
il **pollo,**	chicken	la **polla,**	spring of water
il **porto,**	port	la **porta,**	door
il **testo,**	test	la **testa,**	head
il **tormento**	torment	la **tormenta,**	blizzard
il **torto**	wrong	la **torta,**	cake
il **velo,**	veil	la **vela,**	sail

7. Some nouns change the meaning when changing the gender, but retain the same form in both genders.

il **boa,**	boa	la **boa,**	buoy
il **camerata,**	comrade	la **camerata,**	dormitory
il **capitale,**	account; capital	la **capitale,**	capital city
il **fine,**	aim, purpose	la **fine,**	end; close
il **pianeta**	planet	la **pianeta**	chasuble
il **radio,**	radium; radius	la **radio,**	radio
il **tema,**	theme, subject, topic	la **tema,**	fear

Plural of Nouns

1. Nouns ending in "*-o*" or "*-e*" form the plural in *-i*.

il maestro, the teacher	**i maestr***i*, the teachers
il quaderno, the notebook	**i quadern***i*, the notebooks
la stazione, the station	**le stazion***i*, the stations
la lezione, the lesson	**le lezion***i*, the lessons

2. Nouns ending in *-a* form the plural in *-e* if they are feminine, and in *-i* if they are masculine.

la mela, the apple	**le mel***e*, the apples
la pagina, the page	**le pagin***e*, the pages
il poeta, the poet	**i poet***i*, the poets
il telegramma, the telegram	**i telegramm***i*, the telegrams

But:

l'ala, the wing	**le al***i*, the wings
l'arma, the weapon	**le arm***i*, the weapons
il vaglia, the money order	**i vagli***a*, the money orders
il procaccia, the mail carrier	**i procacci***a*, the mail carriers

3. Some nouns have irregular plurals.

il dio, the god	**gli d***ei*, the gods
il bue, the ox	**i bu***oi*, the oxen
l'uomo, the man	**gli uom***ini*, the men

4. Some nouns ending in *-o* are *masculine* in the singular and *feminine* in the plural.

il braccio, the arm	**le braccia,** the arms
il dito, the finger	**le dita,** the fingers
il labbro, the lip	**le labbra,** the lips
il miglio, the mile	**le miglia,** the miles
il muro, the wall	**le mura,** the walls
il paio, the pair	**le paia,** the pairs
l'uovo, the egg	**le uova,** the eggs

Many of these nouns have a regular masculine plural form in *-i*, usually denoting a figurative meaning. For example, *i bracci del mare* means "the arms of the sea," while *le braccia* means "the arms of a human being."

5. Nouns ending in *-ca* or *-ga* form the plural in *-che* or *ghe* if they are feminine, and in *-chi* or *-ghi* if they are masculine.

la monaca, the nun	**le mona***che*, the nuns
la paga, the salary	**le pa***ghe*, the salaries
il monarca, the monarch	**i monar***chi*, the monarchs
il collega, the colleague	**i colle***ghi*, the colleagues

6. Nouns ending in -*cia* or -*gia* (with the stressed *i)* retain the stressed *i* in the plural.

la farmacia, the pharmacy   **le farmac***ie***,** the pharmacies
la bugia, the lie   **le bug***ie***,** the lies
la tecnologia, technology   **le tecnolog***ie***,** technologies

7. Nouns ending in -*cia* or -*gia* (with the unstressed *i)* retain the unstressed *i* in the plural if *c* or *g* is preceded by a vowel. However, they drop the unstressed *i* in the plural if *c* or *g* is preceded by a consonant.

la camicia, the shirt   **la camic***ie***,** the shirts
la ciliegia, the cherry   **le cilie***gie***,** the cherries

But:
la pioggia, the rain   **le piog***ge***,** the rains
la roccia, the rock   **le roc***ce***,** the rocks

Note:

     a. In modern usage the unstressed *i* tends to disappear and the following spellings are also admitted: *ciliege, camice, valige,* etc.

     b. The unstressed *i* must be retained to avoid ambiguity between a noun and an adjective. For example, *audacia,* pl. *audacie (audace* is an adjective); *tenacia,* pl. *tenacie (tenace* is an adjective).

8. Nouns ending in -*scia* (with the unstressed *i)* form the plural in -*sce.* Nouns ending in -*scìa* (with the stressed *i)* form the plural in -*scìe.*

l'ascia, the axe   **le a***sce***,** the axes
la scia, the trail   **le sc***ìe***,** the trails

9. Nouns ending in -*co* or -*go* that are stressed on the next-to-last syllable *generally* form the plural in -*chi* or -*ghi.*

il cuoco, the cook   **i cuo***chi***,** the cooks
il fico, the fig   **i fi***chi***,** the figs
il falco, the hawk   **i fal***chi***,** the hawks
l'ago, the needle   **gli a***ghi***,** the needles
il luogo, the place   **i luo***ghi***,** the places
il mago, the magician   **i ma***ghi***,** the magicians

But:
l'amico, the friend   **gli ami***ci***,** the friends
il nemico, the enemy   **i nemi***ci***,** the enemies
il Greco, the Greek   **i Gre***ci***,** the Greeks
il porco, the pig   **i por***ci***,** the pigs

10. Nouns that end in -*co* or -*go* that are stressed on the second syllable from the last, *generally* form the plural in -*ci* or -*gi*.

il **portico,** the portico	i **porti**ci, the porticoes
il **parroco,** pastor	i **parro**ci, the pastors
l'**asparago,** the asparagus	gli **aspara**gi, the asparagus
il **radiologo,** the radiologist	i **radiolo**gi, the radiologists
il **teologo,** the theologian	i **teolo**gi, the theologians

But:

il **carico,** the load	i **cari**chi, the loads
il **catalogo,** the catalogue	i **catalo**ghi, the catalogues
il **dialogo,** the dialogue	i **dialo**ghi, the dialogues
l'**epilogo,** the epilogue	gli **epilo**ghi, the epilogues
il **girovago,** the vagrant	i **girova**ghi, the vagrants
l'**obbligo,** the obligation	gli **obbli**ghi, the obligations
il **profugo,** the refugee	i **profu**ghi, the refugees
il **prologo,** the prologue	i **prolo**ghi, the prologues
il **valico,** the pass	i **vali**chi, the passes

11. Nouns ending in -*io* form the plural in -*ii* if the *i* is stressed in the singular, but in -*i* if the *i* is unstressed in the singular.

lo **zio,** the uncle	gli **z**ii, the uncles
addio, good-bye	**add**ii, good-byes
pendio, slope	**pend**ii, slopes
lo **studio,** the study	gli **stud**i, the studies
il **premio,** the prize	i **prem**i, The prizes
il **figlio,** the son	i **figl**i, the sons

But:

l'**assassinio,** the murder	gli **assassin**ii, the murders
il **conio,** the coin	i **con**ii, the coins
il **direttorio,** the executive board	i **direttor**ii, the executive boards
il **tempio,** the temple	i **templ**i, the temples

Note: The following nouns ending in -*io* form the plural in *ii* or in -*i* preceded by an accent on the next-to-the-last syllable.

il **beneficio,** the benefit	i **benefic**ii or **benefi**ci
il **condominio,** the condominium	i **condomin**ii or **condomì**ni
il **principio,** the beginning, principle	i **princip**ii or **princì**pi

12. Certain nouns have the same form in the singular and the plural:

a. Nouns ending in a consonant
    il gas, the gas **i gas,** the gasses

b. Nouns ending in an accented vowel
    la città, *the city* **le città,** the cities

c. Nouns ending in *-i* or *-ie*
    la sintesi, the synthesis **le sintesi,** the syntheses
    la specie, the species **le specie,** the species

d. Nouns of one syllable
    la gru, the crane **le gru,** the cranes

e. Nouns denoting a family
    la famiglia Rossi, the Rossi family **i Rossi,** the Rossis

f. Abbreviations
    la bici, (from **bicicletta**) the bicycle **le bici,** the bicycles

However, there are some exceptions:

l'effigie, the image	**le effigi,** the images
la moglie, the wife	**le mogli,** the wives
la superficie, the surface	**le superfici,** the surfaces

13. Some nouns are only used in the singular:

fame, hunger	**latte,** milk
miele, honey	**pepe,** pepper
sete, thirst	**prole,** offspring

Some others are only used in the plural:

annali, annals	**calzoni,** trousers
occhiali, glasses	**forbici,** scissors
narici, nostrils	**fauci,** jaws

17. Adjectives and Adverbs

Adjectives

The form of an Italian adjective changes to agree in gender and number with the noun it modifies. (See pp. 121–122, *Agreement of Adjectives*.)

Forms of Regular Adjectives

	Adjectives ending in -*o*		Adjectives ending in -*e*	
	Masculine	Feminine	Masculine	Feminine
Singular	content*o*	content*a*	gentil*e*	gentil*e*
Plural	content*i*	content*e*	gentil*i*	gentil*i*

1. Adjectives ending in -*co*, -*go*, -*ca*, -*ga*, or -*io* form the plural as the nouns with similar endings. (See pp. 117–118.)
However, adjectives ending in -*ico* form masculine plurals in -*ci* and feminine plurals in -*che*.

	singular	plural
masculine	**magnifico**	**magnifici**
	generico	**generici**
feminine	**magnifica**	**magnifiche**
	generica	**generiche**

It is always advisable to consult the dictionary for possible *exceptions* such as the following:

	singular	plural
masculine	**dimentico**	**dimentichi**
	carico	**carichi**
feminine	**dimentica**	**dimentiche**
	carica	**cariche**

2. Compound adjectives, such as *chiaroveggente* ("clairvoyant"), *sacrosanto* ("sacrosanct"), *malandato* ("in bad condition"), *variopinto* ("many-colored"), *anglo-americano* ("Anglo-American"), form their plurals by changing only the second part of the word.

E' verità sacrosanta.	It is the pure truth.
I rapporti anglo-americani sono buoni.	Anglo-American relations are good.

Note that adjectives of nationality are *not* capitalized in Italian.

Agreement of Adjectives

1. An adjective (*or* a past participle used as an adjective) agrees in gender and number with the noun or pronoun it modifies, either as a direct modifier or as a predicate adjective. An adjective modifying two or more nouns of *different* gender must be used in the *masculine* plural form.

il libro ross*o*	the red book
la penna ross*a*	the red pen
i libri ross*i*	the red books
le penne ross*e*	the red pens
Il libro è ross*o*.	The book is red.
L*e* penne sono ross*e*.	The pens are red.
Il libro e la penna sono ross*i*.	The book and the pen are red.
Il vetro è rott*o*.	The glass is broken.
I quaderni sono chius*i*.	The notebooks are closed.
La porta e la finestra sono aper*te*.	The door and the window are open.

2. a. Adjectives of color that were originally nouns (*blu, rosa, marrone, lilla, viola,* etc.) are invariable, that is, they do not change form depending on gender and number.

nuvole rosa	pink clouds	**vestiti marrone**	brown suits

   b. When two adjectives of color are used, one qualifying the other, they are both invariable.

cappelli verde-pisello	pea green hats
occhi azzuro-chiaro	light blue eyes

3. A few other adjectives are also invariable such as *dabbene* ("respected"), *dappoco* ("worthless"), *pari* ("equal"), *perbene* ("respected," "decent"), *avvenire* ("future," "to come"), *dispari* ("odd"), *impari* ("unequal"), *altrui* ("other's," "other people's"), *loro* ("their").

un uomo dabbene	a respected man
a pari condizioni	under the same conditions
le generazioni avvenire	future generations
i numeri dispari	the odd numbers
una lotta impari	an uneven struggle
le disgrazie altrui	other people's troubles
la loro figlia	their daughter
il loro figlio	their son

4. Some adjectives like *ogni* ("every"), *qualche* ("some"), *qualunque* ("whatever"), *qualsiasi* ("any"), *qualsivoglia* ("any") are invariable and are only used with *singular* nouns.

ogni uomo e ogni donna	every man and woman
qualche ragazzo e qualche ragazza	some boys and girls
qualunque regalo, qualunque offerta	whatever gift, whatever offering
qualsiasi fiore e qualsiasi pianta	any flower any plant

5. Some adjectives such as *nullo* ("null"), *nessuno* ("no," "not . . . any"), *ciascuno* ("every," "each") only have the masculine and feminine *singular* form. These adjectives have no plural form.

Nessuna nuova, buona nuova.	No news is good news.
Parlammo con ciascuna donna, ciascuna ragazza.	We spoke to each woman, each girl.

Position of Adjectives

The rules for the position of adjectives in Italian tend to be rather fluid. Factors such as emphasis, balance, and rhythm in a sentence may determine whether an adjective precedes or follows the noun it modifies. Nonetheless, though no hard and fixed rules can be laid down, the following key principles will apply in *most* situations.

1. The following descriptive adjectives most often precede the noun in Italian

antico	ancient	**giovane**	young
bello	beautiful, handsome	**grande**	big, large
bravo	fine, good	**lungo**	long
breve	short	**nuovo**	new
brutto	ugly	**piccolo**	little, small
buono	good	**povero**	poor
caro	dear	**stesso**	same
cattivo	bad	**vecchio**	old

2. Numerals, possessive, demonstrative, interrogative and indefinite adjectives usually come before the noun.

Abbiamo visto *quattro* soldati.	We have seen four soldiers.
Mio **fratello studia l'italiano.**	My brother studies Italian.
Questa **casa è vecchia.**	This house is old.
Quali **giornali leggi?**	What newspapers do you read?
Ecco *alcuni* libri rari.	Here are some rare books.

3. In general, descriptive adjectives and those denoting colors, religion, and nationality follow the nouns they modify.

un ragazzo *intelligente*	an intelligent boy
una bestia *selvaggia*	a wild beast
La casa *gialla* **con il tetto** *rosso* **è mia.**	The yellow house with the red roof is mine.
Mi piacciono le rose *rosse.*	I like red roses.
Questa è una chiesa *cattolica*	This is a Catholic church.
Ecco una ragazza *italiana.*	Here is an Italian girl.

4. Participles used as adjectives follow the noun.

Il latino è una lingua *morta.*	Latin is a dead language.
Mi accolse con le braccia *aperte.*	He received me with open arms.
Amo i tuoi occhi *ridenti.*	I love your smiling eyes.
E' l'immagine *vivente* **del padre.**	He is the living image of his father.

5. Certain adjectives have different meanings, depending on whether they precede or follow their noun. If they follow the noun, they usually have a literal or objective meaning. When preceding the noun, they usually have a figurative or subjective meaning.

Tu sei un uomo *alto.*	You are a tall man.
Ho un *alto* **concetto di te.**	I have a high opinion of you.
Ecco una prova *certa.*	Here is certain proof.
Incontrai un *certo* **signor Rossi.**	I met a certain Mr. Rossi.
Visitammo le famiglie *povere.*	We visited the needy families.
Il *povero* **ragazzo annegò.**	The unfortunate boy drowned.
Questi sono panni *vecchi.*	These are old clothes.
Siamo *vecchi* **amici.**	We are old friends.

The most common of these adjectives and their meanings, are listed below:

Adjective	Meaning when following	Meaning when preceding
alto	tall	high
caro	dear, expensive	dear, beloved
certo	definite, reliable	certain
diverso	different	various
galante	gallant	honest
gentile	kind, courteous	noble
grande	large	great
nuovo	(brand) new, not old	another, different
povero	poor, poverty-stricken	unfortunate
proprio	characteristic of	own
puro	pure	sheer
stesso	-self, very	same, very
vario	miscellaneous	several
vecchio	old (age)	old (for many years)

Special Adjectives

The adjectives *bello, quello, buono, nessuno, grande,* and *santo* have: a. special forms when they precede the noun and b. regular forms when they follow the noun or a form of the verb *essere.*

Note that in this latter case *quello* is used as a pronoun.

Special Forms of *bello* and *quello*

The special forms of *bello* and *quello* follow the pattern of the definite article *(il, lo, l', la, i, gli, le)*. Thus:

bel **viaggio**	beautiful trip	*quel* **libro**	that book
bello **stadio**	beautiful stadium	*quello* **zaino**	that knapsack
bell' **orologio**	beautiful watch	*quell'* **alunno**	that student
bella **ragazza**	beautiful girl	*quella* **penna**	that pen
bell' **aula**	beautiful class-room	*quell'* **azione**	that action
bei **fiori**	beautiful flowers	*quei* **soldati**	those soldiers
begli **occhi**	beautiful eyes	*quegli* **orfani**	those orphans
belle **rose**	beautiful roses	*quelle* **mele**	those apples

Il viaggio fu *bello.*	The trip was beautiful.
Questi fiori sono *belli.*	These flowers are beautiful.
Dammi *quello* **specchio.**	Give me that mirror.
Voglio *quelle* **scarpe.**	I want those shoes.

Special Forms of *buono* and *nessuno*

The special forms of *buono* and *nessuno* when they precede the noun follow the pattern of the indefinite article *(un, uno, una, un')* in the masculine and feminine singular. The plural forms of these adjectives are regular. *Nessuno* has two masculine singular forms and two feminine singular forms and *no* plural forms. When *nessuno* means "no one," "nobody," it has only two forms: *nessuno, nessuna.*

un *buon* **libro**	a good book	*nessun* **quaderno**	no notebook
un *buon* **amico**	a good friend	*nessun* **italiano**	no Italian
un *buono* **psichiatra**	a good psychiatrist	*nessuno* **spazio**	no space
una *buona* **parola**	a good word	*nessun* **risposta**	no answer
una *buon'* **abitudine**	a good habit	*nessun'* **assenza**	no absence

Un libro *buono* **è come un amico.**	A good book is like a friend.
Quest' abitudine è *buona.*	This is a good habit.
Essi sono dei *buoni* **ragazzi.**	They are good boys.
C'è *nessuno?*	Is anyone there?
Nessuna **delle ragazze venne alla festa.**	None of the girls came to the party.

Special Forms of *grande* and *santo*

Grande has special forms in the singular only. All its forms are regular in the plural and whenever *grande* follows a noun or a form of the verb *essere*. *Santo* has special forms only when it precedes a *proper name* (masculine or feminine). When *santo* is used with common nouns or when it follows a form of *essere*, the regular forms of this adjective apply. The special forms of both *grande* and *santo* depend on whether the noun after one of these adjectives starts with a vowel, a consonant, or *s impure*.

un *gran* professore	a great professor	*San* **Carlo**	Saint Charles
un *grande* scrittore	a great writer	*Santo* **Stefano**	Saint Stephen
un *grand'* avvocato	a great lawyer	*Sant'* **Antonio**	Saint Anthony
una *grande* paura	a great fear	*Santa* **Maria**	Saint Mary
una *grande* scena	a great scene	*Sant'* **Anna**	Saint Ann
una *grand'* avventura	a great adventure		

Non è un giardino *grande.*	It is not a large garden.
Queste case sono molto *grandi.*	These houses are very large.
L'anno *santo* **è passato.**	The holy year is over.
Egli vive una vita *santa.*	He lives a holy life.

Adverbs

1. An adverb is an invariable word that modifies verbs, adjectives, other adverbs or, occasionally, a noun or an entire sentence.

Luigi parla *lentamente.*	Louis talks slowly.
E' un romanzo *molto* **interessante.**	It is a very interesting novel.
Vive *molto* **allegramente.**	He lives very happily.
Non ho mai incontrato una ragazza *così.*	I never met a girl like her.
Probabilmente **non avete capito niente.**	You probably didn't understand anything.

2. Adverbs can be classified as: adverbs of manner, place, time, quantity, doubt, affirmation, and negation.

Adverbs of manner

1. Adverbs of manner are often formed by adding *-mente* to the *feminine-singular* form of the adjective.

fortunata ──────►	fortunatamente	fortunately
sincera ──────►	sinceramente	sincerely
recente ──────►	recentemente	recently
semplice ──────►	semplicemente	simply

But:

benevola ──────►	benevolmente	benevolently
leggera ──────►	leggermente	lightly
violenta ──────►	violentemente	violently

2. If the feminine adjective ends in *-le* or *-re* and this ending is preceded by a vowel, the final *-e* is dropped before adding *-mente*.

facile ──────►	facilmente	easily
regolare ──────►	regolarmente	regularly

However, if *-le* or *-re* is preceded by a consonant, the final *-e* is not dropped before adding *-mente*.

alacre ──────►	alacremente	readily
folle ──────►	follemente	madly
pedestre ──────►	pedestremente	dully

Note: a. The ending *-mente* may *not* be added to adjectives denoting color and to some others like *buono, cattivo, fresco,* and *vecchio.* It may be added, sometimes, to present or past participles.

incessante	incessantemente	incessantly
abbondante	abbondantemente	abundantly
perduta	perdutamente	hopelessly
disperata	disperatamente	desperately

   b. The adverbs *altrimenti* ("otherwise") and *parimenti* ("likewise") are irregular in form.

3. Other ways of forming adverbs of manner include: a. *con* or *senza* + a noun and b. the use of a preposition + *modo* or *maniera* + an adjective in a prepositional phrase.

Ascoltiamo *con attenzione.*	We listen attentively
Ascoltarono *senza pietà.*	They listened pitilessly
Fu trattato *in modo cortese.*	He was treated kindly.
Noi facciamo tutto *in maniera appropriata.*	We do everything properly.
Vivono *alla maniera antica.*	They live in the old-fashioned way.

4. Adjectives are sometimes used as adverbs.

Vivono *felici.*	They live happily.
Cammina *veloce!*	Walk fast!
Piove *forte.*	It rains hard.
Non risponde mai *giusto.*	He never answers correctly.
Sicuro **che c'ero!**	Sure enough I was there!

5. Several adverbs are formed by adding the ending *-oni* (or *-one)* to the verbal or nominal stem with or without the preposition *a* (or *in).*

Procede *a balzelloni.*	He bounces along.
Il ragazzo dormiva *bocconi* (or *boccone).*	The boy was sleeping face downwards.
Sono stati tutto il giorno *ciondoloni* (or *ciondolone).*	They have been hanging around all day.
Le vecchie pregavano *(in) ginocchioni.*	The old women were praying on their knees.

6. Adverbs and adverbial phrases of manner are also formed in many other ways (by the use of prepositions, by repeating the adjective twice, etc.).

Il malato alza *a mala pena* **la mano.**	The patient can hardly raise his hand.
Il lago si stendeva *a vista d'occhio.*	The lake stretched as far as the eye could see.
Camminava *bel bello* **per la strada.**	He was walking slowly down the street.
Ci sto *giusto giusto.*	I just fit in.

Common Adverbs of Place

altrove	elsewhere	**quaggiù**	down here
dappertutto	everywhere	**quassù**	up here
davanti	in front	**sopra**	on, over
dentro	in, inside	**sotto**	under
dietro	behind, at the back	**su**	up
dovunque	everywhere anywhere	**vicino**	near
fuori	out, outside		
giù	down		
là, lì	there		
laggiù	down there		
lontano	far		
qua (or **qui**)	here		

Common Adverbs of Time

adesso	now	precedentemente	previously
allora	then	presto	quickly, early
ancora	still	prima	before
domani	tomorrow	quando	when
dopo	after	quindi	then, afterwards
finalmente	finally	raramente	rarely
finora	until now	sempre	always
ieri	yesterday	spesso	often
immediatamente	immediately	subito	soon
mai	never	talvolta	sometimes, at
oggi	today		times
ora	now	tardi	late
poi	after		

Common Adverbs of Quantity

abbastanza	enough	parecchio	quite a lot of
appena	just, scarcely, hardly	più	not ... any more no more
assai	much, enough	piuttosto	rather, somewhat
meno	less	poco	not very
molto	much, a lot	troppo	too

Common Adverbs of Doubt, Affirmation, and Negation

appunto	exactly	nemmeno	by no means!
certamente (or certo)	certainly	no (or non)	no (non)
		perfettamente	perfectly
davvero	really	possibilmente	possibly
forse	perhaps	precisamente	precisely
già	of course	probabilmente	probably
giammai	never	sì	yes
naturalmente	naturally	sicuramente (or sicuro)	surely
neanche (or neppure)	certainly not		

Adverbial Expressions

Very often adverbial expressions *(locuzioni avverbiali)* consisting of two or more words are used to modify or to replace simple adverbs.

di tutto punto	completely	di buon'ora	early
di punto in bianco	suddenly	sul momento	at the moment
a poco a poco	little by little	a volte	sometimes

di tanto in tanto	from time to time	**nel frattempo**	in the meantime
adagio adagio	very slowly	**tra breve** *(poco)*	in a short while
ben volentieri	very willingly	**su per giù**	more or less
contro voglia	unwillingly	**senz'altro**	certainly
alla svelta	quickly	**in nessun modo**	in no way
all'impazzata	madly	**nel caso**	in case
per l'appunto	exactly	**per ipotesi**	by supposition
per sempre	for ever	**a bizzeffe**	in a great quantity
alla fine	in the end, finally	**a squarciagola**	at the top of one's voice
all'incirca	about, approximately	**in un batter d'occhio**	in the twinkling of an eye

Position of Adverbs

1. Generally adverbs are placed immediately *after* the verb.

Lo zio di Antonio è arrivato *ieri* **dall'America.**	Antony's uncle came yesterday from America.
Camminava *lentamente* **per le strade della città.**	He was walking slowly through the streets of the city.

Nonetheless, an adverb may *precede* a verb when special emphasis is intended.

Prima **paghi,** *meglio* **è.**	The sooner you pay, the better it is.

Note: *Non* ("not") is always placed *before* the verb.

Non **correre, per piacere.**	Please, don't run.

2. If an adverb modifies an adjective or another adverb, it is placed *before* the adjective or adverb.

Tu sei *sempre* **contento.**	You are always happy.
Sei arrivato *troppo* **tardi.**	You came too late.

3. In a compound tense the adverb may be placed:
   a. *between* the auxiliary verb and the past participle.

Abbiamo *già* **visto questo film.**	We have already seen this film.
Non ho *ancora* **ricevuto il tuo regalo.**	I haven't received your gift yet.
Avete *sempre* **studiato l'italiano.**	You have always studied Italian.

b. *after* the past participle (for many adverbs of place, time, and manner).

Hai capito *male*!	You have got it wrong!
Nessuno è venuto *qui*.	Nobody came here.
Ho risposto *immediatamente*.	I answered immediately.
Sono partiti *in fretta*.	They left in a hurry.

c. *before* the auxiliary verb, when special emphasis is required.

Ormai **siamo arrivati**.	We are nearly there now.
Spesso **ho telefonato a Marco**.	I often phoned Marc.
Assai **hai rischiato**!	You risked a lot!

18. Possessive Adjectives and Pronouns

1. The forms of the possessive adjectives and pronouns are identical.

	SINGULAR		PLURAL	
Adjective/Pronoun	*Masculine*	*Feminine*	*Masculine*	*Feminine*
my/mine	**il mio**	**la mia**	**i miei**	**le mie**
your/yours	**il tuo**	**la tua**	**i tuoi**	**le tue**
(familiar)				
your/yours	**il Suo**	**la Sua**	**i Suoi**	**le Sue**
(formal)				
his, her/his,	**il suo**	**la sua**	**i suoi**	**le sue**
hers, its				
our/ours	**il nostro**	**la nostra**	**i nostri**	**le nostre**
your/yours	**il vostro**	**la vostra**	**i vostri**	**le vostre**
(familiar)				
your/yours	**il Loro**	**la Loro**	**i Loro**	**le Loro**
(formal)				
their/theirs	**il loro**	**la loro**	**i loro**	**le loro**

2. Possessive adjectives, unlike their counterparts in English, agree in gender and number with the object possessed and *not* with the possessor.

Carlo ha scritto alla su*a* amica.	Carl wrote to his girl friend.
La signora ha venduto i su*oi* gioielli	The lady sold her jewels.
Le tu*e* poesie sono belle, Paolo.	Your poems are lovely, Paul.

3. Possessive adjectives and pronouns are normally preceded by the definite article, which must be repeated before *each* adjective or pronoun.

Dov'è *il mio* **libro e** *il mio* **quaderno?**	Where is my book and notebook?
Ho preso *il mio;* **ecco** *il tuo.*	I took mine; here is yours.

4. The definite article is *not* used:

    a. before nouns denoting family relationships (*padre, madre, figlio, figlia, fratello, sorella,* etc.), if they are used in the singular and are not modified by an adjective or suffix.

Mio **fratello abita in città.**	My brother lives in the city.
Nostro **figlio va all'università.**	Our son goes to college.

But:

I nostri **fratelli non sono ricchi.**	Our brothers are not rich.
Il suo povero **zio è morto ieri.**	His poor uncle died yesterday.
Il mio **cuginetto mi scrive spesso.**	My little cousin often writes to me.

Note that *papà (babbo* in Tuscany), *mamma, nonno,* and *nonna* retain the article.

Il mio papà **lavora in fabbrica.**	My father works in a factory.
La tua nonna **sembra più giovane di sua sorella.**	Your grandmother seems younger than her sister.

    b. When addressing a person directly.

Che fai, figlio *mio?*	What are you doing, my son?
Congratulazioni, *mio* **caro amico!**	Congratulations, my dear friend!

    c. When possessive pronouns are preceded by a form of the verb *essere.*

Questa penna è *mia.*	This pen is mine.
E' *tuo* **questo libro?**	Is this book yours?

However, the article *must* be used when a distinction has to be made or for special emphasis.

Questo è *il mio* **biglietto. Dov'è** *il tuo?*	This is my ticket. Where is yours?
Questa borsa è *la mia.*	This purse is mine.

    d. In a number of idiomatic expressions.

a casa mia	in my house
a vostra disposizione	at your disposal
cara mia	my dear girl
da parte mia	on my part
Dio mio!	my goodness!
E' colpa mia.	It is my fault.
Ho fatto tutto mio.	I grabbed everything.
Il piacere è mio.	The pleasure is mine.
in loro onore	in their honor
in vita nostra	in our life
Mamma mia!	Heavens!
per conto mio	on my account
Sono affari miei!	It's my business!
Tesoro mio!	My darling!
un par mio	one like me

5. The article is always used with the possessive adjective *loro* or *Loro*. Since these forms are invariable, the article allows for distinctions of gender and number.

Lavoro con *il loro fratello.*	I work with their brother.
Viaggio con *la loro* **zia.**	I travel with their aunt.
Come stanno *i Loro* **nonni?**	How are your grandparents?

6. Unlike English, the definite article is used (instead of the possessive adjective) to refer to parts of the body or articles of clothing, whenever they belong to or are part of the subject.

Pietro alza *la* **mano.**	Peter raises *his* hand
Mario, togliti *il* **cappotto.**	Mario, take off *your* coat.
Ho dimenticato *il* **cappello in ufficio.**	I forgot *my* hat in the office.

7. The third-person possessive forms *il suo, la sua, i suoi, le sue* may cause ambiguity or misunderstanding, because they can mean "his," "her," "its," and the polite form "your" all at once. To avoid ambiguity, they should be replaced with *di lui* (for "his"), *di Lei, di Loro* (for the polite "your"), *di lei* (for "her"), and *di loro* (for "their").

Questa è la valigia *di lui,* **non** *di lei.*	This suitcase is his, not hers.
Alessandro ha salutato la mamma *di lei.*	Alexander greeted her mother.
Antonio si è dimesso e Maria ha preso il posto *di lui.*	Anthony resigned, and Mary took his place.
Claudia telefonò al fratello per parlare dei problemi *di lui.*	Claudia phoned her brother to talk about his problems.

8. For the same reasons of clarity, *proprio* replaces *suo* and *loro:* a. when the subject of the sentence is an indefinite pronoun *or* b. when the possessive adjective refers to the subject, as distinguished from some other person mentioned in the sentence.

Ognuno ama la *propria* **patria.**	Everyone loves his own country.
Dopo aver parlato con Teresa, Giuseppe prese i *propri* **libri.**	After he finished talking with Theresa, Joseph took his (own) books.

9. With impersonal constructions, *proprio* must be used instead of *suo.*

Bisogna seguire la *propria* **coscienza.**	One must follow his own conscience.
Si deve fare il *proprio* **dovere.**	One has to do his duty.

Note: Italian can express an English sentence, such as "This book is mine," in three different ways and with three different shades of meaning: *questo libro è mio* ("it is my property"), *questo libro è il mio* ("it is mine and not someone else's"); and *questo è il mio libro* ("this book is mine not *another's*").

19. Demonstrative Adjectives and Pronouns

Demonstrative Adjectives

1. The chart below outlines the forms of Italian demonstrative adjectives "this" and "that" in English).

Forms of Demonstrative Adjectives

Singular		Plural	
questo *(m.)* **questa** *(f.)*	this	**questi** **queste**	these
codesto *(m.)* **codesta** *(f.)*	that	**codesti** **codeste**	those
quello *(m.)* **quella** *(f.)*	that	**quelli** **quelle**	those

2. The demonstrative adjective precedes and agrees in number and gender with the noun it modifies. No article is used.

quest*o* **cappello**	this hat
quest*a* **casa**	this house
quest*i* **fiori**	these flowers
quest*e* **pagine**	these pages

3. Demonstrative adjectives are repeated before each noun.

questi **garofani** e *quelle* **rose**	these carnations and those roses
questa **porta** e *questa* **finestra**	this door and this window

However, when a noun is *preceded* by several descriptive adjectives, the demonstrative adjective is not repeated.

questa **buona e brava signorina**	this good and clever young lady

4. *Questo* and *questa* become *quest'* before singular words beginning with a vowel.

*quest'***orologio**	this watch	*quest'***aula**	this classroom

5. *Quello* follows the pattern of the definite article. (see Chapter 17, p. 124)

6. *Questo* and *quello* are sometimes reinforced with *qui (qua)* and *lì (là)* respectively.

questo ragazzo *qui* (or *qua)*	this boy here
quella ragazza *lì* (or là)	that girl there

7. *Questa,* shortened into *sta,* sometimes is contracted with the noun, as in the following examples.

stamani or **stamane**	**(questa mane)**	this morning
stamattina	**(questa mattina)**	this morning
stanotte	**(questa notte)**	tonight, last night
stasera	**(questa sera)**	this evening
stavolta	**(questa volta)**	this time

8. *Codesto* (or *cotesto)* is used when referring to what is near the person addressed.

Esci con *codeste* **scarpe?**	Are you going out with those shoes?
Giovanni, mi piace *cotesta* **camicia che porti.**	John, I like that shirt you are wearing.
Perchè mangi *codeste* **mele?**	Why are you eating those apples?
Codeste **non sono parole degne di te!**	Those words are not worthy of you!

However, in contemporary Italian, *codesto* tends to be replaced (except in Tuscany) with *quello*.

Note: a. *Quella* takes an apostrophe before feminine nouns beginning with a vowel (except *i* followed by another vowel).

*Quell'***aula è troppo piccola.**	That classroom is too small.

But:

Quella **iole è carina.**	That boat is pretty.

b. *Questi, queste,* and *quelle* never taken an apostrophe.

Questi **ideali sono irraggiungibili.**	These ideals are unattainable.
Queste **ali sono troppo lunghe.**	These wings are too long.
Quelle **armi sono vecchie.**	Those weapons are old.

Demonstrative Pronouns

1. A demonstrative pronoun always refers to someone or something mentioned previously.

When used alone, the forms of the demonstrative adjectives *questo,* *codesto,* and *quello* (p. 134) function as demonstrative pronouns. They agree in gender and number with the noun for which they stand.

Questo **è il mio indirizzo.**	This is my address
E' *quella* **la tua casa?**	Is that your house?
Questi **sono i miei libri e** *quelli* **sono i tuoi.**	These are my books and those are yours.
Questa mela è matura e *quella* **è acerba.**	This apple is ripe and that one is green.

2. The demonstrative pronouns may be followed by the relative pronouns *che, di cui, del quale,* etc. (See Chapter 22, *Relative Pronouns.)*

Ascolta la canzone. E' *quella che* **ti piace?**	Listen to the song. Is that the one you like?
Ecco i dischi italiani: sono *quelli di cui* **ti parlai.**	Here are the Italian records; they are the ones I spoke to you about.

3. *Quello* may be followed by *di* either to indicate possession or to translate "that (those) of," "the one(s) by."

Ecco il mio orologio e *quello di* **mio fratello.**	Here is my watch and the one that belongs to my brother. *(my brother's)*
Accetta il consiglio del saggio e rigetta *quello dello* **stolto.**	Accept the advice of a wise person and reject that of a foolish one.
Hai visto i quadri di Modigliani? No. Ho visto *quelli di* **De Chirico.**	Did you see the paintings by Modigliani? No. I saw those by De Chirico.

4. The forms *questo, questa, questi, queste* may mean "the latter," and *quello, quella, quelli, quelle,* "the former."

Giulia e Rosa sono sorelle; *questa* **è bassa,** *quella* **è alta.**	Julia and Rose are sisters; the latter is small, the former is tall.
Roberto e Giovanni sono amici; *questo* **è ricco,** *quello* **è povero.**	Robert and John are friends; the latter is poor, the former is rich.

Note that, unlike English, Italian usually mentions the latter before the former.

5. *Questo* can mean *questa cosa,* while *quello* can mean *quella cosa.*

Perché mi dici *questo?*	Why are you telling me this?
Capisco *quello* **che vuoi dire.**	I see what you mean.

Additional Demonstrative Pronouns

1. Some other Italian demonstrative pronouns include: *questi, quegli,* *costui, costei, colui, colei, coloro, ciò.*

2. *Questi* ("this one") and *quegli* ("that one") are masculine singular pronouns referring only to people and used only as subject.

Questi **lavora,** *quegli* **dorme.**	This one works, that one sleeps.
Arturo e Claudio sono due studenti; *questi* **è intelligente,** *quegli* **è assiduo.**	Arthur and Claude are two students; the latter is intelligent, the former is diligent.

Note: In contemporary Italian, these two pronouns are often replaced with *questo* and *quello.*

3. *Costui (m.)* ["this one"], *costei (f.)* ["this one"] and *costoro (m. and f.)* ["these"] are used to refer to people, often in questions after the verb. (Sometimes they carry a derogatory connotation.)

E' *costui* **il ragazzo che vende giornali?**	Is this the boy who sells newspapers?
Dove ho visto *costoro?*	Where did I see these people?
Chi è *costei?*	Who is this woman?
Carneade, chi era *costui?*	Carneade, who was that?
Non parlarmi di *costei.*	Don't talk to me about her.
Mai con *costoro!*	Never with them!

4. *Colui (m.)* ["the one who"], *colei (f.)* ["the one who"], *coloro (m. and f.)* ["the ones who"] are used to refer to people and are usually followed by a relative pronoun.

Colui **che farà meglio riceverà il premio.**	The one who does the best will receive the prize.
Colei **che ami è qui.**	The one you love is here.
Coloro **i quali dicono così si sbagliano di grosso.**	The ones who say so are greatly mistaken.

5. *Ciò* means *questa cosa* or *quella cosa.* It is singular, invariable, and refers to things.

Non ho detto *ciò.*	I did not say that.
Ciò **mi è chiarissimo.**	This is very clear to me.
Fa' *ciò* **che ti piace.**	Do whatever you want.

Note: When it is not used as subject, *ciò* may be replaced by *lo, ne* (= *di ciò*), and *ci* (= *a ciò*).

L'hai visto (= *hai visto ciò)?*	Did you see that?
Ha fatto tutto bene e *ne* (= *di ciò)* **è orgoglioso.**	He did everything well, and he is proud of it.
Ci (= *a ciò)* **penso io.**	I'll see to it.

20. Comparison of Adjectives and Adverbs

Comparison of Adjectives

1. To form the comparative, place *più* ("more") or *meno* ("less") before the adjective. To form the superlative, place the appropriate definite article + *più* ("most") or *meno* ("least") before the adjective.

Positive		*Comparative*		*Superlative*	
corto, -a	short	*più* **corto, -a**	shorter	*il più* **corto** *la più* **corta**	the shortest
ricco, -a	rich	*più* **ricco, -a**	richer	*il più* **ricco** *la più* **ricca**	the richest

2. Comparative and superlative adjectives agree in gender and number with the nouns they modify.

pianta *più corta*	shorter plant	*la* **pianta** *più corta*	the shortest plant
racconti *più corti*	shorter stories	*i* **racconti** *più corti*	the shortest stories
gente *meno ricca*	less rich people	*la* **gente** *più ricca*	the richest people
famiglie *meno ricche*	less rich families	*le* **famiglie** *meno ricche*	the least rich families

Comparative Adjectives

Comparisons of Inequality

1. **più ... di** *(che)* more than   **meno ... di** *(che)* less than

Note that *di* ("than") contracts with the definite article.

La luna è *più* **piccola** *della* **terra.**	The moon is smaller than the earth.
Giovanni è *meno* **ricco** *di* **Antonio.**	John is less rich than Anthony.
L'elefante è *più* **forte** *del* **cavallo.**	The elephant is stronger than the horse.
E' *meno* **fortunato** *che* **capace.**	He is less lucky than capable.

2. *Di* is used to mean "than" before nouns, pronouns, or numbers.

Firenze è meno popolosa *di* **Roma.**	Florence is less populated than Rome.
Io sono meno stanco *di* **te.**	I am less tired than you.
Ho ascoltato più *di* **cinque canzoni.**	I listened to more than five songs.

3. *Di* + the definite article *(del, dello, della, dell', dei, degli, delle, degl')* is used to mean "than" before nouns, possessive adjectives, or pronouns.

L'aeroplano è più veloce *del* **treno.**	The airplane is faster than the train
La mia automobile è più vecchia *della* **tua bicicletta.**	My car is older than your bicycle.
La tua casa è più alta *della* **mia.**	Your house is taller than mine.

4. *Che* is used to mean "than" before adjectives, adverbs, participles, gerunds and infinitives in comparisons of quantity, or in comparisons that are followed by a preposition.

Mio fratello è meno bello *che* **intelligente.**	My brother is less handsome than intelligent.
Meglio tardi *che* **mai.**	Better late than never.
Il sindaco è meno amato *che* **temuto.**	The mayor is less loved than feared.
Si ottiene di più implorando *che* **minacciando.**	One achieves more by asking than by threatening.
E' più facile criticare *che* **fare.**	It is easier to criticize than to do.
C'è più pane *che* **vino.**	There is more bread than wine.
Il cielo è più bello in primavera *che* **in estate.**	The sky is more beautiful in spring than in summer.

5. The comparative can be reinforced by the adverbs such as *molto, alquanto, assai, ben,* and *oltremodo* or moderated by the adverbs such as *un po'* and *un tantino.*

La mia casa è *molto* **più grande della tua.**	My house is much bigger than yours.
Tu sei *un po'* **più alto di me.**	You are a little taller than I.

6. When "than" is followed by a clause, it is expressed by *di quello che* + a verb in the indicative, *di quanto* + a verb in the indicative or subjunctive, *che non* + a verb in the subjunctive.

E' più ricco *di quel che pensavo.*	He is richer than I thought.
La visita durò più a lungo *di quello che credevamo.*	The visit lasted longer than we thought.
Impiegai più tempo *di quanto* avevo *(avessi) previsto.*	It took more time than I expected.
Signor Rossi, Lei arriverà lì più presto *che non s'immagini.*	Mr. Rossi, you will arrive there sooner than you think.

Comparisons of Equality

1. **tanto** *(altrettanto)* **... quanto**   as ... as
   così ... come   as ... as
   non meno che   as ... as
   non meno di   as ... as
   al pari di   as ... as

E' *tanto* **largo** *quanto* **lungo.**	It is as wide as it is long.
Giorgio è *così* **bravo** *come* **buono.**	George is as clever as he is good.
La musica è bella *non meno che* **la poesia.**	Music is as beautiful as poetry.
Luigi ha studiato *non meno di* **te.**	Louis studied as much as you did.
Marco è stanco *al pari di* **Claudio.**	Marc is as tired as Claude.

Note that *tanto* and *così* can be omitted.

E' largo *quanto* **lungo.**	It is as wide as it is long.
Giorgio è bravo *come* **buono.**	George is as clever as he is good.

2. *Tanto* and *quanto* generally agree in gender and number with the noun they modify.

C'erano *tanti* **ragazzi** *quante* **ragazze.**	There were as many boys as girls.
Visitammo *tante* **chiese** *quanti* **musei.**	We visited as many churches as museums.

3. When used as adverbs, *tanto* and *quanto* are invariable.

Mi piace il tennis *tanto quanto* **il calcio.**	I like tennis as much as soccer.
Lavorarono *tanto quanto* **noi.**	They worked as much as we did.

Comparisons Involving Ratios

quanto più ...	**tanto più**	the more ...	the more
quanto più ...	**tanto meno**	the more ...	the less
quanto meno ...	**tanto più**	the less ...	the more
quanto meno ...	**tanto meno**	the less ...	the less

Note that *quanto* or *tanto,* or both may be omitted.

Quanto **più legge,** *tanto* **più apprende.**	The more he reads, the more he learns.
Quanto **più guadagna,** *tanto* **meno possiede.**	The more he earns, the less he has.
(Quanto) **meno studia,** *tanto* **più gioca.**	The less he studies, the more he plays.
(Quanto) **meno lavora,** *(tanto)* **meno guadagna.**	The less he works, the less he earns.

Superlative Adjectives

Relative Superlatives

1. The relative superlative "the" + "-est," "most," or "least" + the adjective) is formed by placing the definite article in front of the comparative *più* or *meno.*

L'oro è *il più prezioso* **dei metalli.**	Gold is the most precious metal.
Questo vestito è *il meno costoso* **di tutti.**	This suit is the least expensive of all.
Tu sei *il più vecchio* **di tutti.**	You are the oldest of all.

2. *Di* or *di* + the definite article (sometimes *fra* or *fra* + the definite article) is used to express "in," or "among" after a superlative.

Questo è il palazzo più alto *di* **Napoli.**	This is the tallest building in Naples.
Carlo è l'alunno più intelligente *della* **classe.**	Carl is the most intelligent student in his class.
Tu sei il più ricco *fra* **noi tre.**	You are the richest of the three of us.
Il Po è il più lungo *fra i* **fiumi italiani.**	The Po is the longest of Italian rivers.

Note: a. The definite article that is usually placed in front of *più* or *meno* may *also* be placed in front of the noun.

Giuseppe è *il* **più gentile dei miei amici.**	Joseph is the kindest of my friends.
Giuseppe è *l'***amico mio più gentile.**	

b. In conversational Italian, the definite article is sometimes omitted.

Franco è *(il)* **più alto dei fratelli.**   Frank is the tallest of his brothers.

Absolute Superlatives

The Italian absolute superlative has no corresponding form in English. However, it can be translated by "very," "extremely," "enormously," "quite," "super" + an adjective or an adverb.

This superlative is formed in five ways:

1. By dropping the last vowel of the adjective and adding *-issimo (-issima, -issimi, -issime)* to the stem.

alto ⟶	**altissimo**	very high
caldo ⟶	**caldissimo**	very warm
forte ⟶	**fortissimo**	very strong

Note: a. Adjectives ending in *-co* or *-go* may add an *h* before *-issimo,* while adjectives ending in unstressed *-io* drop the *i* before *-issimo.* (See Chapter 16, pp. 117–118.)

stanco ⟶	**stanchissimo**	extremely tired
simpatico ⟶	**simpaticissimo**	very nice
largo ⟶	**larghissimo**	enormously large
serio ⟶	**serissimo**	quite serious
pio ⟶	**piissimo**	very religious

b. Adjectives ending in *-dico, -fico,* and *-volo* add   *-entissimo (-entissima, -entissimi, entissime)* to the stem.

maledico ⟶	**maledicentissimo**	extremely slanderous
magnifico ⟶	**magnificentissimo**	quite magnificent
benevolo ⟶	**benevolentissimo**	very benevolent

c. Adjectives whose stem ends in *r,* take the ending *-errimo, (-errima, -errimi, -errime).*

celebre ⟶	**celeberrimo**	enormously famous
acre ⟶	**acerrimo**	very harsh
aspro ⟶	**asperrimo**	quite sour (harsh)
misero ⟶	**miserrimo**	very poor

2. By placing an adverb such as *molto, assai, troppo, veramente, incredibilmente, infinitamente, altamente,* or *estremamente* before the adjective or adverb.

Anna è *molto* **contenta.**	Ann is very happy.
Questa casa è *veramente* **grande.**	This house is very large.
Giovanni è *incredibilmente* **avaro.**	John is very stingy.

3. By adding a prefix such as *arci-*, *ultra-*, *extra- (stra-)*, *sopra-*, or *iper-*.

Quell'uomo è *arcimilionario.*	That man is a multimillionaire.
Questo libro è *stravecchio.*	This book is very old.
Egli ha dei gusti *sopraffini.*	He has superfine tastes.

4. By repeating the adjective or adverb.

E' un bambino *piccino piccino.*	He is a very small child.
Parlò *piano piano.*	He spoke very softly.
Il cuore mi batte *forte forte.*	My heart is beating very hard.

5. By adding another adjective or expression.

sporco lercio	filthy dirty
bagnato fradicio	soaking wet
pieno zeppo	packed full
stanco morto	dead tired
secco allampanato	as lean as a rake
buono come il pane	a heart of gold
lento come una tartaruga	slow as a turtle
puro al cento per cento	100% pure

Irregular Comparison

1. The following adjective have irregular comparative and superlative forms.

Positive		Comparative	Relative Superlative	Absolute Superlative
buono	good	**migliore**	**il migliore**	**ottimo**
cattivo	bad	**peggiore**	**il peggiore**	**pessimo**
grande	big, great	**maggiore**	**il maggiore**	**massimo**
piccolo	small, little	**minore**	**il minore**	**minimo**
alto	high, tall	**superiore**	**il supremo**	**supremo/ sommo**
basso	low, short	**inferiore**	**l'inferiore**	**infimo**
esterno	external	**esteriore**	**l'estremo**	**estremo**
interno	internal	**interiore**	**l'intimo**	**intimo**

2. The preceding adjectives have also *regular* forms.

Positive	Comparative	Relative Superlative	Absolute Superlative
buono	più buono	il più buono	buonissimo
cattivo	più cattivo	il più cattivo	cattivissimo
grande	più grande	il più grande	grandissimo
piccolo	più piccolo	il più piccolo	piccolissimo
alto	più alto	il più alto	altissimo
basso	più basso	il più basso	bassissimo
esterno	più esterno	il più esterno	_____
interno	più interno	il più interno	_____

3. The choice between the regular and irregular forms depends on meaning and/or personal preference, style and usage. In general, the irregular forms are used in a *figurative,* rather than literal, sense.

Il monte Bianco è *più alto del monte Cervino.* (literal)	Mont Blanc is higher than the Matterhorn
Conduce una vita *superiore* **ai suoi mezzi.** (figurative)	He lives beyond his means.
Questa collina è *più bassa* **di quella.**	This hill is lower than that one.
Marco è *inferiore* **a Paolo in intelligenza.**	Marc is inferior to Paul in intelligence.

4. The irregular forms of *grande* and *piccolo* are used when they refer to importance or age, rather than to literal size.

Dante è il nostro *maggiore* **poeta.** (importance)	Dante is our greatest poet.
Mio fratello *maggiore* **abita a Napoli.** (age)	My oldest brother lives in Naples.
La tua casa è *più grande* **della mia.** (literal sense)	Your house is bigger than mine
Pulci è un poeta *minore.* (importance)	Pulci is a minor poet.
Mia sorella *minore* **è partita per le vacanze.** (age)	My younger sister went on vacation.
Questa borsa da viaggio è *più piccola* **di quella.** (literal sense)	This traveling bag is smaller than that one.

5. The following are additional examples of the irregular comparative and superlative forms.

La cattedrale è *l'edificio più alto* della città.	The cathedral is the highest building in the city.
Quant'è *il minimo* prezzo?	What is the lowest price?
Mi dispiace, ma questa stoffa è d'*infima* qualità.	I am sorry, but this cloth is of the lowest quality.
Nerone fu un *pessimo* imperatore.	Nero was a very bad emperor.
Questo è *il migliore* racconto che lui abbia mai scritto.	This is the best story he ever wrote.
Essi abitano al piano *superiore*.	They live on the upper floor.
Questo vino è *ottimo*.	This wine is excellent.
Mi trattò con *la massima* pazienza.	He was extremely patient with me.

Note: Some adjectives have *no* comparative or superlative forms. These adjectives express:

a. time—*giornaliero*, daily; *settimanale*, weekly; *annuale*, yearly;
b. what material an object is made of—*aureo*, golden; *bronzeo*, made of bronze; *argenteo*, made of silver; *ferreo*, made of iron;
c. local or national origin—*cittadino*, civic; *campagnuolo*, rural; *francese*, French; *europeo*, European; *africano*, African;
d. position—*principale*, main; *iniziale*, initial; *terminale*, terminal;
e. scientific or geometric concepts—*chimico*, chemical; *nucleare*, nuclear; *lineare*, linear; *triangolare*, triangular; *quadrato*, square; *cubico*, cubic; *cilindrico*, cylindrical; *sferico*, spherical.

Comparison of Adverbs

Adverbs of manner and some others are compared like adjectives, by placing *più, meno, tanto . . . quanto, così . . . come, quanto . . . altrettanto* before the adverb.

Comparisons of Inequality

Quest' anno Riccardo lavora *più* regolarmente dell'anno scorso.	This year Richard is working more regularly than last year.
Il treno corre *meno* velocemente dell'aereo.	The train moves slower than the airplane.
Ritornerò *più* tardi delle 11.	I will return after 11 o'clock.
Io vado al cinema *meno* spesso di tuo fratello.	I go to the movies less often than your brother.
Si comportò molto *più* intelligentemente di quanto pensassi.	He acted much more intelligently than I had thought.

Comparisons of Equality

Alberto studia *tanto* **diligentemente** *quanto* **Tommaso.**	Albert studies as diligently as Thomas.
Lui gioca *altrettanto* **bene** *quanto* **il suo amico.**	He plays as well as his friend.

Superlative Adverbs

Absolute Superlatives

The absolute superlative of an adverb is formed by adding *-mente* to the feminine singular form of the absolute superlative of the adjective. However a more common construction is *molto* (or *veramente, assai, troppo*) followed by an adverb.

La tartaruga cammina *lentissimamente.*	The turtle walks very slowly.
Anna vive *molto allegramente.*	Ann lives very happily.
L'ospite arrivò *veramente tardi.*	The guest arrived very late.
L'ammalato sopportò il dolore *assai pazientemente.*	The patient endured the pain very patiently.

Relative Superlatives

The relative superlatives of an adverb is formed by placing the article *il* (the *only* article that can be used) in front of the comparative forms. The word "possibile" is added, sometimes, to express the idea "as . . . as possible."

Lo farò *al più* **presto.**	I'll do that as soon as I can.
Partirò *il più* **tardi** *possibile.*	I'll leave as late as possible.
Alfredo parlò *il più* **cortesemente** *possibile.*	Alfred spoke as courteously as possible.

Note: The comparative followed by *che* + verb *potere* is equivalent to the relative superlative followed by *possibile*. Thus the last sentence above could have been written: *Alfredo parlò più cortesemente che potè.*

Irregular Comparison

1. Certain adverbs have irregular comparative, relative superlative, and absolute superlative forms. Here are the most common.

Adverb		*Comparative*	
bene	well	**meglio**	better
male	badly	**peggio**	worse
molto	much	**più, di più**	more
poco	little	**meno, di meno**	less

Relative Superlative		*Absolute Superlative*	
(il) meglio	the best	**ottimamente**	very well
(il) peggio	the worst	**pessimamente**	very badly
(il) più	the most	**moltissimo**	very much
(il) meno	the least	**pochissimo**	very little

Per fare *meglio* **spesso si fa** *peggio.*	To do better, one often does worse.
Ti senti un po' *meglio?*	Are you feeling any better?
"Come stai?" *"Ottimamente,* **grazie!"**	"How are you feeling?" "Very well, thank you!"
Lo tratta *peggio* **di una bestia.**	He treats him worse than an animal.
Le cose cominciarono *male* **e finirono** *peggio*	Worse was to follow.

2. In the relative superlative, the article *il* is often omitted unless *possibile* is used.

Chi ha fatto *meno* **errori?**	Who made the fewest mistakes?
Lavora *il meno possibile.*	He works as little as possible.

3. The irregular comparatives *più, meno, meglio,* and *peggio* can be used as masculine nouns.

Il peggio **è passato.**	The worst is over.
Il meglio **è nemico del bene.**	Leave well enough alone.
Parlammo *del più* **e** *del meno.*	We spoke about this and that.

4. *I più* and *i meno* correspond to "the majority," "the minority."

I più **la pensano così.**	The majority are of this opinion.
I più **tirano** *i meno.*	The majority leads the minority.

5. *Il più* may be translated as "the greatest quantity" or "the most important thing."

Il più è **fatto.**	Most of it is done.
Il più è **cominciare.**	The most important thing is to get started.
Il più è **che non gli piace lavorare.**	And moreover, he does not like to work.

6. *Più . . . più* and *meno . . . meno* are equivalent to "the more . . . the more" and "the less . . . the less" in English.

Più **studi,** *più* **impari.**	The more you study, the more you learn.
Meno **mangi,** *meno* **ingrassi.**	The less you eat, the less you gain weight.
Meno **si dice,** *meglio* è.	The less you say, the better.

Note: *Più* and *meno* can also be used as adjectives, as well as adverbs.

Mi piace con *meno* **sale.**	I like it with less salt.
Non ne voglio *più.*	I don't want any more.

21. Personal Pronouns

Personal pronouns can be divided into two groups: 1. stressed (or *disjunctive)* pronouns and 2. unstressed (or *conjunctive)* pronouns, depending on whether or not tonic accent falls on them.

Stressed and unstressed pronouns may be further classified according to their function. Thus a stressed pronoun functions as: a. subject, b. direct object, or c. indirect object (after a preposition), while an unstressed pronoun may serve as: a. direct object or b. indirect object.

		Stressed Pronouns			Unstressed Pronouns	
		Subject	Direct Object	Indirect Object (after preposition)	Direct Object	Indirect Object
Singular	1	io	me	me	mi	mi
	2	tu	te	te	ti	ti
	3	egli, lui, esso	lui	lui, esso	lo	gli, ne
		ella, lei, essa	lei	lei, essa	la	le, ne
			Lei	Lei	La	Le
			sè	sè		
(Reflexive)			sè	sè	si	si
Plural	1	noi	noi	noi	ci	ci
	2	voi	voi	voi	vi	vi
	3	essi, esse, loro	loro	essi, esse, loro	li, le	loro (gli), ne
			Loro	Loro		Loro
			sè	sè		
(Reflexive)			sè	sè	si	si

Note: The other forms of the reflexive pronouns are the same as those of the unstressed direct-object pronouns.

Subject Pronouns

1. A subject pronoun is the subject of a verb. Note that the speaker is called the *first person* ("I," "we"); the one addressed, the *second person* ("you"); and the one spoken of, the *third person* ("he," "she," "it," "they")

	Singular			Plural	
1st person	**io**	I	**noi**	we
2nd person	**tu**	you *(informal)*	**voi**	you *(informal)*
3rd person	**Lei**	you *(formal)*	**Loro**	you *(formal)*
	egli, lui, esso	he	**loro**	they *(m.)*
	ella, lei, essa	she	**loro**	they *(f.)*
	esso	it *(m.)*	**essi**	they *(m.)*
	essa	it *(f.)*	**esse**	they *(f.)*

2. Subject pronouns are usually omitted in Italian except when they are necessary for clarity, emphasis, or contrast, and when the subject is separated from the verb.

Leggiamo il giornale.	We are reading the newspaper.
Sperava che *tu* **venissi.**	He hoped that you would come.
Andrò *io.*	I will go.
Tu **lavori e** *lei* **dorme.**	You work and she sleeps.
Tu, **figlio mio, sei il mio conforto.**	You, my son, are my consolation.

3. The first-person singular *io* is written with a lowercase letter in Italian, *not* with a capital letter as in English.

4. *Tu* and its plural form *voi,* called the *familiar form* of "you," are used in the family, among intimate friends and fellow students, or when speaking to children, servants, and animals. *Voi* is also used in political speeches and in business letters.

Tu, **mamma, sei il mio amore.**	You are my love, mom.
Voi, **bambini, dovete andare a dormire.**	You, children, have to go to bed.
Voi, **cittadini, dovete votare.**	You, citizens, must vote.
Desideriamo entrare in relazione d'affari con *voi.*	We would be glad to enter into business relations with you.

5. *Lei* and its plural *Loro,* called the *polite form* of "you," are used when speaking to strangers, superiors, and people one is not well acquainted with. *Lei* and *Loro* (not to be confused with *lei,* "she," and *loro,* "they") are normally capitalized. *Lei* always takes a third-person singular verb while *Loro* always takes a third-person plural verb.

Desidererei parlare con *Lei,* **professore.**	I would like to talk with you, professor.
Dottoressa Cardillo, *Lei* **è una signora veramente gentile.**	Doctor Cardillo, you are a very kind woman.
Care signore, quando partono *Loro* **per New York?**	Dear ladies, when are you leaving for New York?

Note: Loro is frequently replaced by the less formal *voi*.

Egregi signori, *(voi)* **state per assistere ad uno spettacolo meraviglioso.**	Dear sirs, you are about to see a wonderful show.

6. *Egli* and *ella* are used mainly in the written language. In conversational Italian, they are generally replaced by *lui* and *lei*.

Ella **si è diplomata presso questa scuola.** (written)	She graduated from this school.
Egli **presta il servizio militare.** (written)	He is serving in the army.
Lei **mangia con me oggi.** (conversational)	Today she is eating with me.
Lui **mi telefona ogni giorno.** (conversational)	He phones me every day.

7. *Esso, essa, essi* and *esse* are used to refer to animals and inanimate objects. However, they are generally omitted.

Hai visto il cavallo da corsa? *(Esso)* **è molto veloce.**	Did you see the race horse? He is very fast.
Non compro questa casa: *(essa)* **è molto cara.**	I am not buying this house. It is very expensive.

Stressed Direct-Object Pronouns

Stressed direct-object pronouns receive the action of the verb. They have the following forms.

	Singular		*Plural*
me	me	**noi**	us
te	you *(informal)*	**voi**	you
lui	him	**loro**	them *(m.)*
lei	her	**loro**	them *(f.)*
Lei	you *(formal, m. and f.)*	**Loro**	them *(formal, m. and f.)*
sè	himself, herself	**sè**	themselves *(m. and f.)*

These pronouns are used:

1. For emphasis (often with *anche,* "also," *proprio,* "just," and *solamente,* "only" or contrast. Note that these pronouns *always* follow the verb.

Accolsero *noi* **come liberatori** (emphatic form). **Ci accolsero come liberatori.**	They received us as liberators.
Egli ha chiamato proprio *te* (emphatic form). **Egli ti ha chiamato.**	He called you.
Voglio *te,* **non** *lui.*	I want you, not him.
Cerca di scusare *sè* **ed accusa gli altri.**	He tries to excuse himself while accusing others.
Per non danneggiare *sè,* **scappò via.**	He ran away not to harm himself.

2. In comparisons and after *tranne,* meaning "except."

Riccardo è italiano *come me.*	Richard is Italian like me.
Vennero tutti, *tranne lei.*	Everybody came, except her.

3. After a verb governing two or more objects (direct or indirect).

Vedo *lui e Franco.*	I see him and Frank.
Ho parlato *con lui e con lei.*	I spoke with him and with her.
Ho dato un libro *a te e a Giacomo.*	I gave you and James a book.

4. In exclamations, after some adjectives.

Disgraziato *me!*	Unlucky me!
Beato *te!*	Lucky you!
Felice *lui!*	Happy him!

5. In the case of *lui, lei,* and *loro,* as predicate nominatives after a form of the verb *essere.*

E' *lui.*	It is he.
E' *lei.*	It is she.
Sono *loro.*	It is they.

Stressed Indirect-Object Pronouns

The stressed indirect-object pronouns have the following forms:

Singular		*Plural*	
me	me	**noi**	us
te	you *(informal)*	**voi**	you *(informal)*
lui, esso	him, it *(m.)*	**loro, essi**	them *(m.)*
lei, essa	her, it *(f.)*	**loro, esse**	them *(f.)*
Lei	you *(formal)*	**Loro**	you *(formal)*
sè	yourself, oneself, itself	**sè**	yourselves, themselves

These pronouns have the following uses.

1. Stressed indirect-object pronouns are used after prepositions such as *a*, "to"; *con*, "with,"; *da*, "by," "from"; *di*, "of," "about"; and *per*, "for."

Studio *con lui* **e con suo cugino.**	I am studying with him and his cousin.
Siamo fieri *di te* **e di tuo fratello.**	We are proud of you and your brother.
Vuoi venire *con me?*	Do you want to come with me?
Ama parlare *di sè.*	He likes to talk about himself.

Note the repetition of the preposition in the first two examples.

2. The third-person reflexive pronoun *sè* generally refers to people, but sometimes to animals or things. It can be masculine or feminine, singular or plural.

Caterina era fuori di *sè* **per l'ira.**	Catherine was beside herself with anger.
Roberto e Giacomo si preoccupano solo di *sè.*	Robert and James only worry about themselves.
La luce si spegne da *sè.*	The light goes out by itself.

3. *Sè* replaces *lui, lei, loro* when it refers to the subject of the sentence.

Il maestro condusse gli alunni con *sè.* **(= con** *lui*).	The teacher took the students with him.
Giuseppe e Giovanni lavorano per *sè* **(= per** *loro).*	Joseph and John work for themselves.

Note the difference between *sè* and *lui, lei, loro.*

Si preoccupa di *sè.*	He is worried about himself.
Si preoccupa di *lui (di lei, di loro).*	He is worried about him (her, them).

4. *Sè* can be reinforced by *stesso (-a, -i, -e)*. The accent on *sè* is then generally omitted.

Ha pensato solo a *se stesso.*	He only thought about himself.
Fanno male a *se stessi.*	They hurt themselves.

Note: *Sè* and *se stesso* can only be used as objects and *not* as subjects. Thus, the English "She said that herself" is rendered in Italian by *L'ha detto lei* (or *lei stessa).*

5. Many prepositions add *di* before a disjunctive pronoun. These prepositions include: *contro,* "against"; *dentro,* "inside"; *dietro,* "behind"; *dopo,* "after"; *fra,* "among"; *fuori,* "outside"; *presso,* "at"; "near"; *prima,* "before"; *senza,* "without"; *sopra,* "above"; *sotto,* "under"; *su,* "on"; *verso,* "to", "toward."

Non so perchè è *contro di me.*	I do not know why he is against me.
Non dice a nessuno cosa ha *dentro di sè.*	He does not tell anyone what he has inside of him.
Arrivarono *dopo di noi.*	They arrived after us.
Viviamo *fra di loro.*	We live among them.
Partì *prima di te.*	He left before you.
La responsabilità cade tutta *sopra di noi.*	The responsibility lies entirely on us.

Note: The use of *di* after *dopo, fra,* and *senza* is optional.

6. *Da* followed by a disjunctive pronoun may mean "at," "to," "in someone's house" or "all by oneself."

Come puoi vivere *senza (di)* **me?**	How can you live without me?
Mario e Giorgio vengono *da me.*	Mario and George come to my house.
Hai imparato a suonare il piano *da te.*	You learned how to play the piano by yourself.

Unstressed Direct-Object Pronouns

Unstressed direct-object pronouns, like the stressed, receive the action of the verb. They have the following forms:

	Singular		*Plural*
mi	me	**ci**	us
ti	you *(informal)*	**vi**	you *(informal)*
La	you *formal m.* and *f.)*	**Li, Le**	you *(formal, m.* and *f.)*
lo	him, it *(m.)*	**li**	them *(m.)*
la	her, it *(f.)*	**le**	them *(f.)*

These pronouns have the following uses.

1. An unstressed direct-object pronoun is normally placed *in front of* the verb of which it is the direct object.

Lo **tratto come un fratello.**	I treat him as a brother.
Non *ci* **rispettano più.**	They do not respect us any more.
"Mi **capisci quando parlo italiano?" "Sì,** *ti* **capisco."**	"Do you understand me when I speak Italian?" "Yes, I understand you."

2. An unstressed direct-object pronoun agrees in gender and number with the noun it replaces. When the pronoun replaces nouns of different genders, the masculine-plural pronoun *(li)* is used.

"Conosci *il signor Rossi?***"**	"Do you know Mr. Rossi?"
"Non *lo* **conosco."**	"I do not know him."
"Conosci *la signora Rossi?***"**	"Do you know Mrs. Rossi?"
"Non *la* **conosco."**	"I do not know her."
"Conosci *il signor Rossi e la signora Rossi?***"**	"Do you know Mr. and Mrs. Rossi?"
"Non *li* **conosco."**	"I do not know them."

Note: In compound tenses conjugated with *avere*, the past participle agrees in gender and number with the direct-object pronoun.

Il signor Cotugno **è arrivato, ma noi non** *l'***abbiamo vist**o.	Mr. Cotugno has arrived, but we did not see him.
La signora Cotugno **è arrivata, ma noi non** *l'***abbiamo vist**a.	Mrs. Cotugno has arrived, but we did not see her.

3. *Lo, la, mi, ti, vi* may drop their final vowel before another vowel or the letter *h. Ci* may drop the *-i* only before *e* or *i*.

*L'***aiutano sempre.**	They always help him.
*T'***aspetto (or** *Ti* **aspetto) da circa un'ora.**	I have been waiting for you almost an hour.
Roberto? *L'***ho visto ieri sera.**	Robert? I saw him last night.
*C'***elessero consiglieri delegati.**	They appointed us managing directors.
Quelle domande *c'***imbarazzarono.**	Those questions puzzled us.
Ci **avvisarono del tuo arrivo.**	They informed us of your arrival.

4. *Li, Le, La, li,* and *le* never drop their final vowel.

Quando *Li* **ascolteremo di nuovo?**	When will we be listening to you again?
Chi *La* **aiuta, dottor Monaco?**	Who is helping you, doctor Monaco?
Non *li* **importuniamo mai.**	We never bother them.
Non *le* **incontrai più.**	I never met them again.

5. An unstressed direct-object pronoun generally follows an infinitive and is attached to it. Note that the infinitive drops the final *e*

Sono contento di *vederti.*	I am glad to see you.
Sei venuto ad *aiutarmi?*	Did you come to help me?
Abbiamo cercato di *difenderlo.*	We tried to defend him.

6. When the infinitive depends on the verbs *dovere, potere, preferire, volere,* or *sapere,* the object pronoun may *either* be attached to the infinitive *or* be placed in front of the conjugated verb.

Dobbiamo incoraggiar*li.* ⎫ *Li* **dobbiamo incoraggiare.** ⎭	We must encourage them.
Voglio salutar*ti.* ⎫ *Ti* **voglio salutare.** ⎭	I want to say hello to you.
Sai guidar*la?* ⎫ *La* **sai guidare?** ⎭	Can you drive it?

7. With the affirmative imperative (second-person singular [*tu*] or plural [*voi*] or first-person plural [*noi*], the unstressed direct-object pronoun *follows* the verb and is *attached* to it.

Ama*mi* **sempre.**	Love me always.
Ecco il nonno. Salutate*lo,* **bambini.**	Here is grandpa. Say hello to him, children.
Questa è la nostra bandiera. **Rispettiamo***la.*	This is our flag. Let's respect it!.

However, if the affirmative imperative is in the third-person singular (*Lei*) or plural (*Loro*), the pronoun *precedes* the verb.

E' un ottimo libro. *Lo* **compri!**	It is a very good book. Buy it!
Ecco il documento, signori. *Lo* **leggano, per piacere.**	Here is the document, gentlemen. Please, read it!

8. With the negative imperative, the unstressed direct-object pronoun generally *precedes* the verb.

E' una stoffa scadente. Non *la* **comprare.**	It's poor-quality cloth. Don't buy it.
Non *mi* **spingere. (or Non** **spinger***mi*).	Do not push me.

Note: a. *Lo* can be a neuter pronoun meaning *ciò* or may refer to a whole sentence.

Lo **credo** (= **credo** *ciò*).	I believe that.
Sai che Claudio ha vinto la **partita?** *Lo* **supponevo.**	Do you know that Claude has won the game? I thought so.

b. *Lo* is also used as a neuter pronoun to represent an idea that has been previously mentioned.

E' furbo Paolo? Sì, *lo* **è e come!**	Is Paul shrewd? Yes, he is (*shrewd*) and how!
Pensavo che fossero ricchi, ma non *lo* **sono.**	I thought they were rich, but they are not (*rich*).

c. *La* can also be a neuter pronoun. It may be used in idiomatic phrases such as:

Se *la* **passa bene.**	He lives quite well.
Non te *la* **prendere.**	Don't take it amiss.

Unstressed Indirect-Object Pronouns

The unstressed indirect-object pronoun denotes the person "to," "for," or "from whom" an action is performed. The forms of these pronouns are as follows:

Singular		*Plural*	
mi	to me	**ci**	to us
ti	to you (informal)	**vi**	to you
Le	to you (formal)	**Loro**	to you
gli	to him		
le	to her	**loro**	to them

Unstressed indirect-object pronouns have the same forms as the unstressed direct-object pronouns, *except* in the third-person singular and plural forms.

1. The indirect-object pronoun normally *precedes* the conjugated verb. However, *loro* and *Loro* usually *follow the verb*.

Gli **scrisse una lettera.**	He wrote him a letter.
Le **mandai un mazzo di fiori.**	I sent her a bunch of flowers.
Hai inviato *loro* **il pacco?**	Did you send them the package?

Note: In colloquial Italian *loro* is frequently replaced by *gli*, which *precedes* the verb.

I miei vicini? *Gli* **sto facendo un favore.**	My neighbors? I am doing them a favor.

2. The indirect-object pronoun agrees in gender and number with the noun it replaces.

Ecco *il ragazzo.* **Raccontagli la storia.**	Here is the boy. Tell him the story.
Ecco *la ragazza.* **Raccontale la storia.**	Here is the girl. Tell her the story.
Ecco *i ragazzi.* **Racconta** *loro* **la storia.**	Here are the boys. Tell them the story.
Ecco *le ragazze.* **Racconta** *loro* **la storia.**	Here are the girls. Tell them the story.

Note: In compound tenses conjugated with *avere*, the past participle does *not* agree with the indirect-object pronoun and always ends in *-o*.

Gli **ho offerto una tazza di caffè.**	I offered him a cup of coffee.
Le **ho offerto una tazza di caffè.**	I offered her a cup of coffee.
Ho offerto *loro* **una tazza di caffè.**	I offered them a cup of coffee.

3. *Mi, ti,* and *vi* may become *m', t',* and *v'* before a vowel or the letter *h. Ci* becomes *c'* only before *e* or *i.*

*M'*inviarono una cartolina da **Roma.**	They sent me a postcard from Rome.
*C'*elargirono cure ed affetto.	They lavished care and affection on us.
Ci augurarono la buona notte.	They wished us a good night.

4. The pronouns *Le* and *Loro* are capitalized when they are used in the polite form.

Dottor Lanzotti, *Le* **auguro una felice giornata.**	Doctor Lanzotti, I wish you a very good day.

5. An indirect-object pronoun generally *follows* an infinitive and is *attached* to it. However *loro* and *Loro* follow the infinitive, but they are not attached to it. Note that an infinitive drops its final *e* with an indirect-object pronoun.

Desidererei *parlargli.*	I would like to talk to him.
Ho cercato di *dar loro* **tutto quello che avevo.**	I tried to give them whatever I had.

6. When the infinitive depends on the verbs *dovere, potere, preferire, volere,* or *sapere,* the object pronoun may *either* be attached to the infinitive *or* be placed in front of the conjugated verb. However *loro* and *Loro* must follow the infinitive.

Devo scriver*gli.* \ *Gli* **devo scrivere.**	I must write to him.
Posso offrir*Le* **un gelato?** \ *Le* **posso offrire un gelato?**	May I offer you some ice cream?
Preferisci scrivere *loro* **in italiano?**	Would you like to write to them in Italian?

7. With the affirmative imperative [second-person singular (*tu*) or plural (*voi*) or first-person plural (*noi*)], an unstressed indirect-object pronoun *follows* the verb and is *attached* to it. *Loro* and *Loro* follow the verb, but are *not* attached to it.

Compra*gli* il libro.	Buy him the book.
Spedite*mi* una cartolina.	Send me a postcard.
Date *loro* la risposta.	Give them the answer.

8. With the negative imperative, the unstressed indirect-object pronoun generally *precedes* the verb. However, *loro* and *Loro* come *after* the verb.

Non *gli* date niente più.	Do not give him anything anymore.
Non *gli* offrire il tuo posto.	Do not give him your seat.
Non rispondete *loro* neanche una parola.	Do not answer them, not even a word.

9. With a gerund or a past participle standing on its own, the unstressed indirect-object pronoun *follows* the verb and is *attached* to it.

Dicendogli: **"Buona sera," chiusi la porta.**	Saying "Good night" to him, I closed the door.
Consegnatole **il libro, me ne andai.**	Having given her the book, I went away.

10. The unstressed indirect-object pronoun sometimes replaces the possessive adjective, when referring to parts of the body or clothing.

Gli **fa male la testa.**	His head hurts.
La camicetta *le* va un po' stretta di spalle.	Her blouse is a bit tight in the shoulders.

11. Some verbs that take a direct object in English take an indirect object in Italian. The following are the most common of these verbs.

bastare to be sufficient; to last	**piacere** to please
chiedere to ask	**ricordarsi** to remember
dire to say, to tell	**rispondere** to answer
dispiacere to displease	**somigliare** to resemble
domandare to ask	**telefonare** to phone
far male to hurt	**voler bene** to love
far sapere to let know	

Chiedi*gli* dove abita.	Ask him where he lives.
Le **farò sapere ogni cosa.**	I'll let you know everything.
Non ti ricordi *di lui?*	Don't you remember him?
Mia madre? *Le* **voglio tanto bene.**	My mother? I love her very much.

Double-Object Pronouns

When two object pronouns are governed by the same verb, the indirect object always *precedes the direct object. Note the patterns in the chart below.*

Indirect Object Pronouns	Direct Object Pronouns				
	lo	la	li	le	ne
mi	me lo	me la	me li	me le	me ne
ti	te lo	te la	te li	te le	te ne
gli, le, Le	glielo	gliela	glieli	gliele	gliene
ci	ce lo	ce la	ce li	ce le	ce ne
vi	ve lo	ve la	ve li	ve le	ve ne
si	se lo	se la	se li	se le	se ne

1. Note that, before *lo, la, li, le,* and *ne, mi, ti, si, ci,* change to *me, te, se, ce, ve.* Note also that *gli* and *le* change before *lo, la, li, le,* and *ne* to *glie* and form one word with the pronoun that follows. In combined forms no distinction is made between "to him," "to her," "to you."

Lisa *me lo* **disse.**	Lisa told me that.
Filippo *te lo* **diede.**	Phillip gave it to you.
Il pacco? *Ce l'***ha mandato la zia.**	The package? Our aunt sent it to us.
Ti piacciono le mie scarpe nuove? *Me le* **ha comprate la mamma.**	Do you like my new shoes? My mother bought them for me.
Saggia queste paste. *Ce le* **ha offerte Luisa.**	Taste these pastries. Louise offered them to us.
Se lo **portò con sè.**	He took it with him.
Tommaso *glielo* **portò.**	Thomas brought it to him.
Hai ancora le chiavi di Arturo? No, *gliele* **mandai subito.**	Do you still have Arthur's keys? No, I sent them to him immediately.

2. The pronouns *loro* and *Loro* follow the verb but they are not attached to it.

Vendi*lo a loro.*	Sell it to them.
Racconta*lo a loro.*	Tell it to them.

3. The double-object pronouns are placed in the same position as the single object pronouns, that is, they come *before a conjugated verb and after an infinitive.*

Guarda il quadro. Guglielmo *te lo* **sta mostrando.**	Look at the painting. William is showing it to you.
Preferisco dir*glielo* **personalmente.**	I prefer to tell him personally.

4. When the infinitive depends on the verbs *dovere, potere, sapere* or *volere,* double-object pronouns may be placed *either* after the infinitive *or* before the auxiliary verbs.

Dobbiamo dir*glielo* al più presto. *Glielo* **dobbiamo dire al più** **presto.**	We must tell him as soon as possible.
Posso vender*telo* allo stesso **prezzo.** *Te lo* **posso vendere allo stesso** **prezzo.**	I can sell it to you at the same price.
Qual è la strada per Napoli? **Sapresti indicar*cela*.** **Qual è la strada per Napoli?** *Ce* *la* **sapresti indicare?**	What is the way to Naples? Could you show it to us?

The Pronoun *ne*

1. *Ne* is a useful pronoun that covers all genders, as well as both singular and plural. It has a variety of meanings: "of it," "of him," "of her," "of them," "some of it," "some of them," etc.

2. The pronoun *ne* may replace a partitive construction.

"Ho *molte matite. Ne* vuoi?" **"No, grazie. *Ne* ho."**	"I have many pencils. Would you like some of them" "No thank you. I've got some (of them)."
"Hai *dei fiammiferi?"* "Non *ne* **ho."**	"Have you got any matches?" "I haven't any (of them)."

3. *Ne* may also replace a noun preceded by numerals or an adjective of quantity.

Hai *tre* fratelli?" "No, *ne* ho due."	"Do you have three brothers?" "No, I have two (of them).
"Quanti cugini avete?" *"Ne* **abbiamo** *quattro."*	"How many cousins do you have?" "We have four (of them)."

Note that *ne* is *never* omitted in Italian, whereas its English equivalents are often implied *or* expressed by a possessive adjective.

Non *ne* conosco il prezzo.	I don't know its price (= the price *of it*).
Mario è un buon lavoratore. *Ne* **conosco le capacità.**	Mario is a good worker. I know his ability (= the ability *of* *him*).

4. Often, *ne* replaces prepositional phrases introduced by *di* (followed by a noun or an entire clause) or by *da* (followed by a place).

Parliamo spesso *di Alberto. Ne* **parliamo spesso.**	We often talk about Albert. We often talk about him.
"Hai bisogno del vocabolario?" **"Sì,** *ne* **ho bisogno."**	"Do you need the dictionary?" "Yes, I need it."
"Volete parlare *del vostro viaggio* **in Italia?" "Sì, voglio** **parlar***ne."*	"Would you like to talk about your trip to Italy?" "Yes, I would."
"Torni *da scuola*?" **"Sì,** *ne* **torno ora."**	"Are you coming back from school?" "Yes, I am just coming back (from there)."
"E' uscito il treno *dalla* *galleria*?" **"***Ne* **uscirà in cinque minuti."**	"Did the train come out of the tunnel?" "It will come out (of there) within five minutes."

5. *Ne* has the same position in a sentence as the object pronoun.

Prendi del formaggio. *Ne* **prendo.**	Take some cheese. I'll take some.
Vuoi parlare dell'emigrazione **italiana? Voglio parlar***ne* **(***Ne* ***voglio parlare***.)	Would you like to talk about Italian emigration? I would.

6. In compound tenses *ne* precedes the verb. When replacing a partitive, it requires *agreement* with the past participle.

Abbiamo discusso a lungo di **politica.** *Ne* **abbiamo discuss***o* **a lungo.**	We discussed politics for a long time. We discussed it for a long time.
Hai visto degli alunni in giro? **Si,** *ne* **ho vist***i* **cinque.**	Have you seen any students around? Yes, I have seen five.

The Adverbs of Place *ci* and *vi*

1. Besides being object pronouns, *ci* and *vi* are used as unstressed adverbs of place and mean "here" or "there". They are practically interchangeable, although *ci* is more common in everyday speech.

A Maurizio piace il mio paese. *Ci* **viene a passare le vacanze** **ogni anno.**	Maurice likes my town. He comes here every year to spend his vacation.
Vai in Italia quest'estate? Sì, *ci* **vado.**	Are you going to Italy this summer? Yes, I am going there.

2. *Ci* and *vi*, followed by a form of the verb *essere*, are equivalent to the English "there is," "there are."

C'è un vino migliore di questo. **Ci (or** *Vi***) sono molti alunni in** **questa classe.**	There is a finer wine than this one. There are many students in this class.

3. *Ci* and *vi* are replaced by *lì* or *là* when the speaker wishes to emphasize the place mentioned.

Il dottore era *lì*.	The doctor was there.

4. *Ci* and *vi* replace prepositional phrases introduced by:

a. *a, in, su,* or *da* followed by a place.

Vai mai *al cinema*? **Sì,** *ci* **vado.**	Do you ever go to the movies. Yes, I do.
Sei mai stato *in Francia*? **Sì,** *ci* **sono stato.**	Have you ever been to France? Yes, I have.
Siete andati *sul balcone*? **No, non** *ci* **siamo andati.**	Have you gone up to the balcony? No, we have not.
Marco è *dal dentista*? **No, non** *ci* **va più.**	Is Mark at the dentist's. No, he does not go there any more.

b. *a* or *su* followed by a noun denoting things.

Pensi ancora *al denaro perduto*? **Sì,** *ci* **penso ancora.**	Do you still think about the money you lost? Yes, I do.
Giochi tutto *su questa carta*? **Sì,** *ci* **gioco tutto.**	Do you bet everything on this card? Yes, I bet it all.

c. *a* followed by an entire clause.

Hai provato *a dormire un po' di più*? **Sì,** *ci* **ho provato.**	Have you tried sleeping a little longer? Yes, I have.
Non credi più *a quello che ti ho detto*? **No, non** *ci* **credo più.**	Do you no longer believe what I told you? No, I do not.

5. *Ci* and *vi* are placed before or after the verb, according to the rules for object pronouns.

Ci **andammo tutti insieme.**	We went there all together.
Andiamo*ci* **tutti insieme.**	Let us go there all together.

22. Relative Pronouns

A relative pronoun joins a dependent clause to the main clause and refers back to a noun or a group of words previously mentioned in the sentence (the *antecedent*). The relative pronouns in English are "that," "who," "whom," "whose," and "which." They are often omitted but *never* in Italian. The relative pronouns in Italian are: *che, il quale, cui, chi.*

Il *ragazzo che* vedi è mio fratello.	The *boy (that)* you see is my brother.

The relative pronoun may serve as: 1. the subject, 2. the direct object, or 3. the object of a preposition.

L'alunno *che* studia impara. (subject)	The student that studies learns.
Il libro *che* leggo è interessante. (direct object)	The book that I am reading is interesting.
L'amico *di cui* ti ho parlato è un medico. (object of a preposition)	The friend I spoke to you about is a doctor.

Che

1. *Che* ("who," "whom," "that," "which") is an invariable pronoun. It may be used both as subject and direct object for persons, animals, and things, as well as for both genders and numbers. *Che* cannot be used with prepositions.

L'uomo *che* venne a pranzo è molto simpatico.	The man who came to dinner is very nice.
La ragazza *che* incontrai ieri è italiana.	The girl (whom) I met yesterday is Italian.
Ecco i biglietti *che* non sono stati venduti.	Here are the tickets that were not sold.
Il cane *che* hai appena visto è mio.	The dog (that) you saw just now is mine.

2. *Che* may drop the *e* before words starting with a vowel.

La casa *ch'*aveva comprato era grande.	The house (that) he had bought was big.
Ho preso il libro *ch'*era sul banco.	I took the book that was on the table.

3. In a relative clause introduced by *che*, the agreement of the past participle of a transitive verb with the noun that *che* refers to is optional.

La ragazza che hai *visto* (or *vista*) **è mia cugina.**	The girl (that) you have seen is my cousin.
Le scarpe che abbiamo *comprato* (or *comprate*) **sono nuove.**	The shoes we bought are new.

Il quale

Il quale (*la quale, i quali, le quali*), meaning "who," "which," "that," is a variable pronoun. It can be used for persons, animals, or things. This form is often replaced in every day speech by *che*. However it is used after prepositions for emphasis, greater clarity, or to avoid repetition.

La signora con *la quale* **viaggio è mia zia.**	The lady with whom I am traveling is my aunt.
Il soldato, *il quale* **muore per la patria, è un eroe.**	The soldier who dies for his country is a hero.
Ho salutato la figlia di Alberto, *la quale* **partirà domani.**	I said goodbye to Albert's daughter who is leaving tomorrow.
Io credo che Antonio, *il quale* **è un uomo onesto, non penserà che io gli faccia del male.**	I believe that Anthony, who is an honest man, will not think that I will do him any wrong.

Note: **Quale** without an article means "such as."

Poeti *quali* **Dante e Petrarca sono conosciuti in tutto il mondo.**	Poets such as Dante and Petrarch are known around the world.

Cui

1. *Cui* ("that," "which," "whom") is invariable and is used as an indirect object (normally after a preposition) for persons, animals, and things and for both genders and numbers. *Cui* can be replaced by a form of *il quale.*

Ecco la ragazza *di cui* (or *della quale*) **stavo parlando.**	Here is the girl I was speaking of.
Questo è il paese *in cui* (or *nel quale*) **sono nato.**	This is the town where I was born.
L'Italia è il paese *da cui* (or *dal quale*) **provengo.**	Italy is the country I come from.

2. When *cui* is used without a preposition, it means *a cui*.

L'avvocato *cui* (= *a cui*) **parlai di questa faccenda, agì immediatamente.**	The lawyer to whom I talked about this matter acted immediately.
La medicina *cui* (= *a cui*) **ricorsi, fu efficace.**	The medicine to which I resorted was effective.

3. When *cui* is preceded by the definite article, it means "whose," "of which."

Incontrammo la signora *il cui figlio* (or *il figlio della quale*) **lavora con noi.**

We met the lady whose son works with us.

Il libro, *le cui pagine* (or *le pagine del quale*) **sono strappate, appartiene a Giacomo.**

The book whose pages are torn belongs to James.

Chi

1. *Chi* is an invariable, singular pronoun. It is used in reference to people (both genders) and as either the subject or object (direct or indirect) of a subordinate clause. It means: "the one who(m)," "he who(m)," "she who(m)," "anyone who(m)," "someone who(m)," "who(m)ever," 'those who(m)," etc.

Chi **disse questo fu tuo fratello.**

The one who said this was your brother.

Chi **m'informò fu tua zia.**

The one who informed me was your aunt.

Rispetto *chi* **ci rispetta.**

I respect whoever respects us.

Raccontalo a *chi* **vuoi.**

Tell whomever you want.

Dobbiamo aiutare *chi* **soffre.**

We must help anyone who suffers.

Chi **s'aiuta, il ciel l'aiuta.**

God helps those who help themselves.

2. In negative sentences, *chi* means "nobody who."

Non c'è *chi* **mi aiuti.**

There is nobody who can help me.

Non vedo *chi* **possa farlo.**

I see no one who can do it.

3. *Chi*... *chi* means "one ... another," "some ... some," "some ... others."

Ho visto Giulio e Michele. *Chi* **suonava,** *chi* **cantava.**

I saw Julius and Michael. One was playing, the other was singing.

Chi **dice una cosa,** *chi* **ne dice un'altra.**

Some say this, some say that.

Other Relative Pronouns

1. *Quello che, quel che, ciò che,* and *quanto,* meaning "that which" or "what," are used when the antecedent is not precise or is understood. These forms generally refer to things. They can be either the subject or the direct object of the verb.

Non so *quello che* **vuoi.**	I do not know what you want.
Quel che **dicono non m'interessa.**	I am not interested in what they say.
Ascolta *ciò che* **ti dico.**	Listen to what I am telling you.
Ecco *quanto* **ho trovato.**	Here is what I found.

Note: With *tutto,* these forms express the idea of "all that" or "everything."

Non è oro *tutto ciò che* **brilla.**	All that glitters is not gold.
Ti darò *tutto quello che* **vuoi.**	I will give you everything you want.

2. *il che, la qual cosa,* meaning "which," refers back to a whole statement.

Non venne a tempo, *il che* **mi sorprese.**	He did not come on time, which surprised me.
Viaggeremo insieme, *la qual cosa* **mi rallegra.**	We will travel together, which pleases me.

The same idea can be expressed also by two independent clauses.

Non venne a tempo, e questo mi sorprese.	He did not come on time, and that surprised me
Viaggeremo insieme, e questo mi rallegra.	We will travel together, and that pleases me.

23. Interrogatives and Exclamations

All the relative forms presented in the preceding chapter, except *cui*, can be used as interrogative or exclamatory adjectives or pronouns. (Note that *chi* can only be used as a pronoun.)

Interrogatives

Interrogative Pronouns

1. The interrogative pronouns in Italian are as follows.

che? che cosa? cosa?   what?

chi?   who? whom?

quale? quali?   which one? which ones?

quanto? (-a, -i, -e)   how much? how many?

Che **è successo?**	What happened?
Che cosa **aspetti?**	What are you waiting for?
Da che **proviene questa malattia?**	What is the cause of this disease?
Chi **parla?**	Who is speaking?
Chi **hai incontrato?**	Whom did you meet?
Con chi **lavori?**	Whom do you work with?
Quali **scegliamo?**	Which ones should we choose?
Quale di **voi desidera partire?**	Who among you wants to leave?
Qual è **il mio cappello?**	Which one is my hat?
Quanti **verranno?**	How many will come?
A quanti **hai scritto?**	How many did you write to?

2. *Che* means *quale cosa*. It is invariable and is used as the subject or the object (direct or indirect) of the verb.

Che **fai?**	What are you doing?

3. In colloquial or Tuscan usage, *cosa* often replaces *che cosa?*

Cosa **vuoi?**	What do you want?

4. *Chi* means *quale persona*. It is invariable and is used as the subject or the object (direct or indirect) of the verb. Note that as the subject of the verb, *chi* is only used in the singular.

Chi **l'ha fatto?**	Who did it?

5. The prepositions such as *di, a,* and *per* are always placed before *chi.*

Di chi **hai paura?**	Whom are you afraid of?
A chi **stai scrivendo?**	Whom are you writing to?
Per chi **hai votato?**	Whom did you vote for?

6. When *di chi* is used to mean "whose," the verb *essere* follows immediately.

Di chi è **questa casa?**	Whose house is this?
Di chi sono **i giornali?**	Whose newspapers are they?

7. *Quale* as an interrogative pronoun loses the article. It is variable and *never* elides before a vowel. *Quale* followed by *essere* is used to ask for information.

Quali sono **i tuoi amici?**	Who are your friends?
Qual è **la capitale della Francia?**	What is the capital city of France?

8. The interrogative pronouns can also be in *indirect* questions, which generally depend on verbs such as *domandare,* "to ask," *chiedere,* "to ask," *dire,* "to tell," *sapere,* "to know."

Gli domandai *chi* **aveva vinto la partita.**	I asked him who won the game.
Vorrei sapere *cosa* **fai.**	I would like to know what you are doing.
Dimmi *quanti* **figli hai.**	Tell me how many children you have.

Interrogative Adjectives

1. The following are the interrogative adjectives in Italian.

che? what? what kind of?	**quanto?** (-a, -i, -e) how much?
quale? quali? which? what?	how many?

Che **rivista compri?**	What magazine are you buying?
Che **notizie mi hai portato?**	What news did you bring me?
A quale **famiglia appartiene?**	What family do you belong to?
Quali **fiori vuoi?**	Which flowers do you want?
Quanta **pasta hai mangiato?**	How much pasta did you eat?
Quante **mele hai venduto?**	How many apples have you sold?

Che is used for both singular and plural.

2. *Quale?, quali?* agree in number and gender with the nouns they modify. *Quale* refers to a choice between two or more alternatives, whereas *che* is less precise. However, in today's usage, *quale* and *che* are interchangeable.

Che (or *quali*) **giornali leggi?**	What newspapers do you read?

Interrogative Adverbs

The interrogative adverbs in Italian are as follows.

come? how?	**quando?** when?
come mai? how come?	**perchè?** why?
dove? where?	

Come **stai?**	How are you?
Come mai **non mi telefoni più?**	How come you don't call me anymore?
*Dov'*è **la scuola?**	Where is the school?
Quando è **partito?**	When did he leave?
Perchè **non mi scrivi?**	Why don't you write to me.

Exclamations

1. The following are the most common exclamatory words.

che! what (a[n]) ... !
chi! who!
quale! what (a[n]) ... !
quanto! how ... !
come! how ... !

2. *Che* and *quale* are not used as pronouns, but as an adverb (= *quanto*) and an adjective respectively.

Che **vergogna!**	What a shame!
Quale **paesaggio!**	What a landscape!

3. *Quale* never elides because the *e* can be omitted both before a vowel or a consonant.

Qual **artista!**	What an artist!
Qual **dolore!**	What a pain!

4. Unlike English usage, *quanto* is immediately followed by the verb.

*Quant'*è **bella quella ragazza!**	How beautiful that girl is!
Quanto è (or *Quant'*è) **grande questo stadio!**	How big this stadium is!

5. In colloquial Italian, *che* followed by an adjective is the equivalent of the English "how" followed by an adjective.

Che **bello!**	How beautiful!
Che **antipatico!**	How nasty!

The construction is normally considered ungrammatical. The recommended construction is *come* followed by a verb and an adjective.

*Com'*è **bello!**	How beautiful it is!
*Com'*è **antipatico!**	How nasty he is!

24. Negatives

1. *No* is the adverb of negation most commonly used in Italian. It can replace a whole sentence.

Ascoltate la radio? *No.* (= *Non ascoltiamo la radio.*)	Do you listen to the radio? No.
Avete visto la partita ieri sera? *No.* (= *Non abbiamo visto la partita ieri sera.*)	Did you watch the game last night? No.

Note: Generally, *no* is followed by *signore* ("sir"), *signora* ("madam"), or *signorina* ("miss").

Avete letto il giornale? No, signore.	Did you read the newspaper? No, sir.

2. A sentence is made negative by placing *non* ("not") before the verb.

Arturo scrive una lettera.	Arthur writes a letter.
Arturo *non* **scrive una lettera.**	Arthur does not write a letter.
Tu studi l'italiano.	You are studying Italian.
Tu *non* **studi l'italiano.**	You are not studying Italian.

Note: a. The verb "to do," in English negative sentences, is not used in Italian.

Lui non guadagna soldi abbastanza.	He *does* not earn enough money.

b. In the *tu* form, a positive command is made negative by changing the imperative to the infinitive and placing *non* before it.

Dormi! *Non dormire!*	Sleep! Don't sleep!
Mangia! *Non mangiare!*	Eat! Don't eat!

3. *Non* can be reinforced by the adverbs of quantity *affatto, mica, per niente* (= "at all").

Non capisce *affatto!*	He does not understand at all!
Non costa *mica tanto!*	It is not expensive at all!
Non è vero *per niente!*	It is not true at all!

Note: In negative responses only, *affatto* may also reinforce *niente,* "nothing," to mean "not at all." In these cases, *affatto* may stand alone.

"Hai studiato la lezione?"	"Did you study the lesson?" "Not
"Niente affatto."	at all."
"Hai fame?" *"Affatto."*	"Are you hungry?" "Not at all."
"Hai capito?" *"Affatto."*	"Did you understand?" "Not at all."

4. *Non* can be used in combination with other words to form negative expressions. The following are the most common of these expressions:

non ... alcuno (*adjective*)	not ... any, no (*adjective*)
non ... ancora	not yet
non ... che	only
non ... mai	never
non ... nè ... nè	neither ... nor ... nor
non ... neanche (or **nemmeno,** or **neppure**)	not ... even
non ... nessuno (*pronoun*)	nobody, no one, not ... anybody
non ... nessuno (*adjective*)	no, not ... any
non ... niente (or **nulla**)	nothing, not ... anything
non ... più	no longer, no more, not ... again, not ... anymore

Non c'è *alcun* **giornale.**	There isn't any newspaper.
La posta *non* è *ancora* **arrivata.**	The mail did not come yet.
Non **mi telefona** *mai.*	He never calls me.
Non **ho** *nè* **carta** *nè* **penna.**	I have neither paper nor pen.
Non **mi saluta** *nemmeno.*	He doesn't even say hello to me.
Non è *più* **qui.**	He is no longer here.

5. A negative sentence in Italian must always have a negative word before the verb. This may result in a double negative, which, unlike English, does *not* make the meaning affirmative. It expresses a single negative idea.

Non **vedo** *nessuno.*	I don't see anybody.
Non **abbiamo** *nessuna* **intenzione di partire.**	We have no intention of leaving.
Non c'è *niente* **di più bello.**	There is nothing more beautiful.

Note: Three or more negative words can be used in the same sentence.

Non **intendo** *mica* **offendere** *nessuno.*	I don't intend to offend anybody.
Non **dire** *mai* *nulla* **a** *nessuno.*	Don't you ever say anything to anybody.

6. *Non* is omitted when negative words, such as *neanche, nemmeno, neppure, nessuno,* or *niente, precede the verb.*

Nessuno **l'ha visto.**	Nobody saw him.
Nemmeno **Giovanni è venuto.**	John has not come either.
Nè **tu** *nè* **tuo fratello avete pagato il biglietto.**	Neither you nor your brother have paid for the ticket.

7. *Non* is omitted when negative words are used in a question.

Neanche **tu sei d'accordo con me?**	Not even you are in agreement with me?
Nessuno **parla?**	Nobody is talking?
Niente **ti commuove?**	Nothing moves you?

8. *Non* is also omitted in connection with the preposition *senza*, "without."

E' **partito** *senza neanche* (or *nemmeno,* or *neppure*) **salutarmi.**	He left without even saying good-bye to me.
E' **arrivato** *senza* **aver avvertito** *nessuno.*	He arrived without informing anybody.
E' **rimasto** *senza niente.*	He was left with nothing.

9. *Mai* always requires the negative *non* when it is placed after the verb. It can stand alone (without *non*) only when it is placed at the beginning of the sentence in the emphatic position, *or* when *non* is incorporated into a pronoun.

Non **legge** *mai.*	He never reads.
Non **studia** *mai* **la lezione.**	He never studies the lesson.
Mai **ho visto uno spettacolo più bello di questo!**	I have never seen a more beautiful show than this one!
Mai **una volta che arrivi a tempo!**	He never once arrives on time!
Nessuno mai **mi scrive.**	Nobody ever writes to me.

10. *Mai* can stand alone as a negative expression in elliptical sentences.

Questo *mai.*	This will never happen (*or* I will never do this.)
Mai **e poi** *mai.*	Never.

11. *Mai, niente (nulla), nessuno,* and other negative words may also be used to replace a whole sentence. In these cases *non* is omitted.

Quante volte sei andato al cinema? *Mai.*	How many times did you go to the movies? I never went.
Che cosa vi ha detto il professore d'italiano? *Niente.*	What did the Italian professor tell you? Nothing.
Chi ha letto il giornale? *Nessuno.*	Who has read the newspaper? Nobody.

12. In compound tenses, the second part of the negative expression generally follows the past participle.

Non **abbiamo visto** *che* **Giovanni.**	We only saw John.
Non **ho accusato** *nessuno.*	I did not accuse anyone.

However, adverbs such as *affatto, ancora, mica, neanche, nemmeno, neppure,* and *più,* may precede or follow the past participle, depending on emphasis, style, or personal preference.

Non ho *affatto* bisogno di voi.⎫ *Non* ho bisogno *affatto* di voi.⎭	I don't need you at all.

Non abbiamo *ancora* ricevuto sue
    notizie. ⎫
Non abbiamo ricevuto *ancora* sue ⎬
    notizie. ⎭
	We haven't received news from
	    him yet.

13. Direct or indirect object pronouns are placed between *non* and the verb.

Non *li* ho ancora incontrati.	I haven't met them yet.
Non *gli* telefonerò più.	I will not call him anymore.

25. Indefinite Adjectives and Pronouns

Indefinite Adjectives

1. The following are the indefinite adjectives in Italian.

ogni every, each	**qualsiasi** (or **qualsivoglia**) any, any sort of
qualche some	**qualunque** any, any sort of

All the above indefinite adjectives are invariable. They are used for persons, animals, and things.

2. *Ogni* always precedes the noun and is used in the singular only. To modify plural nouns, the forms *tutti* or *tutte* are used.

Giorgio va a scuola *ogni* **mattina.**	George goes to school every morning.
Ogni **ragazza ha una penna.**	Every girl has a pen.
Ogni **animale deve mangiare per vivere.**	Every animal has to eat to live.
Ogni **stanza deve essere pitturata.**	Each room has to be painted.
Tutti **i dischi nuovi costano molto.**	All new records are expensive.
Tutte **le barche stanno nel porto.**	All the boats are in port.

3. *Qualche* always precedes the noun. It is used with both the singular and plural forms of nouns. However, with nouns that normally are not used in the plural (*caffè, farina, burro*, etc.), *un po' di* replaces *qualche*.

Dammi *qualche* **consiglio.**	Give me some advice.
Deve avere *qualche* **motivo.**	He must have some reason.
Vuoi *un po' di* **latte?**	Do you want some milk?
Voglio *un po' di* **pane.**	I'd like some bread.

Note: In negative, interrogative, and negative-interrogative sentences *qualche* means "any."

Non so se ci sia ancora *qualche* **biglietto.**	I don't know if there are *any* tickets left.
Hai *qualche* **sigaretta?**	Do you have *any* cigarettes?
Non avete *qualche* **parente a Roma?**	Don't you have *any* relatives in Rome?

4. *Qualunque* and *qualsiasi* have the same meaning ("any," "any sort of"). Generally, they are used with singular nouns and precede them. When they are placed after a noun, they mean "common," "ordinary." They may be used with a plural noun if they follow it.

Lo compro a *qualunque* **prezzo.**	I will buy it at any price.
Farò *qualsiasi* **sacrificio.**	I will make any sacrifice.
Era un uomo *qualunque.*	He was just an ordinary man.
Dammi una tazza *qualunque.*	Give me any old cup.
Compra dei giornali *qualsiasi.*	Buy any papers you like.
Luisa indossa dei vestiti *qualsiasi.*	Louise wears common clothes.

Note: a. *Qualunque* and *qualsiasi* can govern either the indicative or the subjunctive, depending on the certainty or uncertainty they denote.

Qualunque **ragazzo che** *va* **a scuola si dice alunno.**	Every boy that goes to school is called a student.
Qualsiasi **cosa tu** *faccia,* **falla bene.**	Whatever you do, do it well.

b. When used with a form of *essere*, *qualunque* may be separated from the noun and immediately precedes the verb.

Qualunque sia **la tua opinione, cerca di andare d'accordo con i tuoi colleghi.**	Whatever your opinion may be, try to get along with your colleagues.
Qualunque fosse **la proposta, non l'accetterei mai.**	Whatever the proposal, I would never accept it.

Indefinite Pronouns

1. The following are the forms of indefinite pronouns in Italian.

Ognuno, ognuna everyone	**qualcosa (qualche cosa)** something, anything
uno, una one	**altri** another person
chiunque anyone	**chicchessia** anyone, anybody
niente (nulla) nothing, anything	**qualcuno, qualcuna** someone

2. *Ognuno* (-*a*) is used in the singular only and may be followed by *di*.

Ognuno **lo sa.**	Everyone knows that.
Ognuna di **quelle città ha un'università.**	Every one of those cities has a university.

3. *Uno (-a)* is used both in the singular and in the plural (*gli uni, le une*). This pronoun refers to people.

C'è *uno* **che ti cerca.**	There is someone who is looking for you.
Una **delle ragazze è assente oggi.**	One of the girls is absent today.
Ho parlato con *una* **che conosceva mia madre.**	I spoke with a woman who knew my mother.
Conosco bene *gli uni e gli altri.*	I know all of them well.
Le une **criticano** *le altre.*	Some of the women are criticizing the others.

4. *Chiunque* is invariable and singular. It is used only to refer to people.

Chiunque **può farlo.**	Anyone can do that.
Parla con *chiunque.*	He speaks with anyone.

Note: *Chiunque* may introduce a relative clause using the subjunctive.

Chiunque venga, **digli di aspettare.**	Whoever comes, tell him to wait.
Chiunque lo trovi, **deve restituirmelo.**	Anyone who finds it should give it back to me.

5. *Niente* and *nulla* have the same meaning. Both are invariable and singular. They are used to refer to things.

Non **ho fatto** *niente.*	I did not do anything.
Questo *non* **significa** *nulla.*	This does not mean anything.

Note: In interrogative sentences *niente* and *nulla* have a positive meaning.

Vuoi *niente* (= *qualcosa*)?	Do you want anything?
Vedi *nulla* (= *qualcosa*)?	Do you see anything?

6. *Qualcosa* and *qualche cosa* have the same meaning. Both are invariable and singular. They are used to refer to things.

Perchè non fai *qualcosa* **a proposito?**	Why don't you do something about it?
Dammi *qualche cosa* **da mangiare.**	Give me something to eat.

Note: a. *Qualcosa* and *niente* are followed by *di* in constructions like:

qualcosa (niente) di bello (nuovo, interessante, moderno)	something (nothing) beautiful (new, interesting, modern)

b. *Qualcosa* and *niente* are considered masculine for agreement purposes.

Mi è capitato qualcosa di strano.	Something strange happened to me.
E' avvenuto qualcosa?	Did anything happen?
Non è arrivato niente.	Nothing came.
Non è successo niente.	Nothing happened.

7. *Altri* (not to be confused with the plural of *altro*) is invariable and singular. It refers to people and may serve as the subject or object of the verb.

Altri **potrebbe pensare che tu abbia mentito.**	Another person might think that you lied.
Non vedo *altri* **che possa parlargli.**	I don't see anybody else who could talk to him.

8. *Chicchessia* is invariable and singular. It is used to refer to people.

Non mi sento inferiore a *chicchessia.*	I don't feel inferior to anybody.
Risponderebbe a *chicchessia.*	He would answer back to anybody.

9. *Qualcuno, qualcuna* is only used in the singular. It refers to people and may serve as the subject or object of the verb.

Qualcuno **ti cercava.**	Someone was looking for you.
Vedo *qualcuno* **uscire dalla banca.**	I see someone coming out of the bank.

Note: *Qualcuno* may also mean "anyone."

Se viene *qualcuno,* **fammelo sapere.**	Let me know if anyone comes.

Indefinite Adjectives and Pronouns

The following forms can be used as adjectives or pronouns. When used as adjectives, they agree with the noun in gender and number.

tutto	every; whole; everyone
nessuno	any, no on, none
altro	other
alcuno	some, any; some people
molto	much, a lot of, many
parecchio	a lot of, many, several
poco	little, few
certo	some, certain; some people
troppo	too much, too many
tanto	so much, so many

Ho visitato *tutta* **la città** (Adjective)	I visited the whole city.
Tutti **ti cercano.** (Pronoun)	Everyone is looking for you.
Te lo dirò un'*altra* **volta** (Adjective)	I will tell you another time.
Vi sono *altri* **che non verranno.** (Pronoun)	There are others who will not come.

E' partito con *alcuni* **suoi amici.** (Adjective)	He left with some friends of his.
Alcuni **vogliono uscire.** (Pronoun)	Some people want to go out.
Abbiamo *molti* **amici** (Adjective)	We have many friends.
Molti **guardano la televisione.** (Pronoun)	Many people watch television.
Hai mangiato *parecchia* **carne.** (Adjective)	You ate a lot of meat.
Parecchi **partirono per le vacanze.** (Pronoun)	A lot of people went on vacation.
Questo libro ha *poche* **pagine.** (Adjective)	This book has few pages.
Pochi **lo videro.** (Pronoun)	Few people saw him.
Venne dopo un *certo* **tempo.** (Adjective)	He came after some time.
Certi **lo salutarono.** (Pronoun)	Some people greeted him.
Non ha *troppe* **possibilità** (Adjective)	He does not have too many chances.
Troppi **lo ascoltano.** (Pronoun)	Too many people listen to him.
Ho speso *tanto* **denaro.** (Adjective)	I spent so much money.
Tanti **credono che non sia vero.** (Pronoun)	Many people think it is not true.

Note: a. *Alcuno* is used mostly in the plural. In the singular, it is generally replaced by *qualche* in affirmative sentences or questions. In negative sentences, it is replaced by *nessuno*.

Hai *qualche* **dubbio?**	Do you have any doubt?
Non ho *nessuna* (or *alcuna*) **rivista italiana.**	I do not have any Italian magazines.

b. *Alcuni* and *qualcuno* (or the adjective *qualche*) are used only when "some" or "any" stand for "several," or "a few." To express the meaning of "a little," *un po'* is used.

"Quante persone hanno comprato il biglietto?" *"Alcune."*	"How many people bought tickets?" "Some."
"Hai incontrato qualche americano a Roma?" "Sì, *qualcuno.***"**	"Have you met any Americans in Rome" "Yes, some."
"Conosci l'italiano?" "Sì, *un po'.***"**	"Do you know Italian?" "Yes, a little."

c. *Senza* + *nessuno* or *senza* + *alcuno* translates "without any."

senza nessuna responsabilità	without any responsibility
senza alcun dubbio	without any doubt

d. Some indefinites such as *molto, poco, quanto, tanto, troppo,* may be used as adverbs.

Sono molto contento.	I am very happy.
E' poco intelligente.	He is not very intelligent.
Quanto sei bella!	How beautiful you are!
Loro sono tanto ricchi.	They are so rich.
Sei ancora troppo giovane.	You are still so young.

26. Prepositions

A preposition is a word placed before a noun, a pronoun, a verb, an adverb, or a phrase to make clear its relation to another word (or group of words) in the sentence. Like adverbs and conjunctions, prepositions are invariable.

The Preposition *a*

1. The preposition *a* may follow a verb to introduce an infinitive. (See the list of verbs that take *a* before an infinitive in Chapter 14.)

Alberto comincia *a scrivere.*   Albert is beginning to write.

2. The preposition *a* is used in some common expressions: *vicino a,* near; *fino a,* until; *davanti a,* in front of; and *dietro a,* behind; *alla radio,* on the radio; *al telefono,* on the phone, *alla televisione,* on T.V., and so on.

3. *A* may introduce an indirect object.

Scrivo *a Maria.*   I am writing to Mary.
Diceva *a te,* **non** *a me.*   He was saying that to you, not to me.

The Preposition *con*

Con, usually means "with."

Vado *con* **lei.**   I am going *with* her.

However it often has additional meanings.

E' sempre gentile *con* **me.**   He is always kind *to* me.
Il vino si fa *con* **l'uva.**   Wine is made *from* grapes.

The Preposition *da*

Da usually means "from" or "by." However it also has uses:

  a. In the passive construction.
  La lettera fu scritta *da* me.   The letter was written by me.

  b. For indicating place.
  Domani andrai *dal* dentista.   Tomorrow you are going to the
                                      dentist's office.
  c. For indicating manner.
  Morì *da* vecchio.   He died as an old man.

  d. For indicating a quality.
  Rosa è una bimba *dagli* occhi   Rosa is a girl with blue eyes.
  azzurri.

Note: *Da* is always used before an infinitive governed by *molto, niente, nulla, poco, qualcosa,* and *tanto.*

  Non ho niente *da* fare.   I have nothing to do.
  Hai qualcosa *da* leggere?   Do you have something to read?

The Preposition *di*

1. *Di* can follow a verb and precede an infinitive. (See the list of verbs that take *di* before an infinitive in Chapter 14.)

  Il poliziotto gli ordinò *di*   The policeman ordered him to stop.
  fermarsi.

2. *Di* can be used to form an adverb: *di buon'ora,* early; *di certo,* certainly; *di fretta,* in a hurry; *di qui,* from here.

3. *Di* can be used to form an adjective: *società di costruzione,* building society; *un vassoio d'argento,* a silver tray, *metodo di recitazione,* acting method.

4. *Di* can be used to express possession: *la pagina del libro,* the page of the book; *il libro di Carlo,* Carlo's book.

5. *Di* follows nouns of quantity, measure, and collective nouns: *un paio di scarpe,* a pair of shoes; *un litro di latte,* a liter of milk; *una diecina d'uova,* about ten eggs.

Note: There is a difference in meaning between the expressions using a noun + *di* and those using a noun + *da:*

  un bicchiere *di* vino   a glass of wine
  un bicchiere *da* vino   a wine glass

6. *Di* is used to denote English expressions of time, dimensions, and differences in measurement and age:

Sono le sette *del mattino.*	It is 7 a.m.
La stanza ha quattro metri *di lunghezza.*	The room is four meters long.
Giorgio è più alto di Franco *di due centimetri.*	George is taller than Frank by two centimeters.
Egli è maggiore *di due anni.*	He is two years older.

7. *Di* is used in many adjectival phrases: *una multa di 10 dollari,* a 10 dollar fine; *un carico di due tonnellate,* a two-ton load.

8. *Di* is used before the complements of some adjectives: *degno di fiducia,* worthy of confidence; *pieno d'entusiasmo,* full of enthusiasm; *duro d'orecchio,* hard of hearing.

The Prepositions *fra* and *tra*

Fra and *tra* have the same meaning. They usually mean "between" or "among."

Questo è un incontro *fra* **amici.**	This is a reunion among friends.
C'è una casa *tra* **le due vie.**	There is a house between the two roads.

However they can also mean "in" or "within."

Partiremo *fra* **due ore.**	We will leave in (*or* within) two hours.

The Preposition *in*

Usually the preposition *in*, has the same meaning as the English "in."

Il dottore è *in* **ufficio.**	The doctor is in his office.
Accadde *in* **ottobre.**	It happened in October.

However there are many exceptions:

Andiamo *in* **città.**	We are going to the city.
E' una statua *in* **bronzo.**	It is a bronze statue.
Eravamo *in* **pochi.**	There were only a few of us.
Se fossi *in* **te.**	If I were you.

The Preposition *per*

Usually, *per* means "for."

Partono *per* **Palermo.**	They are leaving for Palermo.
Io leggo *per* **diletto.**	I read for pleasure.

However it can also mean "to."

Questo è comodo *per* **me.**	This is useful to me.

The Preposition *su*

Su usually means "on top" of something.

Il libro è *sul* **tavolo.**	The book is on the table.

However it has other meanings as well.

Arrivò *sul* **mezzodì.**	He arrived about noon.
La Marcia *su* **Roma.**	The March on Rome.
Scrisse un libro *sulla* **vecchiaia.**	He wrote a book on old age.

Other Prepositions

1. Prepositions generally *not* followed by *a* or *di*.

avanti   before, in front of, ahead
contro   against, opposite to
dopo   after
eccetto (or **salvo**)   except, save
malgrado   notwithstanding
mediante   by means of
oltre   besides, beyond
secondo   according to
sopra   on, upon, over
sotto   under
verso   toward(s)

2. Prepositions generally followed by *a*.

accanto a   beside
attorno a   around
conforme a   as
circa a   about
davanti a (dinanzi, innanzi)   before
dentro a   inside
dietro a   behind
fino a   till, as far as
intorno a   around, about
vicino a   near

3. Prepositions generally followed by *di*.

a causa di   by reason of
a forza di   by dint of
a ragione di   on account of
a seconda di   according to
al di là di   on the other side
al di qua di   on this side
al di sopra di   above
fuori di   outside
per mezzo di   by means

27. Conjunctions

Like prepositions and adverbs, conjunctions are invariable. Conjunctions connect two or more clauses, words, or groups of words that perform the same function in a sentence. There are two classes of conjunctions: *conjunctions of coordination* and *conjunctions of subordination.*

Conjunctions of Coordination

Connective Conjunctions

Positive		*Negative*	
e (ed)	and	**nè**	
anche	also	**neanche**	
inoltre	besides, moreover	**nemmeno**	nor, neither, not ... either
altresì	likewise, also	**neppure**	

Gli dissi *altresì* **che tu eri arrivato.**	I likewise told him that you had arrived.
E' troppo tardi *e, inoltre,* **sono stanco.**	It is too late, and besides, I am tired.
Non sa parlare italiano *e neanche* **io.**	He can't speak Italian, nor can I.
"Non fumo." "*Nemmeno* **io."**	"I don't smoke". "Neither do I".

Conjunctions of Alternative

o	or
oppure	
piuttosto	rather
altrimenti	likewise
ovvero	or
ossia	or, that is, rather

Note that *ovvero* and *ossia* may also express a correction or a clarification.

Essere *o* **non essere: questo è il problema.**	To be or not to be: that is the question.
Preferirei morire *piuttosto* **che fare una cosa simile.**	I would rather die than do such a thing.
Ovvero **si potrebbe far questo.**	On the other hand, we could do this.
La filologia, *ossia* **la scienza della lingue.**	Philology, that is, the science of languages.

Conjunctions of Opposition

ma   but
però   but
anzi   rather, on the contrary
invece   instead of
tuttavia   still, nevertheless, yet
non di meno   (or **nondimeno**) ⎫
nonostante ciò   ⎬ nevertheless
con tutto ciò   ⎭

Mi piacerebbe venire, *ma* **non posso.**	I would like to come, but I can't.
Non si sentiva bene, *tuttavia* **voleva partire.**	He did not feel well, yet he wanted to leave.

Conjunctions of Explanation or Clarification

infatti (difatti)   indeed, in fact
cioè   that is
invero   indeed

Dissero che venivano e *infatti* **sono venuti.**	They said they would come and they have indeed.
Silvia, *cioè* **la mamma di Carlo, abita qui.**	Sylvia (that is, Carl's mother) lives here.

Conjunctions of Consequence

dunque ⎫
pertanto ⎪
perciò ⎬ thus, therefore, so
quindi ⎪
ebbene ⎭
di conseguenza   in consequence
per il che ⎫ that's why, wherefore
per la qual cosa ⎭
in conclusione ⎫ in conclusion
insomma ⎭

Hai mentito, *perciò* **non ti credo.**	You lied; therefore I don't believe you.
Lo hai promesso e, *dunque,* **fallo.**	You promised that; so do it.

Conjunctions of Relation

e ... e both ... and
nè ... nè neither ... nor
o ... o either ... or
sia ... sia whether ... or
quanto ... tanto just as
ora ... ora now ... now, now ... then
prima ... poi first ... then
quale ... tale just as, exactly like
non solo ... ma anche not only ... but also
non solo non ... ma neppure not ... either, neither
quanto più ... tanto più the more ... the more
talmente ... che to such an extent that, so ... that

O **devi dire la verità** *o* **tacere.** You must either tell the truth or
say nothing.
Ora **piange,** *ora* **ride.** Now he cries, now he laughs.
E' *talmente* **piccolo** *che* **non** It is so small that I can't see it.
riesco a vederlo.

Conjunctions of Subordination

The conjunctions of subordination serve to connect a dependent clause to
the main clause.

Connective Conjunctions

che that
come as, like; that; how; how much

Penso *che* **lavori.** I think that you are working.
E' **necessario** *che* **tu vada.** It is necessary that you go.
Sapevo *come* **studiava.** I knew that (how much) he was
studying.

Conjunctions of Cause

perchè
poichè
chè
giacchè } because, since
siccome
dal momento che

Siccome **non c'eri, ritornai a** Because you were not in, I
casa. returned home.
Dal momento che **non abbiamo** Since we have no money, we
denaro, non possiamo cannot buy it.
comprarlo.

Conjunctions Expressing Goals

affinchè ⎫
perchè
acciocchè ⎬ in order that, so that
al fine di
con l'intento di ⎭

Parlo forte *perchè* mi sentano.   I speak loudly so that they can
                             hear me.

Ti mando il libro, *affinchè* tu lo   I send you the book, so that you
legga.   can read it.

Conjunctions of Time

quando when
mentre while
allorchè when
dopo che after that
prima che before that
ogni volta che every time that
da quando since when

Uscirai *quando* avrai finito.   You will go out when you have
                             finished.

Mentre lui studiava, io leggevo il   While he was studying, I was
giornale.   reading the newspaper.

Conjunctions of Concession

quantunque ⎫
sebbene
benchè ⎬ though, although
per quanto ⎭

Lisa andò a scuola, *sebbene*   Lisa went to school, though she
fosse ammalata.   was ill.
Non vuole rispondere, *per quanto*   He would not answer, though I
l'abbia pregato.   begged him.

Conjunctions of Opposition

mentre ⎫
al contrario ⎬ while, whereas
e invece ⎭

Sei felice, *mentre* Rodolfo   You are happy, whereas Rudolph
piange.   is crying.
Io sono rimasto povero, *e invece*   I have remained poor, while you
tu hai fatto fortuna.   have made a fortune.

Conjunctions of Consequence

cosicchè
tanto che
di modo che } so that, that
talmente che
al punto che

I soldati diedero la loro vita per la patria, *cosicchè* noi potessimo vivere.	The soldiers gave their lives for their country, so that we might live.
Arrivai tardi, *di modo che* non trovai posto.	I arrived late, so I could not find a seat.

Conjunctions of Manner

come   how
quasi   almost, as if
comunque   however

Mostrò *come* l'avrebbe fatto.	He showed how he would do it.
Correva *quasi* lo portasse il vento.	He was running as if the wind were carrying him.

Conjunctions of Exception

fuorchè
tranne che } except, but
eccetto che

Farei qualunque cosa, *fuorchè* scrivere quella lettera.	I would do anything, but write that letter.
Farò tutto, *tranne che* fumare.	I will do anything, but smoke.

Conjunctions of Condition

se   if
purchè   provided (that)
qualora   in case, if
a patto (condizione) che   on condition that
a meno che   unless

Purchè non ci sia nessun pericolo, puoi andare.	Provided that all is safe, you may go.
Qualora ti piaccia, compralo pure.	If you like it, just buy it.

28. Numbers and Units of Measure

Cardinal Numbers

0	zero	32	trentadue
1	uno	33	trentatrè
2	due	34	trentaquattro
3	tre	38	trentotto
4	quattro	40	quaranta
5	cinque	41	quarantuno
6	sei	45	quarantacinque
7	sette	50	cinquanta
8	otto	51	cinquantuno
9	nove	60	sessanta
10	dieci	70	settanta
11	undici	80	ottanta
12	dodici	90	novanta
13	tredici	100	cento
14	quattordici	101	centouno(centuno)
15	quindici	200	duecento
16	sedici	300	trecento
17	diciassette	400	quattrocento
18	diciotto	500	cinquecento
19	diciannove	600	seicento
20	venti	700	settecento
21	ventuno	800	ottocento
22	ventidue	900	novecento
23	ventitrè	1,000	mille
24	ventiquattro	1,001	mille (e) uno
25	venticinque	1,980	millenovecentottanta
26	ventisei	2,000	duemila
27	ventisette	1,000,000	un milione
28	ventotto	2,000,000	due milioni
29	ventinove	1,000,000,000	un miliardo
30	trenta	2,000,000,000	due miliardi
31	trentuno		

1. Cardinal numbers (*except milione* and *miliardo*) are adjectives. Normally placed before the noun, cardinal numbers are invariable in form (except for *uno* and *mille*).

2. *Uno,* when followed by a noun, follows the rules for the indefinite article.

un **quaderno**	one notebook
uno **studente**	one student
una **sorella**	one sister
*un'***aranciata**	one orangeade

3. There is elision in *venti, trenta, quaranta, cinquanta, sessanta, settanta, ottanta, novanta* before combining with *uno* and *otto.*

ventuno turisti	twenty-one tourists
trentotto sedie	thirty-eight chairs
quarantuno palazzi	forty-one buildings
cinquantotto cavalli	fifty-eight horses

The elision is optional in the following cases: *cento ottanta* (or *centottanta*), *cento uno* (less common, *centuno*), *cento otto* (less common, *centotto*). There is no elision in *milleotto.*

4. Numbers ending in -*uno* (21, 31, 41, etc.) may drop the final -*o* before a vowel or a single consonant.

ventun **amici**	twenty-one friends
trentun **pagine**	thirty-one pages
quarantun **matite**	forty-one pencils

5. *Uno* may change the final -*o* into an -*a* when it is written separately from another number. In modern Italian this usage is very common.

Cento e uno pagine or **Cento e una pagina**	One hundred and one pages
Mille e uno case or **Mille e una casa**	One thousand and one houses

6. *Tre* does not take an accent because it is monosyllabic. In combination with *venti, trenta, quaranta, cinquanta,* etc., *tre* becomes part of a polysyllabic word and thus takes an accent on the final *è.*

ventitrè dollari	twenty-three dollars
trentatrè studenti	thirty-three students

7. Unlike its English counterpart *uno* is never used before *cento* and *mille.*

cento fogli	one hundred sheets of paper
mille soldati	one thousand soldiers

8. The plural of *mille* is *mila.*

tre*mila* **bambini**	three thousand children
quattro*mila* **soldati**	four thousand soldiers

9. *Milione* and *miliardo* and their plurals (*milioni, miliardi*) take the preposition *di* before a noun.

un milione *di* **abitanti**	one million inhabitants
un miliardo *di* **stelle**	one billion stars

But: If there is another number between *milione* (or *miliardo*) and the noun, *di* is dropped.

un milione (e)	one million one hundred fifty
centocinquantamila lire.	thousand lira.

10. Compound numbers are generally written as one word. Those beyond one thousand may be broken down into thousands, hundreds, etc.. No conjunction is needed to connect them.

centotrentacinque giorni	one hundred thirty-five days
quattrocentoventitrè dollari	four hundred twenty-three dollars
quarantacinquemilacin-	
quecentosessantanove	
or	forty-five thousand five hundred
quarantacinquemila cinquecento	sixty-nine
sessanta nove	

11. In Italian, a period, not a comma, separates thousands, and a comma, not a period, separates decimals.
   15.234 = 15,234   **24,50** = 24.50   **38,5%** = 38.5%

12. From the thirteenth century on, the centuries are generally called *il Duecento* ("thirteenth century"), *il Trecento* ("fourteenth century"), *il Quattrocento* ("fifteenth century"), *il Cinquecento* ("sixteenth century"), and so on.

13. Eleven hundred," "twelve hundred," etc. are always expressed as "one thousand one hundred," "one thousand two hundred," etc.

millecento (or mille e cento)	eleven hundred
milleduecento (mille e duecento)	twelve hundred

14. "Both" is expressed as *tutti e due* (*tutte e due*); "all three," as *tutti e tre* (*tutte e tre*), and so on. If a noun follows, it takes the definite article.

tutti e due i ragazzi	both boys
tutte e due le ragazze	both girls

Odd and Even Numbers

dispari	odd	**per cinque**	by fives
pari	even	**per dieci**	by tens

I numeri *dispari* sono 1, 3, 5, 7, etc.	The odd numbers are 1, 3, 5, 7, etc.
I numeri *pari* sono 2, 4, 6, 8, etc.	The even numbers are 2, 4, 6, 8, etc.
Contare *per cinque,* **da cinque a cento.**	Count by fives from five to one hundred.

Collective Numbers

un paio   two, a pair of, a couple
una diecina   ten, about ten
una dozzina   a dozen, about twelve
una quindicina   fifteen, about fifteen
una ventina   twenty, about twenty
una novantina   ninty, about ninty
un centinaio   a hundred, about one hundred
un migliaio   a thousand, about one thousand
un milione   a million, about one million
un miliardo   a billion, about one billion

1. The above collective numbers are all accompanied by *di.*

Ci saranno stati *una trentina di* **passeggeri.**	There must have been about thirty passengers.
C'erano alcune *migliaia di* **turisti a Roma.**	There were several thousand tourists in Rome.

Note the difference between *tremila soldati,* ("three thousand soldiers") and *tre migliaia di soldati* ("about three thousand soldiers").

2. The above collective numbers are often used to express age.

Lisa è sulla trentina.	Lisa is about thirty.
Luca si avvicina *alla quarantina.*	Luke is approaching forty.
Carlo ha superato *la cinquantina.*	Carl has passed fifty.

Ordinal Numbers

1st	primo (a,i,e)	18th	diciottesimo
2nd	secondo (a,i,e)		(decimottavo)
3rd	terzo	19th	diciannovesimo
4th	quarto		(decimonono)
5th	quinto	20th	ventesimo
6th	sesto	21th	ventunesimo
7th	settimo	22th	ventiduesimo
8th	ottavo	30th	trentesimo
9th	nono	40th	quarantesimo
10th	decimo	50th	cinquantesimo
11th	undicesimo (undecimo,	60th	sessantesimo
	decimoprimo)	70th	settantesimo
12th	dodicesimo (duodecimo,	80th	ottantesimo
	decimosecondo)	90th	novantesimo
13th	tredicesimo (decimoterzo)	100th	centesimo
14th	quattordicesimo	500th	cinquecentesimo
	(decimoquarto)	1,000th	millesimo
15th	quindicesimo (decimoquinto)	1,000,000th	milionesimo
16th	sedicesimo (decimosesto)		
17th	diciassettesimo		
	(decimosettimo)		

1. Ordinal numbers are adjectives and agree in gender and number with the nouns they modify. They generally precede nouns, but follow the names of popes and kings, or articles of law.

il *quarto* **posto**	the fourth place (seat)
la *quinta* **fila**	the fifth row
Pio *nono*	Pius the ninth
Filippo *secondo*	Philip the second
l'articolo *quarto* **della** **Costituzione**	article 4 of the Constitution

2. Ordinal numbers can be abbreviated by using a figure and adding°.

Il 5° foglio.	The fifth sheet of paper
Il 7° giorno.	The seventh day

3. The first ten ordinal numbers each have a distinct form. However, from "eleventh" on, the ordinal number is formed by simply dropping the final vowel of the cardinal number and adding -*esimo* or -*esima*. If the cardinal number ends in -*è*, it loses its accent but retains the final vowel.

trentatrè	thirty-three ────────▶	**trentatr**eesimo	thirty-third
ottantatrè	eighty-three ────────▶	**ottantatr**eesimo	eighty-third

4. The Latinisms *undecimo, duodecimo,* etc. only rarely replace *undicesimo, dodicesimo,* etc., but are common when referring to kings, or popes.

il *quattordicesimo* **secolo** (or *il* — The 14th century
  Trecento)
Luigi XII (*decimosecondo*) — Louis the 12th
Giovanni XXIII (*vigesimoterzo*) — John the 23rd

5. Ordinals are always written as one word.

il quarantanovesimo giorno — the forty-ninth day
il centocinquantesimo — the one hundred and fifth
  anniversario — anniversary

Fractions

1. Fractions are expressed by using cardinal and ordinal numbers. Cardinal numbers are employed for the numerator of the fraction. Starting with *terzo*, masculine forms of the ordinal numbers express the denominator.

1/3	**un terzo**	1/11	**un undicesimo**
1/4	**un quarto**	1/12	**un dodicesimo**
1/5	**un quinto**	· 1/13	**un tredicesimo**
1/6	**un sesto**	1/14	**un quattordicesimo**
1/7	**un settimo**	1/20	**un ventesimo**
1/8	**un ottavo**	1/100	**un centesimo**
1/9	**un nono**	1/100	**un millesimo**
1/10	**un decimo**	3/8	**tre ottavi**
		4/9	**quattro noni**
		6/13	**sei tredicesimi**
		%	**per cento**

2. "One-half" is *un mezzo.*

3. If *mezzo* ("half") is used as an adjective it agrees with the noun to which it refers and it is placed before it.

mezza giornata di lavoro — a half day of work
mezzo chilo di pane — a half kilo of bread

4. If *mezzo* functions as a noun, it is invariable and follows the noun to which it refers.

Ho comprato due chili e *mezzo* — I bought two and a half kilos of
  di patate. — potatoes.
Sono le tre e *mezzo.* — It is 3:30.

5. The noun for "half" is (*la*) *metà,* used sometimes as an adjective.

Ho preso soltanto *metà* **della torta.** — I only took half the cake.
La metà **di dodici è sei.** — Six is half of twelve.
Verrò a *metà* **settimana** — I will come by midweek.
C'incontreremo a *metà* **strada.** — We will meet half way.

Arithmetic Signs

addizione	+ e, più	2 + 2 = 4 Due più (*or* e) due fanno quattro.
sottrazione	− meno	9 − 4 = 5 Nove meno quattro fanno cinque.
moltiplicazione	× (moltiplicato) per	2 × 3 = 6 Due per (*or* moltiplicato per) tre fanno sei.
divisione	: diviso (per)	20 : 5 = 4 Venti diviso (per) cinque fanno quattro.

addizionare	to add	**moltiplicare**	to multiply
sottrarre	to subtract	**dividere**	to divide

Dimensions

Nouns		*Adjectives*	
l'altezza	height	**alto, -a**	high, tall
la larghezza	width	**largo, -a**	wide
la lunghezza	length	**lungo, -a**	long
la profondità	depth	**profondo, -a**	deep
lo spessore	thickness	**spesso, -a**	thick

1. *Avere* is often used to express dimensions (*avere . . . di* + noun).

La torre *ha* **25 metri** *di altezza.*	The tower is 25 meters high.
Il fiume *ha* **38 chilometri** *di lunghezza.*	The river is 38 kilometers long.
Il muro *ha* **35 centimetri** *di spessore.*	The wall is 35 centimeters thick.

2. *Essere* is also used to express dimensions.

L'albero *è alto* **3 metri.**	The tree is 3 meters high.
La sala *è larga* **4 metri.**	The room is 4 meters wide.
La profondità di questo pozzo *è di* **12 metri.**	The depth of this well is 12 meters.

3. *Misurare* is also used to express dimensions (*misurare . . . di* + noun).

Il campanile *misura* **62 metri** *di altezza.*	The bell tower is 62 meters high.
Questa stoffa *misura* **76 centimetri** *di larghezza.*	This fabric is 76 centimeters wide.
Questo libro *misura* **3 centimetri** *di spessore.*	This book is 3 centimeters thick.

Units of Measure
(*Metric System*)

l'ettaro	hectare	(*about 2½ acres*)
il chilo (chilogrammo)	kilogram	(*2.2 pounds*)
il metro	meter	(*39.37 inches*)
il chilometro	kilometer	(*about ⅝ of a mile*)
il centimetro	centimeter	(*0.39 inches*)
il litro	liter	(*a little more than a quart*)
la tonnellata	ton	(*1000 kilos*)

Other Units of Measurement

il pollice	inch	(*2.54 centimeters*)	la pinta	pint	(*0.47 liters*)
il piede	foot	(*30 centimeters*)	il gallone	gallon	(*3.78 liters*)
la iarda	yard	(*91.44 centimeters*)	la libbra	pound	(*454 grams*)
il miglio	mile	(*1.61 kilometers*)			

Geometrical Terms

Plane Surfaces

la linea	line	il rettangolo	rectangle
l'angolo	angle	il rombo	rhomboid
l'angolo retto	right angle	il pentagono	pentagon
il triangolo	triangle	l'esagono	hexagon
il quadrato, quadro	square	il cerchio	circle
		il diametro	diameter
		il raggio	radius

Solids

il cubo	cube	la piramide	pyramid
il cilindro	cylinder	il cono	cone
la sfera	sphere	il prisma	prism
l'emisfero	hemisphere		

29. Time

Days of the Week

lunedì	Monday
martedì	Tuesday
mercoledì	Wednesday
giovedì	Thursday
venerdì	Friday
sabato	Saturday
domenica	Sunday

Except for *domenica,* the days of the week are masculine. They are *not* capitalized. Days of the week are not preceded by a definite article, except to express a habitual action. The preposition "on" is not expressed in Italian.

Oggi è *lunedì.*	Today is Monday
E' partita *martedì.*	She left on Tuesday.
La domenica **vado in chiesa.**	I go to church on Sundays.

Months of the Year

gennaio	January	luglio	July
febbraio	February	agosto	August
marzo	March	settembre	September
aprile	April	ottobre	October
maggio	May	novembre	November
giugno	June	dicembre	December

1. The months of the year are masculine and are *not* capitalized. No article is necessary with them.

2. To express "in" with months, either *a* or *in* is used.

Sono nato *a* (or *in*) **maggio.**	I was born in May.
A (or *in*) **luglio fa caldo.**	It is warm in July.

3. *On* + days of the month is expressed by the masculine definite article + a *cardinal* number (*due, tre, quattro,* etc.), except for "the first," which is translated by *il primo.*

il *primo* **maggio**	on May first (the first of May)
il *due* **maggio**	on May second
il *tre* **maggio**	on May third

Note the following forms for asking and answering questions about the day of the month.

Qual è la data di oggi?	
Quanti ne abbiamo oggi?	What is the date?
Oggi è *il primo (di) giugno.*	Today is the first of June.
Il primo.	The first.
Oggi ne abbiamo *tre.*	Today is the third.

Note: Italians write dates in the following manner: *il 4 novembre 1985* or *4 11 1985 = (il 4 novembre 1985.)* Notice that the day precedes both the month and year.

Seasons of the Year

la primavera	spring	**l'autunno**	fall, autumn
l'estate (*f.*)	summer	**l'inverno**	winter

1. The names of the seasons are not capitalized. They are generally preceded by the definite article.

Odio l'autunno.	I hate fall.
Mi piace l'estate.	I like summer.

2. However, to indicate "in" with seasons, either *in* or *di* (*d'*) without the definite article is used.

In **inverno** (or *D'*î**nverno**) **vado a sciare.**	I go skiing in the winter.

Years

When referring to years, the masculine-singular definite article is always used, since the word *anno* is understood. The preposition "on" is not expressed with years in Italian.

Il 1945 **segnò la fine della guerra.**	1945 marked the end of the war.
Dante morì *nel 1321.*	Dante died in 1321.
Nacque *il 20 maggio 1938.*	He was born on May 20, 1938.

Divisions of Time

il secondo	second	la sera, la serata	evening
il minuto	minute	la notte, la nottata	night
l'ora	hour	il giorno, la giornata	day
la mezz'ora	half an hour	la settimana	week
la mattina (il mattino), la mattinata	morning	il mese	month
		la stagione	season
		l'anno, l'annata	year
il pomeriggio	afternoon	il secolo	century

Note: *La mattina (il mattino), la sera, la notte, il giorno,* and *l'anno* are used when talking about a precise time. *La mattinata, la serata, la nottata, la giornata, l'annata* indicate a duration of time.

La domenica è *il giorno* **di riposo.** (precise time).	Sunday is the day of rest.
Oggi è *una bella giornata.* (duration)	Today is a beautiful day.
Abbiamo passato *un anno* **a Roma.** (precise time)	We spent a year in Rome.
Abbiamo avuto *una buona annata.* (duration)	We had a good year.

Expressions of Time

ora, adesso now
proprio ora (or **adesso**) right now
oggi today
questa mattina / **stamattina, stamani** this morning
questo pomeriggio this afternoon
questa sera (or **stasera**) this evening, tonight
questa notte (or **stanotte**) tonight
ieri notte (or **la notte scorsa**) last night
avantieri notte the night before last
ieri yesterday
avantieri (or **l'altro ieri**) the day before yesterday
domani tomorrow
al mattino, alla mattina / **di mattino, di mattina** in the morning
nel (di) pomeriggio in the afternoon
nella (di) sera in the evening
nella (di) notte at night
domani mattina tomorrow morning

ieri pomeriggio yesterday afternoon
la settimana scorsa ⎫
la settimana passata ⎭ last week
la settimana prossima ⎫
la settimana che viene ⎭ next week
il mese scorso ⎫
il mese passato ⎭ last month
sabato scorso ⎫
sabato passato ⎭ last Saturday
giovedì prossimo ⎫
giovedì che viene ⎭ next Thursday
tutto il giorno ⎫
tutta la giornata ⎭ all day
ogni giorno every day
per tutto il tempo all the time
all' inizio (or al principio) del mese at the beginning of the month
verso la metà del mese about the middle of the month
verso la fine del mese toward the end of the month
verso la metà della settimana about the middle of the week
al principio (or all'inizio) dell'anno at the beginning of the year
verso la metà dell'anno about the middle of the year
alla fine dell'anno at the end of the year
qualche volta (or talvolta) sometime
(per) pochi giorni a few days
verso la metà di settembre about mid-September

Telling Time

1. Note the following patterns for telling the time of day in Italian.

Che ora è? ⎫ **Che ore sono?** ⎭	What time is it?
E' l'una.	It is one o'clock.
Sono le due (tre, quattro, etc.).	It is two (three, four, etc.) o'clock.
E' mezzogiorno.	It is noon.
E' mezzanotte.	It is midnight.
A che ora?	At what time?
Alle sei (precise, in punto).	At six o clock (sharp).
Alle sette e cinque.	At five after seven
Alle otto e un quarto.	At quarter past eight.
Alle nove e mezzo.	At nine-thirty.
Alle dodici e mezzo.	At half past noon.
Alle dieci meno un quarto.	At quarter to ten.
Alle ventuno e quarantacinque.	At quarter to ten (P.M.) (9:45).
Alle undici meno dieci.	At ten to eleven.
Alle ventidue e cinquanta.	At ten to eleven (P.M.) (10:50).

2. If it is not the exact hour, determine the nearest hour, making the half hour the dividing point. Then add or subtract the number of minutes, as follows:

Sono le due *e* **venticinque.**   It is twenty five after two.
Sono le otto *meno* **venti.**   It is twenty minutes before eight.

3. The verb *mancare* can be used to express time before the hour.

Mancano **venti minuti alle otto.**   It is twenty minutes before eight.

4. A.M. is expressed by *di mattina* or *del mattino* (della mattina).

Sono le nove *di mattina.*   It is nine o'clock A.M.

5. P.M. can also be expressed by *del pomeriggio, di sera (della sera), or di notte (della notte).*

Sono le tre *del pomeriggio.*   It is three o'clock P.M..
Sono le otto *di sera.*   It is eight o'clock P.M..
Sono le undici *di notte.*   It is eleven o'clock P.M.

Note: The 24-hour clock is used in Italy for train, plane, bus, and theater schedules, and often for appointments.

alle tredici = 1 P.M. (13:00)
alle sedici e venticinque = at 4:25 P.M. (16:25)
alle diciotto meno venti = 5:40 P.M. (17:40)

Directions

(il) nord   north
(il) sud   south
(l') est (*m.*)   east
(l') ovest (*m.*)   west

(il) nord-est   northeast
(il) sud-est   southeast
(il) nord-ovest   northwest
(il) sud-ovest   southwest

30. Prefixes and Suffixes

Common Italian Prefixes

Italian has developed a large number of prefixes that can change the meaning of a word. The most common are:

a- *to* (doubling the following consonant)
  *ac*correre, to run
  *al*legare, to enclose

a- *without* (without doubling the following consonant)
  *a*morale, amoral
  *a*normale, abnormal

ante-, anti- *before*
  *ante*fatto, antecedents
  *anti*camera, anteroom

anti- *against*
  *anti*comunista, anticommunist
  *anti*ruggine, antirust

arci- *arch-* or *very, extremely*
  *arci*vescovo, archbishop
  *arci*contento, supremely happy
  *arci*noto, very well known

bi-, bis- *twice*
  *bi*mensile, twice a month
  *bis*nonno, great-grandfather

co-, con- *with, between*
  *co*abitare, to live together
  *co*editore, copublisher
  *con*dividere, to divide between or among

contra-, contro- *against*
  *contr*attacco, counterattack
  *contro*vento, against the wind

de-, di- *away from, arising form*
  *de*portare, to deport
  *de*viare, to deviate
  *di*mettere, to remove, to discharge
  *de*tronizzare, to dethrone

dis- *un-*
  *dis*fare, to undo
  *dis*occupato, unemployed

extra-, estra-, stra- *above, outside of*
  *extra*urbano, out-of-town
  *estra*dare, to extradite
  *stra*ordinario, extraordinary
  *stra*ricco, immensely rich

fra-, tra-, infra- *between, among*
  *fra*pporre, to interpose
  *tra*passare, to pierce, to run through
  *infra*settimanale, midweek (*adj.*)

in- *in, un* (as negative)
  *in*esperto, inexpert
  *in*civile, uncivilized

in- *in-* (used in the formation of verbs from nouns or adjectives)
  *in*fiammare, to inflame
  *in*tenerire, to soften

infra-, inter- *in, between*
  *infra*mmezzare, to interpolate
  *inter*porre, to interpose

iper- *very, extremely*
  *iper*critico, very critical
  *iper*sensibile, very sensitive

mis- *mis-*
  *mis*fatto, misdeed

po-, pos-, post- *after*
  *pos*domani, the day after tomorrow
  *post*bellico, postwar (*adj.*)

pre- *pre-* (generally with the idea of "before")
  *pre*avviso, forewarning
  *pre*annunziare, to announce in advance
  *pre*fabbricato, prefabricated

pro- *for*
  *pro*console, proconsul (*one acting "for" the consul*)
  *pro*sindaco, promayor (*one acting "for" the mayor*)

re-, ri- (a repeated action *or* an action in response to another)
*ri*leggere, to read again
*ri*studiare, to study again
*re*azione, reaction

s- (the contrary *or* intensity of action)
*s*fortunato, unfortunate
*s*montare, to dismount
*s*cancellare, to erase
*s*beffeggiare, to mock

semi- or **emi-** *half* or *almost*
*semi*cerchio, semicircle
*emi*sfero, hemisphere
*semi*aperto, half-open

sopra- or **sovra-** *above, beyond, upon, super-* (doubling the following consonant)
*sopra*nnotato, above mentioned
*sopra*ppeso, overweight
*sopra*ffino, superfine

sotto-, sott- *under, below*
*sotto*segretario, undersecretary
*sotto*prezzo, below (the normal) price
*sotto*valutare, to underestimate
*sott*inteso, understood

tra-, trans-, tras- *trans-*
*tra*lucente, translucent
*trans*atlantico, transatlantic
*tras*portare, to transport

vice *instead of*
*vice*rè, viceroy
*vice*presidente, vice president

Common Italian Suffixes

Italian is also rich in suffixes that add different shades of meaning to words. At times, they may be confusing to the nonnative speaker.

Thus, the noun *paese*, "village" can be modified to *paesino, paesetto, paesello, paesuccio, paesucolo, paesotto, paesone, paesaccio* to express smallness, niceness, affection, endearment, ugliness, contempt, commiseration, pity, and so on.

Students should not create or pick their own suffixes, but should follow the usage of Italian authors or educated native speakers.

Diminutive Suffixes

The following suffixes convey the idea of smallness, prettiness, and affection. They are added to the noun after dropping the final vowel and they are given in the masculine singular form; for the feminine form change the -o into -a.

-ino	**gatto,** cat	**gatt***ino,* little cat
	piede, foot	**pied***ino,* little foot
-cino	**cartone,** pasteboard	**carton***cino,* thin pasteboard
-icino	**lume,** lamp	**lum***icino,* little lamp
-ello	**vino,** wine	**vin***ello,* thin wine
	storia, story	**stori***ella,* funny story, fib, joke
-erello	**vecchio,** old man	**vecchi***erello,* poor old man
-icello	**vento,** wind	**vent***icello,* breeze
	fiume, river	**fium***icello,* little river
-etto	**giovane,** young man	**giovan***etto,* little young man
	libro, book	**libr***etto,* little book
-atto	**lupo,** wolf	**lup***atto,* wolf-cub
-otto	**ragazzo,** boy	**ragazz***otto,* strong boy
-uccio	**re,** king	**re***uccio,* little king
	bocca, mouth	**bocc***uccia,* cute, little mouth
-uolo (-olo)	**figlio,** son	**figli***uolo* (**figli***olo*), dear son
-icciuolo	**porto,** port	**port***icciuolo* (**port***icciolo*), little port
(icciolo)	**strada,** road	**strad***icciola,* little road
-olino	**pesce,** fish	**pesci***olino,* little or cute fish
-uzzo	**labbro,** lip	**labbr***uzzo,* cute lip
	via, street	**vi***uzza,* small street

Note: a. Sometimes the diminutives indicate contempt or commiseration.

casa, house	**cas***uccia,* shanty house
podere, farm	**poder***etto,* miserable little farm
viso, face	**vis***uccio,* pale face

b. Two dimunitives are often added to the same word.

giovane, young man	**giovan***ottino,* fine, strong young man
signorina, young lady	**signor***inella,* fine young girl

c. Some nouns change gender *and* meaning when a suffix is attached.

la camera, room	**il camer*ino*,** little room, dressing room, cabin, lavatory, toilet
la bocca, mouth	**il bocch*ino*,** cigarette holder, mouthpiece
la coda, tail	**il cod*ino*,** pigtail, reactionary, die-hard

Augmentative Suffixes

The following suffixes (given in the masculine singular form) convey an idea of largeness.

-one	**libro,** book	**libr*one*,** big book
	parola, word	**parol*ona*,** big word

Note: Some feminine nouns change gender when the suffix **-one** is attached.

la bottiglia bottle	**il bottigl*ione*** big bottle
la casa house	**il cas*one*** big house
la donna woman	**il donn*one*** big woman
la febbre fever	**il febbr*one*** high fever
la nebbia fog	**il nebb*ione*** dense fog
la palla ball	**il pall*one*** soccer ball
la porta door	**il port*one*** main door
la stanza room	**lo stanz*one*** large room

-zone	**villano,** countryman, rude person	**villan*zone*,** boor, lout
-cione	*(used when the noun already ends in* **-one***)*	

padrone, master	**padron*cione*,** important master
bastone, stick	**baston*cione*,** big stick

Depreciative Suffixes

The following suffixes (given in the masculine singular form) convey an idea of ugliness or bad and despicable quality.

-accio	**ragazzo,** boy	**ragazz*accio*,** bad boy
	donna, woman	**donn*accia*,** bad woman
-acchione	**frate,** friar, monk	**frat*acchione*,** stupid monk
-accione	**uomo,** man	**om*accione*,** big, ugly man
-astro	**poeta,** poet	**poet*astro*,** poor poet
-iciattolo	**mostro,** monster	**mostr*iciattolo*,** horrible monster
-ipola	**casa,** house	**cas*ipola*,** ugly house
-occio	**bimbo,** child	**bim*boccio*,** ugly child

-onzolo	medico, doctor	mediconzolo, inexperienced doctor
-otto	signore, master	signorotto, despicable master
-ozzo	predica, sermon	predicozzo, long-winded sermon
-ucolo	maestro, teacher	maestrucolo, inept teacher
-uncolo	uomo, man	omuncolo, ugly little man, "shrimp"
-upola	casa, house	casupola, ugly house

Note: a. Many of the above suffixes may be added to proper names and adjectives.

Carlo Charles	*Carletto,* Charlie
Giuseppe, Joseph	**Pepp***ino,* Joey **Pepp***one,* big Joe
caro, dear	car*ino,* pretty, cute
intelligente, intelligent	intelligent*one,* "a brain"
verde, green	verd*astro,* greenish
dolce, sweet	dolci*astro,* unpleasantly sweet

b. Some nouns in Italian end in one of the preceding suffixes. However, they are *not* altered nouns, but *new* words with their own meaning. The following are some examples:

avo, grandfather, ancestor	**avello,** tomb
balzo, leap	**balzello,** heavy tax
banco, desk, bench	**banchetto,** banquet
baro, cardsharp, swindler	**barone,** baron
basto, packsaddle	**bastone,** stick
becco, beak	**becchino,** gravedigger, undertaker
bega, dispute, quarrel	**beghina,** bigot
bocca, mouth	**boccone,** morsel, bite
bolla, bubble	**bolletta,** bill
botte, barrel	**bottone,** button
brando, sword	**brandello,** shred, rag
bricco, jug	**briccone,** rascal
burro, butter	**burrone,** ravine
cappa, cape, mantel	**cappella,** chapel
carato, carat	**caratello,** keg
carta, paper	**cartuccia,** cartridge
cavallo, horse	**cavalletto,** easel
cervo, dear	**cervello,** brain
ciclo, cycle	**ciclone,** cyclone
colla, glue	**colletta,** collection
drappo, cloth, fabric	**drappello,** squad, platoon
fante, infantryman	**fantino,** jockey
fava, broad bean	**favella,** speech, tongue
fede, faith	**fedina,** (police) record
filo, thread	**filetto,** border, fillet
foca, seal	**focaccia,** bun
gazza, magpie	**gazzella,** gazelle
matto, crazy person	**mattone,** brick
minestra, soup	**minestrone,** vegetable soup, minestrone

monte, mountain	**montone,** ram, mutton
mulo, mule	**mulino,** mill
occhio, eye	**occhiello,** buttonhole
paglia, straw	**paglietta,** straw hat
polpa, pulp, flesh	**polpetta,** meatball
posto, place	**postino,** mailman
tacco, heel	**tacchino,** turkey
tifo, typhus fever, fanaticism	**tifone,** typhoon
torre, tower	**torrone,** nougat
verme, worm	**vermicello,** thin kind of spaghetti

Other Suffixes

-aggine   a. is sometimes equal to English "-ness."
   cretin*aggine,* foolishness
      b. also expresses a particular act.
   cretin*aggine,* foolish act, piece of foolishness

-aglia (**-aia, -ame, -eto, -io, -ume**) indicate "a group" or "a crowd of."
   (Note that *-aglia* often has a disparaging meaning.)
   nuvol*aglia,* mass of cloud
   gent*aglia,* rabble, despicable people
   ris*aia,* rice field
   poll*ame,* poultry
   aranc*eto,* orange grove
   calpest*io,* stamping (Note that *-io* is added only to verbal stems.)
   lord*ume,* filth (Note that *-ume* is added only to adjectives.)

-aio   indicates the "maker," "dealer," or "one in charge of something."
   forn*aio,* baker
   libr*aio,* bookseller
   lampion*aio,* lamplighter

-aiuolo, -aiolo, -aro denote occupations.
   barc*aiolo,* boatman
   legn*aiuolo,* carpenter, cabinet maker
   benzin*aro* or (**benzin***aio*), service-station attendant

-anza is used to form abstract nouns.
   fratell*anza,* brotherhood
   adun*anza,* meeting
   lontan*anza,* distance, remoteness

-ario is often equal to the English "-ry."
   mission*ario,* missionary
   vision*ario,* visionary

-ata a. is sometimes equal to the English suffix "-ful."
pal*ata*, shoveful
cucchia*iata*, spoonful
    b. often indicates "the act of striking" or "a blow."
man*ata*, a blow with the hand
pugnal*ata*, a stab with a dagger
test*ata*, butt or blow with the head
    c. often expresses an action.
passeggi*ata*, walk, stroll
vir*ata*, tacking

-enza, -ezza are suffixes added respectively to verb and adjective stems to
    form abstract nouns.
conosc*enza*, knowledge
part*enza*, departure
bell*ezza*, beauty

-eria a. denotes a place where something is made or sold.
panett*eria*, bakery
libr*eria*, bookstore
gelat*eria*, ice-cream parlor
pesch*eria*, fishmarket
salum*eria*, delicatessen
    b. indicates a profession, business, or occupation.
ingegn*eria*, engineering
edit*oria*, publishing
    c. may mean "a collection."
cancell*eria*, stationery articles
chincagli*eria*, knickknacks
argent*eria*, silverware
    d. is sometimes equivalent to the English suffixes "-ry" and "-ness."
fess*eria*, foolery, foolishness
furb*eria*, astuteness
diavol*eria*, deviltry

-ia a. is the ending of the names of many arts and sciences
filosof*ia*, philosophy
teolog*ia*, theology
geometr*ia*, geometry
biolog*ia*, biology
    b. is the ending of many abstract nouns.
allegr*ia*, happiness
pazz*ia*, craziness
fantas*ia*, imagination

-iccio denotes a resemblance, or a tendency to.
malat*iccio*, sickly
ross*iccio*, reddish

-iere   denotes a person who makes, sells, or is in charge of.
panett*iere*, baker
stall*iere*, stableman
inferm*iere*, male nurse

-oso   is an adjective-forming suffix that generally means "having," "full of," "characterized by."
torment*oso*, stormy
fam*oso*, famous
fang*oso*, muddy
meravigli*oso*, marvelous
fall*oso*, faulty
erb*oso*, grassy

-tà   is equivalent to the English "-ty."
universi*tà*, university
cit*tà*, city
facol*tà*, faculty
generosi*tà*, generosity
regolari*tà*, regularity
passivi*tà*, passivity

-tore (-sore)   a. is equivalent to the English suffixes "-or" and "-er," and indicates an agent or doer.
conquista*tore*, conqueror
scrit*tore*, writer
inci*sore*, engraver
　　　b. may also be used to form adjectives.
premoni*tore*, premonitory
regola*tore*, regulating

-tura (-sura, -ura)   are used to form abstract and also concrete nouns.
mieti*tura*, harvesting
ar*sura*, parching thirst, drought
cal*ura*, sultriness, heat

-uto   is an adjective-forming suffix that generally means "having" or "characterized by."
oss*uto*, bony
lan*uto*, wool-covered
barb*uto*, bearded.

31. Letters

Parts of a Letter

l'intestazione   heading
l'indirizzo ⎱ address
la direzione ⎰
la formula iniziale   salutation, greeting
la data   date
l'oggetto   subject
il contenuto ⎱ body
il corpo ⎰
il riferimento   reference
la chiusa ⎱ ending
la conclusione ⎰
i saluti   salutation (end)
la firma   signature
il poscritto   postscript
l'allegato   enclosure
la postilla   marginal note, footnote
il codice d'avviamento postale (*CAP*)   postal code
la casella postale   P.O. box

Heading Style

Roma, 20 maggio 1986   Milano, 30 aprile 1986
Torino, 4 novembre 1985   Venezia, 27 settembre 1986

Address Format

Al Signor Arcangelo Cardillo   Alla Signora Claudia Mariani
Via Roma n. 377   Casella Postale 345
83100 Avellino   10100 Torino
Italia   Italia

Salutations

Business Letters

Egregio (or **Pregiato**) **Signore:**   Sir:, Dear Sir:
Egregi (or **Pregiati**) **Signori:**   Sirs:, Dear Sirs:
Egregia (or **Stimata**) **Signora:**   Dear Madam:

More Formal Letters

Signor Presidente: Mr. President
Chiarissimo: (*to a professor or a lawyer*)
Gentilissimo Direttore: (*to a male director*)
Gentilissima Direttrice: (*to a woman director*)

Note: When you do not know whether a woman is married or not, use *Signora.*

Personal Letters

Caro amico, Cara amica,	Dear friend,
Caro Paolo, Cara Silvia,	Dear Paul, Dear Sylvia,
Mio caro cugino, Mia cara cugina,	My dear cousin,
Mia cara Elisa,	My dear Elise,

Note: **Caro (cara)** should only be used with persons one knows well.

Endings

Formal or Business Letters

Vi prego di gradire (or **Vogliate accettare**), **signore (signora, signorina), l'espressione dei miei (nostri) devoti (distinti, rispettosi) sentimenti.**	*Literally:* Please accept Sir (Madam, Miss, or Ms.) the expression of my (our) devoted (distinguished, respectful) sentiments.

Personal Letters

Con amicizia,   With friendship,
Con amichevoli saluti,   With friendly greetings,
Affettuosamente,   Affectionately,
Affettuosi saluti,   With best wishes,
Suo (Sua) affezionatissimo (-a),   Yours with best regards,
Tuo compagno,   Your pal,
Tuo amico,   Your friend,
Baci affettuosi,   Affectionate kisses,
Ti abbraccio,   I embrace you,
Spero di rivederti (risentirti, riparlarti) al più presto.   I hope to see (hear from, speak to) you as soon as possible.

Abbreviations

Sig.	**Signor**	Mr.
Sig.ra	**Signora**	Mrs.
Sig.na	**Signorina**	Miss
Ill.mo	**Illustrissimo**	most illustrious
Preg.mo	**Pregiatissimo**	highly esteemed
Stim.mo	**Stimatissimo**	highly esteemed
Spett.le	**Spettabile**	respectable
Aff.mo (-a)	**Affezionatissimo (-a)**	very affectionate
Obbl.mo	**Obbligatissimo**	very grateful
Dev.mo	**Devotissimo**	very obedient
C.V.	**curriculum vitae**	résumé
c.c.	**copia conforme**	carbon copy
All.	**allegato**	enclosures
P.S.	**postscriptum**	postscript (P.S.)
n.	**numero**	number
Egr.	**Egregio**	distinguished
p.v.	**prossimo venturo**	next + *time period* (day, month, year)
c.m.	**corrente mese**	of this month
c.a.	**corrente anno**	of this year
u.s.	**ultimo scorso**	last + *time period* (day, month, year)
N.B.	**Nota Bene**	note well
v.	**vedi**	see

32. Idioms and Expressions

A

a bassa voce in a low voice
acqua in bocca! keep silent!
ad alta voce aloud
allungare il passo to walk faster
andare: andare coi piedi di piombo to proceed with great caution
andare pazzo to go crazy
aspettare al varco to be on the lookout for
a tutta birra at top speed
avere: avere ... anni to be ... years old
   avere bisogno di to need
   avere caldo to be warm (*of person*)
   avere fame to be hungry
   avere freddo to be cold
   avere fretta to be in a hurry
   avere intenzione di to intend
   avere la bontà di + *infin.* to be kind enough
   avere la luna di traverso to be in a bad mood
   avere l'aria di to seem, to look as if
   avere luogo to take place
   avere paura to be afraid
   avere pazienza to be patient
   avere ragione to be right
   avere sete to be thirsty
   avere sonno to be sleepy
   avere tempo di to have time
   avere torto to be wrong
   avere vergogna to be ashamed
   avere voglia di to feel like
avvenga quel che vuole come what may

B

bastare a se stesso to be self-sufficient
battere a macchina to type
bellezza: che bellezza! how wonderful!
bello: bell'e fatto ready-made; taken care of
   il bello è che the funny thing is
benestare: dare il benestare to approve
benvenuto welcome **dare il benvenuto** to welcome
bere: darla a bere a qualcuno to take somebody in
biglietto: biglietto d'andata e ritorno round-trip ticket
   biglietto di visita business card
bocca: in bocca al lupo! good luck!
bravo! well done! bravo!
bruciare le tappe to go straight ahead
brutto: farla brutta a to play a mean trick on
   vedersela brutta to foresee trouble
buono: alla buona plainly

C

cadere: cadere a proposito to come in handy, to come at the right moment
   cadere dalle nuvole to be dumbfounded
cane: menar il can per l'aia to beat around the bush
casella postale Post Office Box
cavare: cavarsi uno d'attorno to get rid of one
   cavarsi la voglia to satisfy one's wishes
chiedere scusa to beg pardon
colpi di testa sudden decision
condizione: a condizione che provided that
corre l'uso it is the fashion
crisi: in crisi in difficulties
cucirsi la bocca to keep one's mouth shut
cuore: di cuore gladly, heartily
   stare a cuore to be important

D

dare: dare alla luce to give birth
dare fastidio to bother, to annoy
deciditi! make up your mind!
deposito bagagli baggage room
Dio ci scampi! God forbid!
diventare di tutti i colori to blush, to be embarrassed
divieto: divieto di parcheggio no parking
divieto di sosta no stopping
domani l'altro the day after tomorrow
dormire tra due guanciali to be safe and secure
dovere: a dovere properly
dozzina: da (or di) dozzina common, ordinary
drizzare le gambe ai cani to do the impossible
dubitare: non dubitare! don't worry!
durare fatica a to find it hard to
duro: duro di orecchio hard of hearing
tener duro: to stick to it, hold out

E

ecco: ecco fatto that's it
eccomi here I am
elenco telefonico telephone directory
entrare in contatto to establish contact
errore: errore di lingua slip of the tongue
errore di stampa misprint
essere (used idiomatically):
  ci (or vi) sono molti fiori nel giardino there are many flowers in the garden
  Io sono di Napoli I am a native of Naples
  che c'è? What is it?
  che sarà di lui? what will become of him?
  la sua casa è fra due colline his house stands between two hills
  quando fu ciò? when did this happen?
  di chi è questo libro? to whom does this book belong?
  non è da tanto he is inadequate to the task

sono stato a scuola I have been in school
c'è da far subito questo lavoro this work has to be done immediately
età: mezza età middle age
evenienza: per ogni evenienza just in case
eventualità: nell'eventualità che in the event of, in case that

F

faccia tosta gall, impudence
fare: fare alla meglio to do as well as one can
fare amicizia con qualcuno to make friends with someone
fare attenzione to pay attention, to be careful
fare (una) bella figura to cut a fine figure
fare (una) brutta figura to cut a poor figure
fare due passi to go for a stroll
fare (or farsi) il bagno to take a bath, to go swimming
fare il magnifico to spend lavishly
fare il numero to dial
fare (or farsi) la doccia to take a shower
fare la mano a to get used to
fare la spesa to go shopping
fare le cose in grande stile to splurge
fare le valigie to pack the suitcases
fare male to hurt
farsi male to get hurt
fare specie a to amaze
fare una domanda to ask a question
fare una passeggiata to take a walk
fare una visita to pay a visit
fatto a mano handmade
favorire: vuol favorire? won't you please join us (at a meal)?
festa da ballo dancing party
ficcare il naso negli affari altrui to poke one's nose in other people's business
fila via! get out!
fin: in fin dei conti after all
forza! courage!

fuori: fuori commercio   not for sale
   fuori luogo   untimely, out of
   place

G

genere umano   the human race
gente di mal affare   riff-raff
gettare la colpa addosso a
   qualcuno   to lay the blame on
   someone
ghingheri: in ghingheri   dressed up
giocare: giocare d'azzardo   to
   gamble
   giocare di mano   to steal
gioco: prendersi gioco di   to make
   fun of
giorno fatto   broad daylight
giro: a giro di posta   by return mail
   prendere in giro   to poke fun at
grande: fare il grande   to show off
guadagnarsi il pane (or la vita)   to
   earn one's living
guardare dall'alto in basso   to look
   down one's nose at
guastare: guastare le uova nel
   paniere a   to spoil the plans of
guastarsi con qualcuno   to quarrel
   with someone
guastarsi il sangue   to blow one's top
gusto: provare gusto   to have fun

I

idea: idea fissa   fixed idea
   neanche per idea   not in the least
ieri l'altro   the day before yesterday
imbroglio: cacciarsi in un
   imbroglio   to get involved in a
   mess
impicciarsi degli affari propri   to
   mind one's business
indovinare alla prima   to guess
   straight off
infilarle tutte   to succeed all the time
intendere: intendere a rovescio   to
   misunderstand
   intendere a volo   to catch on
   quickly
intendersi di   to be an expert in
interessati degli affari tuoi!   mind
   your own business!
interrotto: la strada è interrotta   the
   road is closed to traffic
intromettere: non intrometterti!
   don't interfere!

italiano: questo si chiama parlare
   italiano   this is plain speaking

L

lampo: un lampo di genio   a stroke
   of genius
lasciare: lascia fare a me!   leave it
   to me!
   lasciarci le penne   to die, to be
   skinned alive
licenza: con licenza parlando
   excuse my language
limite: caso limite   extreme case
liscio: andar liscio   to go smoothly
   l'affare non è liscio   the affair is
   rather tricky
   passarla liscio   to get away with it
lustro: tirato a lustro
   spick-and-span

M

maestro: l'esercizio è un buon
   maestro   practice makes perfect
mandare: che Dio gliela mandi
   buona!   God help him!
mangiare il pane a tradimento   to
   eat unearned bread
metterei la mano sul fuoco!   I would
   swear on it!
mare: promettere mari e monti   to
   promise the moon
meglio: il meglio è nemico del
   bene   leave well alone
memoria: se non mi tradisce la
   memoria   if I remember well
mi meraviglio di lui!   I am
   surprised at him!
mondo: tutto il mondo è paese   it is
   the same all over the world
monte: tutto andò a monte   it all
   came to nothing
morire: chi non muore si rivede!
   look who is here!
mostra: è stato tutto una mostra   it
   was all make-believe
muoviti; è tardi!   hurry up; it is late!
musica: devo dirtelo in musica?   do
   you want me to spell it out for you?

N

nascere con la camicia   to be born
   with a silver spoon in one's
   mouth

naso: menare per il naso to lead by the nose
restare con un palmo di naso to be duped, to be disappointed
negozio di cancelleria stationery store
nervi: avere i nervi (or il nervoso) to be in a bad mood
niente: dal niente from scratch
nocciolo: il nocciolo della questione the crux of the matter
nome e cognome full name
notte bianca sleepless night
nulla osta no objection, permission granted
nuovo di zecca brand-new

O

occhio: a occhio e croce as a rough guess
olio solare sun-tan lotion
ombra: nemmeno per ombra not in the least
opera di consultazione reference work
ora: ora di punta rush hour
ora legale daylight-saving time
orario: il fuso orario time zone
orecchio: fare orecchie da mercante to turn a deaf ear
orto: non è la via dell'orto it is no bed of roses
osso: avere le ossa rotte to be dead tired
un osso duro a hard nut to crack
in carne e ossa in flesh and blood
otto: in quattro e quattr'otto in the twinkling of an eye

P

padronanza: padronanza di se stesso self-control
padronanza di una lingua command of a language
paese: alla paesana according to local tradition
palio: mettere in palio to offer as a prize
palleggiarsi le responsabilità to shift the responsibility
palo: saltare di palo in frasca to digress

papavero: alto papavero big shot
parole di circostanza occasional words
pezzo: un pezzo grosso big shot
pratica: aver pratica con to have practice with
prendere in castagna to catch in the act

Q

quadrare: quadrare a to be satisfactory to
quadrare con to fit
quadro; questo è il quadro della situazione this is how things stand
quarta: partire in quarta to get off to a flying start
quattro: a quattr'occhi in private
questione: venire a questione to quarrel
quota zero point of departure

R

rabbia: che rabbia! I am awfully annoyed!
raccontare: A me la racconti! Don't tell me!
registro: cambiar registro to change one's tune
rendersi conto di to realize
requie: senza requie ceaselessly
resistere alla prova to stand the test
retta: dammi retta! listen to me!
ricorso: presentare un ricorso to appeal
rieccomi here I am again
rientrare in sè to come to one's senses
rifare di sana pianta to do all over again
alla rinfusa at random
riposo: buon riposo! sleep well!
risalire la corrente to go upstream
risentire: a risentirci! until we talk again!
rispetto: con rispetto parlando excuse the word
rispondere picche to say no
rotella: gli manca una rotella he has a screw loose
rotta: essere in rotta con to be at odds with

rovescio: a rovescio (or **alla rovescia**) upside down, backwards

S

sacco: mettere nel sacco to outwit
vuotare il sacco to speak out
santo: tutti i santi giorni day in and day out
sbornia: prendere una sbornia to get drunk
scherzo: stare allo scherzo to take a joke
scrollarsi di dosso to shake off
senso: buon senso common sense
smontare dal servizio to go off duty
spasso: andare a spasso to go for a walk
trovarsi a spasso to be out of work
spremersi il cervello to rack one's brain
sugo: discorsi senza sugo empty talk
sveglia: dare la sveglia to wake up

T

taci! shut up!
tagliare la corda to run away
teatro: che teatro! what fun!
tenersi sulle proprie to keep aloof
tastare il terreno to feel one's way
toccare: toccare il cielo col dito to be in seventh heaven
tocca a lui it is up to him
togliersi di mezzo to get out the way
tornare sulle proprie decisioni to change one's mind
torto: a torto o a ragione rightly or wrongly
tratto in inganno deceived
trovarsi a proprio agio to feel comfortable
tutto: tutt'al più at most
tutto d'un tratto all of a sudden

U

uccello di bosco fugitive
uomo: uomo del giorno man of the hour
uomo di parola man of his word
uomo fatto grown man

uscire: uscire di mente a to escape one's mind
uscire per il rotto della cuffia to barely make it
uscita di sicurezza emergency exit
uso: farci l'uso to get used to it
fuori d'uso worn out, out of commission
utile: venire all'utile to come in handy

V

vaglio: passare al vaglio to sift
vantaggio: essere in vantaggio to have the lead
vedere di to try to
venerdì; mancare di un venerdì to have a screw loose
versare in gravi condizioni to be in serious condition
via: dare il via to start
viaggio d'andata e ritorno round trip
vicenda: a vicenda reciprocally, one another
vigile del fuoco fireman
vinto: darsi per vinto to give in
viso: a viso aperto boldly, frankly
voglia: di buona voglia willingly

Z

zampa: Giù le zampe! Hands off!
zappa: darsi la zappa sui piedi to cut off one's nose to spite one's face
zazzera: portare la zazzera to wear one's hair long
zeppa: metterci una zeppa to make the best of a bad situation
zimbello: essere lo zimbello di tutti he is a laughingstock
zitto! quiet! hush!
zizzania: seminare zizzania to sow discord
zonzo: andare a zonzo to stroll, to loiter
zoppo: un ragionamento zoppo an unsound argument

33. Vocabulary Lists

Territorial Divisions

il capoluogo di provincia chief town of a province
il capoluogo di regione chief town of a region
la circoscrizione (elettorale) (electoral) district
la città city
il comune town
il distretto district
il municipio municipality; city hall
la nazione nation
il paese country, town
la patria homeland
la provincia province
la regione region
lo stato State, country, nation
la terra land, country, rural area
il territorio territory

Commonly Used Words and Phrases

Everyday Greetings and Expressions

Addio. Good-bye.
A proposito. By the way.
Arrivederci (ArrivederLa). Good-bye.
Aspettate un momento. Wait a moment.
Bene (or Benissimo), grazie. (Very) well, thank you.
Buon appetito. Enjoy your meal.
Buona sera (notte). Good evening (night).
Buon giorno (pomeriggio). Good morning (afternoon).
Buon viaggio. Have a good trip.
Che (cosa) vuol dire? What does that mean?
Che desiderate? What do you desire?
Che peccato! What a pity!
Che sfortuna! What a misfortune!
Ciao! Good-bye! Hello!

Ci vediamo (domani, stasera, martedì). See you (tomorrow, tonight, Tuesday).
Come sta (Lei)? How are you?
Come vi chiamate? What is your name?
(Con) permesso. May I come in? Excuse me.
Dov'è il (or la) ...? Where is the ...?
E Lei? And you?
Figuratevi. Don't mention it.
Grazie. Thank you.
In bocca al lupo. Good luck.
(Io) mi chiamo ... My name is ...
Mi dispiace. I am sorry.
Mi fa piacere. I am glad.
No, signore (signora, signorina) No sir (madam, miss).
Non vi capisco. I do not understand you.

Non vorrei disturbarvi. I am sorry to disturb you.

Parlate piano, per favore. Speak slowly please.

Potete farmi un favore (or una cortesia)? Can you do me a favor?

Prego. Don't mention it. You are welcome. Pardon. Please.

Scusi (or Scusa, or Scusate). Excuse me.

Tante (or Mille, or Molte) grazie. Thank you so much.

Tanti saluti. Greetings

Venga qui. Come here.

Responses

Beato lui! Lucky him!

Congratulazioni! Congratulations!

Davvero? Really?

Felicitazioni! Congratulations!

Hai ragione (torto). You are right (wrong).

I miei ossequi. My regards.

Lasciami in pace! Leave me in peace!

Male. Badly.

No. No.

Non importa. It does not matter.

Non lo so. I don't know.

Non mancherò. I won't fail.

Non molto bene. Not so well.

Non ne vale la pena. It is not worth it.

Non posso. I cannot.

Peggio per lui! It serves him right.

Rallegramenti. Congratulations.

Sì. Yes.

Silenzio! Quiet! Silence!

Smettila! Stop it!

Spicciati. Hurry up.

Tanti auguri. Best wishes.

Va bene, d'accordo. That's all right. Okay.

Vattene! Get out!

Volentieri. Gladly. Willingly.

Nationalities and Languages

cinese—il cinese Chinese

francese—il francese French

giapponese—il giapponese Japanese

italiano (-a)—l'italiano Italian

portoghese—il portoghese Portuguese

russo (-a)—il russo Russian

spagnolo (-a)—lo spagnolo Spanish

tedesco (-a)—il tedesco German

Everyday Objects

l'oggetto object

la busta envelope

la carta geografica map

il cestino wastepaper basket

il francobollo stamp

il gesso chalk

la gomma eraser

l'inchiostro ink

la lavagna blackboard

la lettera letter

il libro book

la matita (or il lapis) pencil

la penna pen

il quaderno notebook

Characteristics (*Nouns*)

la caratteristica characteristic

l'altezza height

l'amicizia friendship

il bene goodness, the good

la bontà goodness

la debolezza weakness

la difficoltà difficulty

la distanza distance

la durezza hardness

l'età age

il falso falseness

la fedeltà faithfulness

la forza strength

la gioventù (or la giovinezza) youth

la grandezza greatness

l'industriosità industriousness

la larghezza width

la lunghezza length

il male evil

la noia boredom

l'ostilità hostility

la pace peace

la pazzia craziness, madness

il peso weight

la pigrizia laziness

la povertà poverty

la profondità depth

la ricchezza wealth, richness

la stupidità stupidity
la taglia size
la tensione tension
la verità truth

Characteristics (*Adjectives*)

a buon mercato inexpensive
adirato angry
allegro happy
alto high, tall
amaro bitter
amichevole friendly
aperto open
asciutto dry
avaro stingy
bagnato wet
basso short
biondo blond, fair
bravo clever
bruno brown
brutto ugly
buono good
caldo warm
caro expensive
cattivo bad
chiuso closed
debole weak
difficile difficult
divertente amusing, funny
dolce sweet
duro hard
facile easy
falso false, wrong
fedele faithful
forte strong
generoso generous
gentile kind
giovane young
grande big, great
grasso fat
importante important
intelligente intelligent
interessante interesting
largo large
leggero light
libero free
lontano far
lungo long
magro thin, slim
necessario necessary
noioso boring
nuovo new
pazzo crazy, mad

pubblico public
pulito clean
ricco rich
saggio wise
sano sane
secco dry
sgarbato rude, impolite
simpatico nice, pleasant, agreeable
sporco dirty
stanco tired
triste sad
utile useful
vecchio old, ancient
veloce fast
vicino near

Color

il colore color

arancione orange
azzurro sky blue
bianco white
blu blue
celeste pale blue
chiaro light
giallo yellow
grigio gray
lillà mauve
marrone brown
nero black
rosa pink
rosso red
scuro dark
verde green
viola (or violetto) violet

The Weather (*Nouns*)

il tempo weather

l'acquazzone shower
l'arcobaleno rainbow
la brina frost
il caldo warmth
il calore heat
il clima climate
il diluvio flood
la foschia mist
il fulmine lightning, thunderbolt
il grado degree
la grandine hail
il lampo lightning
la luna moon
la nebbia fog
la neve snow

la **nuvola** cloud
la **nuvolosità** cloudiness
la **pioggerella** drizzle
la **pioggia** rain
il **punto di congelamento** freezing point
la **rugiada** dew
il **sole** sun
la **temperatura** temperature
il **temporale** storm
la **tormenta** blizzard
il **tuono** thunder
l'**umidità** humidity
l'**uragano** hurricane
il **vento** wind

The Weather (*Adjectives*)

afoso sultry
chiaro clear
coperto overcast
freddo cold
fresco cool
gelato frozen
glaciale icy
luminoso bright
nebbioso foggy
nevoso snowy
nuvoloso cloudy
piovigginoso drizzly
piovoso rainy
secco dry
splendido splendid
temperato temperate
tempestoso stormy
umido damp

The Earth

la **terra** earth, soil, ground

l'**aria** air
l'**atmosfera** atmosphere
la **baia** bay
il **bosco** wood
la **campagna** country
il **campo** camp
il **capo** cape
la **collina** hill
il **continente** continent
la **costa** coast
il **deserto** dessert
la **duna** dune
l'**emisfero** hemisphere
il **fiume** large river

la **foresta** forest
il **golfo** gulf
l'**isola** island
il **lago** lake
il **mare** sea
il **mondo** world
la **montagna** mountain
la **natura** nature
l'**oceano** ocean
il **paesaggio** landscape
la **palude** swamp
il **porto** port
il **prato** meadow
la **riva** shore, bank
il **ruscello** small river
la **spiaggia** beach
la **valle** valley

The Family

la **famiglia** family

gli **antenati** ancestors
il **bambino**, la **bambina** baby boy, baby girl
il **bisnonno**, la **bisnonna** great-grandfather, great-grandmother
il **cognato**, la **cognata** brother-in-law, sister-in-law
il **cugino**, la **cugina** cousin (*m.*), cousin (*f.*)
il **fidanzato**, la **fidanzata** boy friend, girl friend
il **figlio**, la **figlia** son, daughter
il **fratello** brother
i **gemelli** twins
il **genero** son-in-law
i **genitori** parents
la **madre** mother
la **mamma** mother, mom
il **marito** husband
la **moglie** wife
il **nipote**, la **nipote** nephew, niece
il **nonno**, la **nonna**, i **nonni** grandfather, grandmother, grandparents
la **nuora** daughter-in-law
il **padre** father
il **parente** relative
la **sorella** sister
lo **sposo**, la **sposa** bridegroom, bride
il **suocero**, la **suocera** father-in-law, mother-in-law
la **zia**, lo **zio** aunt, uncle

The House

la casa house

l'appartamento apartment
l'aria condizionata air conditioning
l'ascensore elevator
l'autorimessa garage
il balcone balcony
il calorifero heating, radiator
la camera (or la stanza) room
la camera da letto bedroom
il camino chimney
la cantina cellar
la chiave key
il corridoio corridor
il cortile courtyard
la cucina kitchen
la cucina a gas gas range
l'entrata entrance
la finestra window
il fornello stove, kitchen range
il giardino garden
il pavimento floor of a room
il piano story, floor
il pianterreno ground floor
la porta door
la sala da pranzo dining room
il salotto living room, parlor
le scale stairs
lo scantinato basement
il soffitto ceiling
il soggiorno living room, den
la stanza da bagno bathroom
lo studio study
il termosifone heating, radiator
la terrazza terrace
il tetto roof
l'uscio entrance, door
la veranda porch, veranda

Furniture

i mobili pieces of furniture
la mobilia furniture

l'armadio clothes closet
il baule trunk, chest
la cassapanca wooden chest
il cassettone chest of drawers
il comodino night table
la credenza sideboard
la cristalliera glass case
il divano (or il sofà) couch, sofa
il frigorifero refrigerator

il guardaroba wardrobe
la lampada da tavolo table lamp
la lampada da terra floor lamp
la lavastoviglie dishwasher
la lavatrice washing machine
la libreria bookcase
la pendola grandfather clock
la poltrona easy chair
il quadro painting, picture
lo scaffale shelf
la scrivania desk
la sedia chair
lo specchio mirror
la stufa stove
il tappeto rug, carpet
il tavolino small table
la tavola table
il tavolo table
le tendine (or le tende) curtains

The Bed

il letto bed
fare il letto to make the bed

la coperta (di lana) (wool) blanket
la coperta elettrica electric blanket
la coperta imbottita quilt
il copriletto bed spread
il cuscino (or il guanciale) pillow
la federa pillow case
il lenzuolo sheet
il materasso mattress
la sponda foot of the bed

The Dressing Table

la toeletta (or la toletta) dressing table

l'abbronzante suntan lotion
l'acqua di Colonia cologne
l'asciugamano towel
il bigodino curler
il casco drier
la cipria powder
la crema da barba shaving cream
la crema di bellezza skin cream
il dentifricio toothpaste
le forbici scissors
le forcine hairpins
la lametta blade
il pennello da barba shaving brush

il **profumo**   perfume
il **rasoio (elettrico)**   (electric) razor
la **retina**   hair net
il **rossetto**   lipstick
il **sapone**   soap
la **spazzola**   brush
lo **spazzolino**   toothbrush
la **spilla**   pin
la **spilla di sicurezza**   safety pin
lo **spillo**   pin
la **tovaglia**   towel

Setting the Table

la **tavola**   table
apparecchiare la tavola   to set the table
sparecchiare la tavola   to clear the table

l'**aceto**   vinegar
l'**argenteria**   silverware
il **bicchiere**   glass
la **bottiglia**   bottle
la **brocca**   pitcher
la **caffettiera**   coffeepot
la **caraffa**   carafe
il **cavatappi**   corkscrew
il **coltello**   knife
il **cucchiaino**   teaspoon
il **cucchiaio**   spoon
la **forchetta**   fork
la **fruttiera**   fruit bowl
l'**insalatiera**   salad bowl
l'**olio**   oil
il **pane**   bread
il **panino**   bread roll
il **pepe**   pepper
la **pepaiola**   pepper shaker
il **piattino**   saucer
il **piatto**   dish
il **piatto di portata**   course
il **sale**   salt
la **saliera**   salt shaker
la **salsa**   sauce
la **scodella**   soup bowl
la **senape**   mustard
la **tazza**   cup
la **tovaglia**   tablecloth
il **tovagliolo**   napkin
il **vasellame**   chinaware
il **vassoio**   tray
la **zuccheriera**   sugar bowl
la **zuppiera**   soup tureen

Meals

il **pasto**   meal

la **cena**   supper
la **colazione**   breakfast
la **merenda**   snack
il **pranzo** (or il **desinare**)   dinner
il **rinfresco**   refreshments
la **seconda colazione**
la **colazione del mezzogiorno**   lunch
lo **spuntino**   snack
lo **spuntino delle undici**   a mid-morning snack

Appetizers

antipasti   appetizers

l'**acciuga**   anchovy
l'**affettato**   sliced ham (salami, etc.)
l'**antipasto misto**   mixed appetizers (cold)
i **capperi**   capers
il **caviale**   caviar
i **fichi con prosciutto**   green figs with Parma ham
il **formaggio**   cheese
i **frutti di mare**   seafood
il **salame**   salami
il **salame affumicato**   smoked salami
il **salame con funghi e carciofini sott'olio**   salami with mushrooms and artichokes in oil
le **sardine**   sardines
sottaceti }
la **giardiniera** }   pickles
il **tonno**   tuna
la **verdura cruda**   raw vegetables

First Courses

la **minestra** (or il **primo piatto**)   soup

gli **agnellotti** (or gli **agnolotti**)   ravioli stuffed with meat
il **brodo**   clear soup
il **brodo di carne**   meat soup
il **brodo di verdura**   clear vegetable soup
i **cannelloni**   pasta with meat-and-cheese filling and tomato sauce

i cappelletti form of ravioli, often served in broth
le fettuccine ribbon noodles
le fettuccine alla romana egg pasta flavored with beef gravy
gli gnocchi Italian dumplings
le lasagne wide, flat noodles
la minestra di pastina noodle soup
la minestra di riso rice soup
il minestrone minestrone (*a thick vegetable soup*)
la pasta asciutta cooked macaroni, generally covered with tomato sauce
la pasta con le sarde pasta with sardines
il pesto a typical Genoese sauce, made with basil leaves and oil
la polenta cornmeal
i ravioli square pieces of dough, filled with cheese or meat
il riso (arrosto, con tartufi) rice (roasted, with truffles)
il risotto alla milanese rice cooked in broth and served with beef
gli spaghetti spaghetti
gli spaghetti al burro spaghetti with butter
gli spaghetti alla carbonara spaghetti with bacon, beaten eggs, and black pepper
gli spaghetti alla marinara spaghetti with mussels, garlic, oil, parsley
gli spaghetti alla matriciana spaghetti with salt pork and tomato sauce
gli spaghetti al pomodoro spaghetti with tomato sauce
gli spaghetti alle vongole spaghetti with clams
la stracciatella broth with beaten egg
lo stufato di manzo beef stew
le tagliatelle noodles
i tortellini (alla bolognese) egg noodles (Bolonia style)
la trippa tripe
la zuppa di pesce fish soup

Meat

la carne meat

l'abbacchio roast suckling lamb

l'agnello lamb
l'arrosto di lepre roast hare
l'arrosto di pernice roast partrige
la bistecca alla fiorentina grilled veal cutlet
la bistecca di manzo beefsteak
la bistecca di vitello veal steak
il bollito stew made of various boiled meats
la braciola rolled slice of beef stuffed with spices
il cappone capon
il capretto goat
il coniglio rabbit
il cosciotto di montone leg of lamb
la costoletta di agnello lamb chop
la costoletta di maiale pork chop
la costoletta di vitello veal chop
il fegato liver
il filetto fillet
il lesso boiled beef, boiled meat
il maiale pork
il manzo beef
l'ossobuco stewed shin of veal
la pancetta bacon
il pollo alla cacciatora chicken cooked in oil, tomatoes, and wine
il pollo alla diavola fried chicken
la porchetta al forno roast suckling pig
il prosciutto prosciutto, ham
i saltimbocca rolled veal with ham
le scaloppine slices of veal cooked in wine with mushrooms, etc.
gli spezzatini veal stew
il tacchino ripieno stuffed turkey
il vitello veal

Fish

il pesce fish

l'anguilla eel
l'aragosta lobster
il baccalà dried salted cod
il calamaro squid
il fritto misto a mixture of fried seafood
i gamberetti all'olio shrimp in oil
il gambero crab
il merluzzo cod
le ostriche oysters

il **polipo**   octopus
il **salmone**   salmon
le **sardine**   sardines
gli **scampi**   shrimp
la **sogliola**   sole
il **tonno**   tuna
la **trota**   trout
la **vongola**   clam

Egg Dishes

le **uova**   eggs

la **frittata**   omelette
la **frittata con prosciutto**   ham
  omelette
le **uova affogate** ⎫ poached
le **uova in camicia** ⎭ eggs
le **uova al guscio**   eggs on the
  half-shell
le **uova al tegame**   fried eggs
le **uova bollite**   boiled eggs
le **uova fritte con pancetta**   bacon
  and eggs
le **uova sbattute**   beaten eggs
le **uova sode**   hard-boiled eggs
le **uova strapazzate**   scrambled
  eggs

Sweets

il **dolce**   sweets

i **biscotti**   biscuits
il **budino**   pudding
le **caramelle**   candies
i **cioccolatini**   chocolate
la **crema**   custard
il **gelato**   ice cream
il **panettone**   sweet bread with
  raisins and orange peel
le **paste**   pastries
la **torta**   cake

Fruit

la **frutta**   fruits

l'**albicocca**   apricot
l'**amarena**   black cherry
l'**ananasso**   pineapple
l'**anguria** (or il **cocomero**)
  watermelon
l'**arachide**   (*f.*) peanut
l'**arancia**   orange
la **banana**   banana
la **castagna**   chestnut
la **ciliegia**   cherry

il **dattero**   date
il **fico**   fig
la **fragola**   strawberry
il **lampone**   raspberry
la **limetta**   lime
il **limone**   lemon
la **macedonia di frutta**   fruit salad
il **mandarino**   tangerine
la **mandorla**   almond
la **mela**   apple
il **melone**   musk melon
il **mirtillo**   cranberry
la **nocciola**   hazel nut
la **noce**   nut
la **pera**   pear
la **pesca**   peach
la **prugna** (or la **susina**)   plum
l'**uva**   grape

Beverages

la **bibita** (or la **bevanda**)   beverage

l'**acqua**   water
l'**acqua di selz**   soda water
l'**acqua minerale**   mineral water
l'**aperitivo**   aperitif
l'**aranciata**   orangeade
la **bibita analcolica**   soft drink
il **caffè con panna**   black coffee
  with cream
il **caffè espresso**   black coffee
il **cappuccino**   white coffee with
  steamed milk
la **cioccolata**   chocolate milk
il **latte**   milk
la **limonata**   lemonade
il **succo di frutta**   fruit juice
il **vino**   wine
il **vino bianco** (**rosso**)   white (red)
  wine

Vegetables

i **legumi** ⎫
gli **ortaggi** ⎬ vegetables
la **verdura** ⎭

l'**aglio**   garlic
l'**asparago**   asparagus
la **barbabietola**   beet
i **broccoli**   broccoli
il **carciofo**   artichoke
la **carota**   carrot
il **cavolfiore**   cauliflower
il **cavolo**   cabbage

il cavolo di Bruxelles brussels
  sprout
il cetriolo cucumber
la cipolla onion
i fagiolini string beans
il fagiolo bean
il fungo mushroom
l'insalata (di lattuga) (lettuce)
  salad
le lenticchie lentils
la melanzana eggplant
l'oliva olive
la patata potato
il peperone pepper
i piselli peas
il pomodoro tomato
il prezzemolo parsley
la rapa turnip
il ravanello radish
il sedano celery
gli spinaci spinach
gli zucchini zucchini

Animals

l'animale (*m.*) animal

l'agnello lamb
l'asino donkey
il cane dog
il cavallo horse
l'elefante (*m.*) elephant
il gatto cat
il leone lion
il lupo wolf
la mucca (or la vacca) cow
l'orso bear
la pecora sheep
il pesce fish
la scimmia monkey
lo scoiattolo squirrel
il serpente snake
la tartaruga turtle
la tigre tiger
il topo mouse
il toro bull
la volpe fox

Birds

l'uccello bird

l'aquila eagle
la colomba dove
la gallina hen

il gallo rooster
la ghiandaia jay
il pappagallo parrot
il passero sparrow
il piccione (or il colombo) pigeon
il picchio woodpecker
la rondine swallow

Insects

l'insetto insect

l'ape bee
la cavalletta grasshopper
la farfalla butterfly
la formica ant
il grillo cricket
la mosca fly
la pulce flea
il ragno spider
la tarma moth
la zanzara mosquito

Trees

l'albero tree

l'abete (*m.*) spruce, fir
l'acero maple
il castagno chestnut
la corteccia (or la scorza) bark
il noce walnut
la palma palm
il pioppo poplar
la quercia oak
la radice root
il ramo branch
il ramoscello twig
il tiglio linden
il tronco trunk

Plants and Flowers

la pianta plant
il fiore flower

la camelia camellia
il caprifoglio honeysuckle
il crisantemo chrysanthemum
la dalia dahlia
il dente di leone dandelion
l'erba grass
la foglia leaf
la gardenia gardenia
il garofano carnation

il **gelsomino** jasmine
il **geranio** geranium
il **giglio** lily
il **lillà** lilac
la **margherita** daisy
il **mazzo di fiori** bouquet
il **mughetto** lily of the valley
il **non ti scordar di me** forget-me-not
l'**orchidea** orchid
il **papavero** poppy
la **rosa** rose
il **tulipano** tulip
la **viola del pensiero** pansy
la **violetta** violet

The City

la **città** city

l'**abitante** inhabitant
l'**albergo** hotel
la **banca** bank
la **biblioteca** library
il **castello** castle
la **cattedrale** cathedral
il **chiasso** noise
la **chiesa** church
il **cimitero** cemetery
il **cinema** movies
la **fabbrica** factory
la **folla** crowd
il **grattacielo** skyscraper
l'**isolato** block
il **marciapiede** sidewalk
il **municipio** city hall
le **mura** walls
il **museo** museum
l'**ospedale** (*m.*) hospital
la **panchina** bench
il **parco** park
la **piazza** square
il **ponte** bridge
il **porto** port
il **quartiere** section
il **semaforo** traffic light
il **sindaco** mayor
lo **stadio** stadium
la **statua** statue
la **strada** (or la **via**) street, road
l'**ufficio postale** (or la **posta**) post office
il **viale** avenue
il **villaggio** village

Stores and Shops

il **negozio** store
la **bottega** shop

il **bar** bar
la **borsa per la spesa** shopping bag
il **caffè** cafè
la **drogheria** grocery store
l'**emporio** emporium, general store
la **farmacia** pharmacy, drugstore
i **grandi magazzini** department stores
la **lavanderia** laundromat
la **libreria** bookstore
la **macelleria** butcher shop
il **mercato** market
(il **negozio di**) **generi alimentari** grocery store
la **panetteria** bakery
la **pasticceria** pastry shop
la **pescheria** fish market
la **polleria** poultry market
la **salumeria** delicatessen
il **supermercato** supermarket

Transportation

i **mezzi di trasporto** means of transport

l'**aeroplano** (or l'**aereo**) airplane
l'**autocarro** truck
l'**automobile** (*f.*) car
l'**autobus** (*m.*) bus
la **barca** boat
la **bicicletta** bicycle
il **camioncino** van
l'**elicottero** helicopter
il **filobus** trolley-bus
la **funicolare** funicular
il **jet** jet
la **motocicletta** motorcycle
la **nave** ship
la **teleferica** cable car
il **transatlantico** liner
il **treno** train

Travel

il **viaggio** trip, journey

l'**agenzia di viaggio** travel agency
il **bagaglio** luggage
il **biglietto** ticket

il biglietto di andata e
ritorno round-trip ticket
la borsa da viaggio traveling bag
Buon viaggio! Have good trip!
controllare i bagagli to check the
luggage
la dogana customs
l'orario schedule
il pacco package
il passaporto passport
il posto (or il sedile) seat
la prenotazione reservation
il soggiorno stay
la valigia suitcase

The Car

l'automobile ⎫
la macchina ⎭ car

l'acceleratore accelerator
l'aria air
avere un guasto (al motore) to
have a breakdown
la batteria battery
la benzina gasoline
la bucatura flat tire
il cruscotto dashboard
il freno brake
il grasso grease
il guasto breakdown
guidare to drive
il motore motor
il parabrezza (m.) windshield
la patente di guida driver's li-
cense
il parcheggio parking lot
il (or lo) pneumatico tire
la ruota wheel
la ruota di riserva spare tire
il serbatoio della benzina tank
lo specchietto retrovisore rear
view mirror
la stazione di servizio service
station
il tergicristallo windshield wiper
la velocità speed
il volante steering wheel

The Human Body

il corpo umano the human body

l'arteria artery
la bocca mouth
il braccio (pl. le braccia) arm

i capelli hair
il capo (or la testa) head
la caviglia ankle
il cervello brain
le ciglia eyelashes
la circolazione del sangue blood
circulation
il collo neck
la colonna vertebrale backbone
la coscia thigh
la costola rib
il cranio cranium
il cuore heart
il dente (pl. i denti) tooth, teeth
le dita del piede toes
il dito (pl. le dita) finger, fingers
la faccia (or il viso) face
il fegato liver
i fianchi hips
la fronte forehead
la gamba leg
il ginocchio (pl. le ginocchia)
knee, knees
la gola throat
il gomito elbow
la guancia cheek
il labbro (pl. le labbra) lip, lips
la lingua tongue
la mano (pl. le mani) hand,
hands
il mento chin
la narice nostril
il naso nose
l'occhio eye
l'orecchio ear
il palato palate
la pelle skin
il petto chest
il piede foot
i polmoni lungs
il polso wrist
il rene kidney
la respirazione respiration
il sangue blood
lo scalpo scalp
la schiena (or il dorso) back
il sistema nervoso nervous system
la spalla shoulder
la spina dorsale spine
lo stomaco stomach
il torso torso
l'unghia nail
la vena vein

il **ventre**   abdomen
lo **zigomo**   cheekbone

Men's Clothing

l'**abbigliamento maschile**   men's clothing

l'**abito completo**   suit
le **bretelle**   suspenders
le **calze**   stockings
i **calzini**   socks
i **calzoni**   pants
la **camicia**   shirt
il **cappello**   hat
la **cintura**   belt
il **colletto**   collar
la **cravatta**   tie
la **cravatta a farfalla**   bow tie
il **fazzoletto**   handkerchief
la **giacca**   jacket
la **giacca a vento**   windbreaker
i **guanti**   gloves
l'**impermeabile** (*m.*)   raincoat
la **maglia**   sweater
le **mutande**   underwear
l'**ombrello**   umbrella
il **panciotto**   vest
i **pantaloni**   pants
il **pigiama**   pajama
le **scarpe**   shoes
la **sciarpa**   scarf
il **soprabito**   overcoat
gli **stivali**   boots

Women's Clothing

abbigliamento femminile   women's clothing

abito a giacca   costume
abito da sera   evening dress
abito intero   dress
la **borsa**   pocketbook, bag
la **borsetta**   purse
le **calze**   stockings
la **camicetta** (or la **blusa**)   blouse
la **camicia da notte**   nightgown
il **cappello**   hat
il **cappotto**   overcoat
la **cintura**   belt
il **costume da bagno**   swimsuit
la **giacchetta**   jacket
la **gonna**   skirt
i **guanti**   gloves
il **mantello**   cape

la **pelliccia**   fur coat
lo **scialle**   shawl, stole
la **sottoveste**   slip
la **vestaglia**   nightgown
la **veste**   dress

Professions and Trades

la **professione**   profession
il **mestiere**   trade

l'**agente** (*m.*) **di polizia**   policeman
l'**annunciatore** ⎫   news
l'**annunciatrice** ⎭   announcer
l'**architetto**   architect
l'**artista** (*m. & f.*)   artist
l'**assistente di volo** (*m. & f.*)   steward, stewardess, flight attendant
l'**assistente sociale** (*m. & f.*)   social worker
l'**attore**   actor
l'**attrice**   actress
l'**autista**   driver
l'**autore** (*m.*)   author
l'**avvocato** ⎫   lawyer
l'**avvocatessa** ⎭
il **banchiere**   banker
il **barbiere**   barber
il **calzolaio**   shoemaker
la **cameriera**   waitress, maid
il **cameriere**   waiter
il **carpentiere**   carpenter
il **centralinista** ⎫   telephone
la **centralinista** ⎭   operator
il **commerciante**   merchant
la **commessa**   salesgirl
il **commesso**   salesman
il **commesso viaggiatore**   traveling salesman
il **contabile**   accountant
il **contadino** ⎫   farmer
la **contadina** ⎭
il **cuoco** ⎫   cook
la **cuoca** ⎭
la **dattilografa**   typist
il (or la) **dentista** (*m. & f.*)   dentist
la **domestica**   maid
il **domestico**   butler, valet
il **dottore** ⎫   doctor
la **dottoressa** ⎭
l'**elettricista** (*m.*)   electrician
il **farmacista**   pharmacist
il **fioraio** ⎫   florist
la **fioraia** ⎭

il **fotografo** photographer
il **giornalista** ⎫
la **giornalista** ⎭ journalist
il **giudice** ⎫
la **giudice** ⎭ judge
l'**idraulico** plumber
l'**impiegato** ⎫ employee, office
l'**impiegata** ⎭ worker
l'**infermiera** nurse
l'**ingegnere** (*m.*) engineer
l'**insegnante** (*m. & f.*) teacher
l'**interprete** (*m. & f.*) interpreter
il **libraio** bookseller
il **macellaio** butcher
il **maestro** ⎫
la **maestra** ⎭ teacher
la **maestra d'asilo** kindergarten
teacher
il **manovale** construction
worker
il **marinaio** sailor
il **meccanico** mechanic
il **medico** doctor
il **musicista** ⎫
la **musicista** ⎭ musician
l'**oculista** (*m. & f.*) eye doctor,
oculist
l'**operaio** worker
il **panettiere** baker
il **parrucchiere** ⎫ hair stylist,
la **parrucchiera** ⎭ hairdresser
il **pilota** pilot
il **pittore** painter
il **poliziotto** ⎫
la **poliziotta** ⎭ police officer
il **postino** mailman
il **prete** (or il **sacerdote**) priest
il **professore** ⎫
la **professoressa** ⎭ professor
il **ragioniere** bookkeeper
il **rappresentante** agent
la **sarta** dressmaker
il **sarto** tailor
lo **scienziato** scientist
lo **scrittore** ⎫
la **scrittrice** ⎭ writer, author
lo **scultore** sculptor
il **segretario** ⎫
la **segretaria** ⎭ secretary
il **soldato** soldier
il **tassista** taxi driver
il (or la) **telescriventista** teletypist
il **tipografo** printer

Education and Academic Sul

l'**istruzione** education
le **materie scolastiche** academic
subjects
le **materie principali** major subjects
le **materie secondarie** minor subjects

l'**asilo infantile** (or l'**asilo
d'infanzia**) kindergarten
la **biologia** biology
la **chimica** chemistry
l'**economia** economics
la **filologia** philology
la **filosofia** philosophy
la **fisica** physics
la **geografia** geography
l'**istituto professionale** vocational
high school
il **greco** Greek
il **latino** Latin
la **laurea** university degree, doc-
torate
la **legge** law
il **liceo** high school
la **lingua e letteratura
italiana** Italian language and
literature
la **lingua straniera** foreign language
la **matematica** mathematics
la **medicina** medicine
la **ragioneria** accounting
la **scuola elementare** elementary
school
la **scuola magistrale** school of
education
la **scuola materna** nursery school
la **scuola media** junior high
school
la **storia** history
l'**università** university

Geometry

la **geometria** geometry

l'**angolo** angle
l'**angolo retto** right angle
il **cerchio** circle
il **cono** cone
il **cubo** cube
il **diametro** diameter
l'**emisfero** hemisphere

la linea   line
la piramide   pyramid
il prisma   prism
il quadrato   square
il raggio   radius
il rettangolo   rectangle
il rombo   rhombus
il semicerchio   semicircle
la sfera   sphere
il triangolo   triangle

Chemistry

la chimica   chemistry

l'elemento   element
il gas   gas
l'idrogeno   hydrogen
il liquido   liquid
il nitrogeno   nitrogen
l'ossigeno   oxygen

Offices and Ranks

la carica   office
il grado (or il titolo)   rank

l'ammiraglio   admiral
il capitano   captain
il cardinale   cardinal
il colonnello   colonel
il deputato   representative
il generale   general
il governatore   governor
il luogotenente   lieutenant
il papa   pope
il prefetto   prefect
il presidente   president
il primo ministro   prime minister
il senatore   senator
il sindaco   mayor
il vescovo   bishop
il vicepresidente   vice president

Materials

il materiale   material

l'acciaio   steel
l'alluminio   aluminum
l'argento   silver
il bronzo   bronze
il carbone   coal
il cemento   cement
la ceramica   ceramic
il cotone   cotton

il cuoio   leather
il ferro   iron
il gesso   plaster
la gomma   rubber
la lana   wool
il legno   wood
il lino   linen
il marmo   marble
il mattone   brick
il metallo   metal
il nailon   nylon
il nichel   nickel
l'oro   gold
l'ottone (*m.*)   brass
la pietra   stone
la pietra calcare   limestone
il piombo   lead
la plastica   plastic
il rame   copper
la seta   silk
lo stagno   tin
la stoffa   fabric
il vetro   glass

Sports

lo sport   sport

l'automobilismo   car racing
le bocce   type of lawn bowling
la caccia   hunting
il calcio   soccer
il canottaggio   boating
il ciclismo   bicycling
la corsa   race, racing
l'equitazione   horseback riding
il footing   jogging
il gioco   game
la lotta libera   wrestling
il motociclismo   motorcycling
il nuoto   diving
la pallacanestro   basket
la partita   game, match
la partita di calcio   soccer game
il pattinaggio   skating
il ping-pong   Ping-Pong
il podismo   running
il pugilato   boxing
la scherma   fencing
lo sci   ski
lo sci acquatico   waterskiing
la squadra   team
il tennis   tennis
la vela   sailing

Holidays and Holiday Greetings

la celebrazione celebration
la festa feast
il giorno festivo holiday

l'Anniversario della Vittoria (*4 novembre*) Victory Day 1918
l'Assunzione (*15 agosto*) Assumption Day
Buon Anno! Happy New Year!
Buona Pasqua! Happy Easter!
Buon Natale! Merry Christmas!
Buone Feste! Happy Holidays!
il Capodanno New Year's Day
l'Epifania (*6 gennaio*) Epiphany
la Festa della Liberazione (*25 aprile*) Liberation Day
la Festa della Repubblica (*2 giugno*) Proclamation of the Republic
La Festa del Lavoro (*1 maggio*) May Day, Labor Day
la Festa dei Santi Pietro e Paolo (*29 giugno*) Saints Peter and Paul
il Ferragosto mid-August holidays
il Giovedì Santo Holy Thursday
il Venerdì Santo Good Friday
l'Immacolata Concezione (*8 dicembre*) the Immaculate Conception
il Mercoledì delle Ceneri Ash Wednesday
il Natale Christmas
la Pasqua Easter
la Pasquetta Monday after Easter
la Pentecoste Pentecost
la Settimana Santa Holy Week
Tutti i Santi (or **Ognissanti**) (*1 novembre*) All Saints' Day
la vigilia di Capodanno
la fine dell'anno } New Year's
la notte di San Silvestro } Eve

Index

a:
  a + indirect object, 181
  the contraction **al,** 110
  verbs requiring **a** before the
    infinitive, 98, 181
abbreviations, 215
accents, 6
active voice, 95
adjectives, 120–125
  agreement of, 121–122
  comparison of, 138–145
  demonstrative, 134–135
  gender and number, 121–122
  indefinite, 175–176, 178–180
  participles used as, 123
  plural of, 120
  position of, 122–123
  possessive, 131–133
  shortened form of, 123–125
adverbs, 125–130
  comparison of, 145–148
  formation of, 126–127
  position of, 129–130
alphabet, 3–5
articles:
  definite, 105, 106–108
  indefinite, 105, 106
  omission of, 108–110
  partitive, 111–112
  with geographical names, 106
  with parts of the body, 107, 133
auxiliary verbs, 27–29
avere, 27–29
  expressions with, 216
  used to express dimensions, 197

body, parts of, 231–232
  use of articles with, 107, 133
buono, 124

che, chi:
  as interrogative pronouns, 168
  as relative pronouns, 164–165, 166

ci (vi), 162–163
ci, vi 149, 154, 155
colui che, colei che, 137
cominciare, 90
commands, *see* imperative
comparison:
  of adjectives, 138–145
  of adverbs, 145–148
conditional mood, 17–19, 85–86
conjunctions, 49–51, 186–190
contractions, 110–111

da:
  since, for, 12
  at the place of, 111
  from, by, 182
dates, 199–200
defective verbs, 81–82
demonstratives:
  adjectives, 134–135
  pronouns, 135–137
di:
  in expressions of quantity, 182
  partitive, 111–112
  possessive, 111
  verbs requiring **di** before an
    infinitive, 99, 182
  with collective numbers, 193
  double consonants, 5
directions, 203
dovere, 89

essere, 28–29
  essere sul punto di, 90
  expressions with, 217
  used to express dimensions, 197
exclamations, 170

fare, 90–91
finire, 90
future tense, 16–17, 84
future perfect tense, 32–33, 84–85

gender:
   adjectives, 120, 121–122
   nouns, 113–115
geographical names, 106
gerunds, 22–23
   past gerunds, 93
grande, 125

idioms and expressions, 221–235
imperative mood, 19–21
imperfect tense, 13–14
impersonal verbs, 46–47, 77–80
indicative mood:
   compound tenses, 27–36
   simple tenses, 8–17
   used after impersonal verbs, 47
infinitives, 21–22
   introduced by **a** and/or by **di,**
     98–100, 181–182
   past infinitives, 92
interrogatives, 168–170
intonation, 6
-issimo, 142

lasciare, 91
letters, 213–215

measurement, 197–198

negatives, 171–174
nessuno, 124
nouns, 113–119
   gender of, 113–115
   plurals of, 116–119
numbers, 191–197

object pronouns, *see* pronouns
orthographic-changing verbs, 54–56

parere, 90
participles:
   present participles, 23–24
   past participles, 29, 93–94
past conditional tense, 33–34
partitive articles, 111–112
passive voice, 95–97
past participles, 29, 93–94
   agreement with preceding direct
     objects, 30–31
   agreement with subjects, 31
perfect tenses, 29–36
piacere, 79–80
place names, *see* geographical names

pluperfect tense, 31
possession:
   di + article, 110–111
   possessive adjectives, 131–133
   possessive pronouns, 131–133
potere, 89
prefixes, 204–206
prepositions, 181–185
   required after certain verbs,
     98–101
present indicative tense, 9–13
present participles, 23–24
preterite perfect tense, 32
progressive form, 23
pronominal verbs, *see* reflexive verbs
pronouns:
   demonstrative, 135–137
   double-object, 160–161
   indefinite, 176–178, 178–179
   interrogatives, 168–170
   ne, 161–162
   personal, 149–161
   possessive, 131–133
   reflexive, 37–38, 149
   relative, 164–167
   stressed direct-object pronouns,
     149, 151–152
   stressed indirect-object pronouns,
     149, 153–154
   subject, 8, 149
   unstressed direct-object, 149,
     154–157
   unstressed indirect-object, 149,
     157–159
punctuation marks, 7

quale, 165
quello, 124

reciprocal use of reflexive verbs,
   38–39
reflexive verbs, 37–40
responses, 222
rhythm, 6

santo (san), 125
sapere, 89
se clause, 51
sembrare, 90
sequence of tenses, 83–87
simple past tense, 15–16
solere, 90
stress, 5–6

subjunctive mood:
  in dependent clauses, 46–47, 86–87
  formation of, 41
  in relative clauses, 52
  tenses of, 41–45
  uses of, 46–53
suffixes, 206–212
superlatives, 141–143, 146
synopses:
  passive voice, 95
  perfect (compound) tenses of the
    indicative, 35
  simple tenses of the indicative, 26
  subjunctive tenses, 45

tenses, *see* individual listings
  sequence of, 83–87
time:
  of day, 202–203
  divisions, 201
  expressions, 201–202

verbs:
  conjugated with **essere**, 36
  followed by a preposition + an
    infinitive, 98–100
  impersonal and defective, 77–82
  irregular, 57–76
  orthographic-changing, 54–56
  regular, 8–26, 27–36
vocabulary lists, 221–235
voice:
  active, 95
  passive, 95–97
volere, 88

weather expressions, 77, 223–224

Verb Index

This verb index will enable you to compare hundreds of commonly used verbs to the book's numerous verb tables. Each of the following groups of regular or irregular verbs provides the page numbers where the various verb tenses are discussed in the book. Each group is then followed by some of the most common verbs—and their definitions—that follow those patterns. By recognizing which verbs follow a certain pattern, you will greatly increase your vocabulary—all at a glance.

Regular *-are* Verbs

Regular *-are* verbs are conjugated in the same way as the verb *parlare*. The various conjugations of *parlare* can be found on the following pages:

present, 9	present conditional, 17
imperfect, 13	past conditional, 33
preterit, 15	present subjunctive, 41
future, 16	past subjunctive, 42
imperative, 19	imperfect subjunctive, 42
present perfect, 27	pluperfect subjunctive, 43
past perfect, 31	past participle, 29
preterit perfect, 32	gerund, 22
future perfect, 32	infinitive, 21

Some common regular *-are* verbs appear in the following list.

Note: Some verbs use the auxiliary *essere* in compound tenses. This is indicated in parentheses.

abitare to live	**assomigliare** to resemble
accomodare to repair	**atterrare** to land (aux. *essere*)
affettare to slice	**attraversare** to cross
aiutare to help	**aumentare** to increase
alzare to lift	**baciare** to kiss
amare to love	**ballare** to dance
arrestare to arrest	**bastare** to suffice (aux. *essere*)
arrivare to arrive (aux. *essere*)	**bisognare** to need (aux. *essere*)
ascoltare to listen to	**cambiare** to change
aspettare to wait	**camminare** to walk
assaggiare to taste	**cantare** to sing

cenare   to have supper
cercare   to look for
chiamare   to call
cominciare   to begin, start
comprare   to buy
conservare   to preserve
consigliare   to advise
contare   to count
continuare   to continue
costare   to cost (aux. *essere*)
cucinare   to cook
curare   to cure
desiderare   to wish
dimenticare   to forget
disegnare   to draw
disturbare   to disturb
diventare   to become (aux. *essere*)
divorziare   to divorce
domandare   to ask
dubitare   to doubt
entrare   to enter (aux. *essere*)
evitare   to avoid
fermare   to stop
festeggiare   to celebrate
firmare   to sign
frenare   to stop
frequentare   to attend
fumare   to smoke
funzionare   to function
gettare   to throw
giocare   to play
girare   to turn
giurare   to swear
gridare   to scream
guadagnare   to gain
guardare   to look at
guidare   to drive
gustare   to taste
illustrare   to illustrate
imbucare   to mail
immaginare   to imagine
imparare   to learn
impostare   to plan
incassare   to cash
incontrare   to meet
indossare   to wear
indovinare   to guess
informare   to inform
ingrassare   to gain weight (aux. *essere*)
inquinare   to pollute
insegnare   to teach
interpretare   to interpret

interrogare   to question
intervistare   to interview
inviare   to send
invitare   to invite
lamentare   to complain
lasciare   to leave
lavare   to wash
lavorare   to work
licenziare   to fire
litigare   to quarrel
lottare   to fight
mancare   to miss
mandare   to send (aux. *avere* and *essere*)
mangiare   to eat
misurare   to measure
mostrare   to show
nevicare   to snow (aux. *essere*)
noleggiare   to rent
notare   to notice
nuotare   to swim
ordinare   to order
pagare   to pay
parcheggiare   to park
parlare   to speak
passare   to pass by (aux. *essere*)
passeggiare   to stroll
pattinare   to skate
pensare   to think
perdonare   to forgive
pesare   to weigh
pettinare   to comb
piantare   to plant
portare   to bring
pranzare   to have lunch
prenotare   to reserve
preparare   to prepare
prestare   to loan
provare   to try
pubblicare   to publish
raccomandare   to recommend
raccontare   to narrate
rallentare   to slow down
rappresentare   to represent
recitare   to recite
regalare   to donate, give
respirare   to breathe
restare   to remain, stay (aux. *essere*)
riattaccare   to hang up
ricordare   to remember
rientrare   to reenter (aux. *essere*)
ringraziare   to thank

rinunciare   to renounce
ripassare   to pass again, revise
riposare   to rest
risparmiare   to save
ritornare   to return (aux. *essere*)
rubare   to rob, steal
saltare   to jump (aux. *avere* and *essere*)
salutare   to greet
sbagliare   to make a mistake
scappare   to escape (aux. *essere*)
scherzare   to joke
sciare   to ski
scusare   to excuse
sembrare   to seem (aux. *essere*)
sistemare   to tidy up, sort out
sognare   to dream
sopportare   to tolerate
sparare   to shoot
sparecchiare   to clear
spaventare   to scare
spazzolare   to brush
sperare   to hope
spiegare   to explain
spogliare   to undress

sposare   to marry
spostare   to move
sprecare   to waste
stampare   to print
stancare   to tire
stirare   to iron
studiare   to study
suonare   to play an instrument
superare   to pass, exceed
svegliare   to wake
tagliare   to cut
telefonare   to call
tirare   to pull
toccare   to touch
tornare   to return (aux. *essere*)
traslocare   to move
trovare   to find
urlare   to shout
viaggiare   to travel
vietare   to prohibit
visitare   to visit
volare   to fly
votare   to vote
vuotare   to empty

Regular -*ere* Verbs

Regular -*ere* verbs are conjugated in the same way as the verb *vendere*. However, many -*ere* verbs are irregular. These will be listed later on. The various conjugations of *vendere* can be found on the following pages:

present, 10
imperfect, 13
preterit, 16
future, 17
imperative, 19
present perfect, 29
past perfect, 32
preterit perfect, 32
future perfect, 32

present conditional, 18
past conditional, 33
present subjunctive, 41
past subjunctive, 42
imperfect subjunctive, 42
pluperfect subjunctive, 43
past participle, 29
gerund, 22
infinitive, 21

Some common regular -*ere* verbs are:

combattere   to fight
credere   to believe
ricevere   to receive

ripetere   to repeat
temere   to fear
vendere   to sell

Regular *-ire* Verbs

Regular *-ire* verbs fall into two groups: 1) those conjugated in the same way as the verb *sentire* and 2) those conjugated similarly to the verb *capire*. The endings are the same for both groups, but verbs of the *capire* group insert *-isc-* before adding the endings for the singular forms and the third person plural.

The various conjugations of *sentire* and *capire* can be found on the following pages.

Note: Sometimes the conjugation is given using another verb, which is indicated in parentheses.

Sentire **Group**	*Capire* **Group**
present, 11	present, 11
imperfect, 14	imperfect, 14
preterit, 16	preterit, 16
future, 17	future, 17
imperative, 20	imperative, 20
present perfect, 34	present perfect, 34
past perfect, 31 (*partire*)	past perfect, 31
preterit perfect, 34	preterit perfect, 32 (*finire*)
future perfect, 34	future perfect, 34
present conditional, 26	present conditional, 18
past conditional, 33 (*partire*)	past conditional, 33
present subjunctive, 41 (*partire*)	present subjunctive, 41 (*finire*)
past subjunctive, 42 (*partire*)	past subjunctive, 42
imperfect subjunctive, 43 (*finire*)	imperfect subjunctive, 43
	pluperfect subjunctive, 45
pluperfect subjunctive, 43 (*partire*)	past participle, 29
past participle, 29 (*dormire*)	gerund, 22 (*sentire*)
gerund, 22 (*sentire*)	
infinitive, 21	

The following is a list of common verbs belonging to the *sentire* group:

avvertire   to notify
conseguire   to achieve
consentire   to consent
convertire   to convert (aux. *essere*)
cucire   to sew
fuggire   to escape (aux. *essere*)
inseguire   to chase

investire   to invest
partire   to leave (aux. *essere*)
seguire   to follow
sentire   to hear, listen
servire   to serve
vestire   to get dressed

These are some common verbs belonging to the *capire* group:

agire   to act
applaudire   to applaud

arrossire   to blush (aux. *essere*)
attribuire   to attribute

capire   to understand
colpire   to hit
condire   to season
contribuire   to contribute
costruire   to build
digerire   to digest
dimagrire   to lose weight (aux. *essere*)
esaurire   to exhaust
esibire   to exhibit
fallire   to fail (aux. *avere* and *essere*)
ferire   to wound
finire   to finish
guarire   to heal (aux. *essere*)
impedire   to prevent
inghiottire   to swallow

istruire   to instruct
preferire   to prefer
proibire   to prohibit
pulire   to clean
punire   to punish
restituire   to return
riunire   to reunite
sostituire   to substitute
sparire   to disappear (aux. *essere*)
spedire   to send, mail, ship
stabilire   to establish
tossire   to cough
tradire   to betray
trasferire   to transfer
ubbidire   to obey
unire   to unite

Irregular *-are* Verbs

There are only four irregular *-are* verbs. The following page numbers show where their conjugations can be found. The compound tenses for the irregular *-are* verbs are conjugated the same as those for regular *-are* verbs or the same as the verbs they originate from, such as *dare—ridare*. The verbs *andare* and *stare* require the auxiliary *essere* in compound tenses.

andare   to go, 57 (aux. *essere*)
dare   to give, 63

fare   to make, do, 65
stare   to stay, 72 (aux. *essere*)

This common verb is conjugated in the same way as the verb *dare*:

ridare   to give back

Other verbs are conjugated similarly to *fare*:

rifare   to do or make again
soddisfare   to satisfy

sopraffare   to overwhelm

Irregular *-ere* Verbs

The majority of *-ere* verbs have some type of irregular form. Most have an irregular preterit tense, past participle, subjunctive, and gerund. The verbs listed below have at least some of these irregular forms. Their various conjugations can be found on the pages indicated next to each verb. It is noted in parentheses when a verb requires the use of the auxiliary *essere* in compound tenses.

accendere   to light, turn on; 57
ammettere   to admit, 66
appartenere   to belong, 73 (aux.
   essere)
appendere   to hang, 58
avere   to have, 27
bere   to drink, 59
cadere   to fall, 59 (aux. *essere*)
chiedere   to ask, 60
commettere   to commit, 66
compiere   to fulfill, 60
comprendere   to comprehend, 69
conoscere   to know (someone), 61
convincere   to convince, 75
corrispondere   to correspond, 70
decidere   to decide, 63
difendere   to defend, 63
discutere   to discuss, 64
distinguere   to distinguish, 64
dividere   to divide, 64
dovere   to have to, must,
   should; 89
eleggere   to elect, 65
essere   to be, 28 (aux. *essere*)
giungere   to arrive, 65 (aux. *avere*
   and *essere*)
mantenere   to maintain, 75

nascere   to be born, 67 (aux.
   essere)
nascondere   to hide, 67
perdere   to lose, 67
piacere   to like, 68 (aux. *essere*)
piangere   to cry, 68
porre   to put, 68
potere   to be able to, 89
proteggere   to protect, 69
raggiungere   to reach, 65
ridere   to laugh, 69
rimanere   to stay, 69 (aux. *essere*)
rispondere   to answer, 70
rompere   to break, 70
sapere   to know, 70
scadere   to expire, 59 (aux.
   essere)
scendere   to descend, 71 (aux.
   avere or *essere*)
scommettere   to bet, 66
scrivere   to write, 71
smettere   to stop, 66
tacere   to be quiet, 72
vedere   to see, 75
vincere   to win, 75
vivere   to live, 75
volere   to want, 76

Irregular -*ire* Verbs

Italian -*ire* verbs have some irregular forms, which can be found on the pages indicated next to each of the following verbs:

apparire   to appear, 58 (aux. *essere*)
aprire   to open, 58
dire   to tell, say; 63
offrire   to offer, 67
salire   to go up, 70 (aux. *avere* or
   essere)

udire   to hear, 74
uscire   to go out, 74 (aux. *essere*)
venire   to come, 75 (aux. *essere*)

These common verbs are conjugated in the same way as the verb *apparire*:

comparire   to appear

scomparire   disappear

Other -*ire* verbs are conjugated similarly to *aprire*:

riaprire   to reopen
coprire   to cover

scoprire   to uncover

These verbs follow the conjugation of *dire*:

ridire   to say again, object to   **predire**   to predict

Still other common *-ire* verbs follow the conjugations used with *venire*:

prevenire   to prevent   **svenire**   to faint

Reflexive and Reciprocal Verbs

Verbs are reflexive when the action reflects back to the person doing it. A reflexive verb is called reciprocal when the action passes from one person or thing to another. Reciprocal verbs are used only in the plural. Reflexive and reciprocal verbs are usually preceded by the pronouns *mi*, *ti*, *si*, *ci*, *vi*, or *si*. Italian makes much greater use of reflexive verbs than English does. These verbs always use the auxiliary *essere* in compound tenses. See pages 37–40 for their conjugations and usage.

Verbs That Are Reflexive in Both Italian and English

alzarsi   to get oneself up
appoggiarsi   to lean oneself
chiamarsi   to call oneself
divertirsi   to enjoy oneself
lavarsi   to wash oneself
mettersi   to put something on oneself

pettinarsi   to comb one's hair
prepararsi   to get oneself ready
svegliarsi   to wake oneself up
tagliarsi   to cut oneself
vestirsi   to get oneself dressed

Verbs That Are Reflexive in Italian But Not in English

accorgersi   to notice
addormentarsi   to fall asleep
fermarsi   to stop
lamentarsi di   to complain about
mettersi a   to start, begin

pentirsi di   to repent of
sedersi   to sit
sentirsi   to feel
sposarsi   to get married

Reciprocal Verbs

Reciprocal verbs indicate an action passing from one person to another. These verbs are only used in the plural.

aiutarsi   to help each other
amarsi   to love each other
guardarsi   to look at each other
incontrarsi   to meet each other
ingannarsi   to deceive each other

odiarsi   to hate each other
parlarsi   to speak to each other
salutarsi   to greet each other
scriversi   to write each other